The Ballad of Johnny Bell

ALSO BY JOHN MORT

Tanks (1987)

The Walnut King (1990)

Soldier in Paradise (1999)

Christian Fiction: A Guide to the Genre (2002)

Read the High Country: A Guide to Westerns (2006)

Goat Boy of the Ozarks (2011)

DONT MEAN NOTHIN: Vietnam War Stories (2011)

The Illegal (2013)

Down Along the Piney (2018)

Oklahoma Odyssey (2022)

The Ballad of Johnny Bell

A Novel

John Mort

Cornerpost Press | 2022

ISBN: 979-8-218-00608-2

Library of Congress Control Number: 2022938440

Edited by Phillip Howerton

Cover design by Ronald Kerns of StudioKerns.

Cover photograph by Phillip Howerton

Interior design by Phillip Howerton

Cornerpost Press
214 West Maple
West Plains, Missouri, 65775
www.cornerpostpress.com

ACKNOWLEDGMENTS

Chapters two and four of this novel appeared in somewhat different form in the journal *New Letters*.

For Patricia

Foreword

Somewhere between the gated communities of Walmart executives and the trashy trailer houses of meth heads exists the real Ozarks. It's a little poorer and a little more rural than the place the average American calls home, but the people who live in the real Ozarks live recognizable and relatable lives. Some prosper, some don't. Some go to church, some don't. Some are mostly good, some mostly ain't. John Mort's fiction inhabits that Ozarks, or at least offers a glimpse of it from the fringes, often through the perspective of the born outsider. Mort's Ozarks seems unassuming and humble but churns with the complexity of the human saga: family dysfunction, class conflict, teen angst, psychological struggle, and economic peril.

The tumultuous year in teenager Johnny Bell's life provides a window into a time and place in the rural Ozarks and into the social and cultural developments affecting that time and place: the looming cloud of Vietnam, the ascendance of corporate poultry processors and the demise of the family farm, the rise of the tourism industry and local efforts to profit off a fascination with the old days. Those forces serve as the backdrop for the characters Mort skillfully brings to life—real people whose failures and triumphs follow you off the page. Mort's ability to bring multi-dimensional characters to full bloom in just a few lines may be his greatest talent, and it's on marvelous display in *The Ballad of Johnny Bell*.

One suspects there is an ample dose of autobiographical material in these pages. No matter how much or how little of the author went into the creation of Johnny Bell, the humanity and hope you'll find herein are without a doubt reflections of John Mort. His is a rare voice shaped both by a boyhood in the rural Ozarks and years of looking back on that place and time from outside the hills. John Mort may focus his energies on the plain people in the Ozarks, but there is nothing ordinary about his storytelling.

Brooks Blevins
February 24, 2022

Preface

"This must be one of the top-ten, never-fail plots—"

So said John "Jack" Leggett, director of the University of Iowa's Writers Workshop, back in 1974. That was the year I submitted my master's thesis, *The Walnut King*, which has now become *The Ballad of Johnny Bell*.

I took several classes from Jack, and he liked me all right, and I learned a lot from him. He was your consummate New Yorker and, probably, would never warm up to something as regional and *humble*—to echo Brooks Blevins in his generous introduction—as *The Walnut King*. The comment he stopped in mid-air was condescending, as if anybody could come up with such a plot and it wasn't, you know, sophisticated.

Jack's comment was also a grudging compliment, or at least I took it that way. In Vietnam, winding through the jungle fifty men back in the column, I developed the art of reading paperbacks. The column would lurch to a halt, I'd prop up my pack on my rifle barrel, and read through the long novels my dear mother sent me. I read Dostoevsky, rather over my head in those days, and Dickens, whose tales of ragamuffin triumph resonated with me. Thus, perhaps, that top-ten, never-fail plot.

My folks were poor, and we were at our poorest in Cabool (Red Buck) and Mountain Grove (Mountain Vale). When I was four, we lived on a small farm south of Cabool. We had a few dairy cattle and chickens but couldn't have paid the bills without the money my dad made as an electrician. Often, he brought in the first service to those remote little farms, down those rough gravel roads. What I remember of those days is like a dream, but then the famous five-year drought hit, and we sold out at auction and moved into town. I finished first grade before we migrated to Florida.

We had a splendid place in Tampa, which was half-rural then. Mammoth grapefruit trees shaded our lot, and a flock of banty chickens roosted in those trees. Our little family drew perilously close to prosperous, but Dad's job, installing attic fans in spring and summer, was brutally hard. Mom's evangelical college credentials were sufficient for teaching second grade at an Ybor City mission school, but anyhow this was city life, and we weren't city people. After a few years, we piled in the pickup and drove back to Missouri, settling on U.S. 60 halfway between Mountain Grove and Cabool, near where the Piney River begins, one-half mile east of Dunn.

Those years, from 1956 to 1962, are where the material for *The Walnut King/Goat Boy of the Ozarks/The Ballad of Johnny Bell* comes from. We maintained a big—small by contemporary standards—broiler house, where Mom and I raised 5000 chicks into three-pound broilers every eight weeks, while Dad went out to wire houses.

The family the Ogletrees are based on lived across a field grown up with oak sprouts. (It was a great place to hunt rabbits.) That family raised goats, not as common a practice then as now, and anyhow these were *milk* goats. The goats were the responsibility of the oldest boy, who let them wander into the woods and go wild, while the father, the always-frustrated patriarch, drove off to far flung regions with his bulldozer and returned filled with rage.

We attended—Mom dragged me, and Dad sat outside in the pickup reading Louis L'Amour—the Assembly of God in Mountain Grove, and sometimes a Freewill

Baptist, way out somewhere on an E or a double-E, where they whooped and hollered, cried and moaned, healed the sick and spoke in tongues what always turned out to be the most banal of prophecies.

Once a year, the Poultry Festival spread out north of Cabool. For me, not quite a teenager, it brought news of the mysterious, wider world, just like Jack Buck, Harry Caray, and Joe Garagiola did broadcasting the Cardinals on KMOX.

There was indeed a feed mill, somewhat like Reverend Larkin's, and an effusive fellow who ran the place and wanted to run Texas County. As for the high school, the tennis scenes are autobiographical. This was the only time I showed any sports ability, and I loved the game. Tennis, like baseball and the Poultry Festival, suggested there was more to the world than chickens and church.

The girls are mostly teenaged fantasy. The family across the field had a daughter my age whom I sort of liked, and I believe she did become a nurse like Suzanne in the novel, but she never paid any attention to me. Jane is almost wholly imagined, though there was a banker's daughter who liked me. I remember how distressed I was when her father was accused of embezzlement, and her family moved, almost overnight, to impossibly far-off Kansas City.

Back to that master's thesis: it was a mess. The characters were much the same as the ones who appear in *The Ballad of Johnny Bell,* but in those first versions they veered off into melodrama, and I couldn't come up with a satisfactory ending. In the late 1970s, I tried a few New York editors (you could still approach them directly in those days), and while several were kind, none saw any profit in working with me.

In the 1980s, I enjoyed some success writing about my Vietnam War experiences. My war stories landed me a good agent for a while—but I was working on a war novel, and I don't believe I even brought up the Ozarks book. She was a consummate New Yorker, too, and I doubt she'd have had much patience with it.

But every so often, I'd return to the manuscript. Eventually, I calmed down the characters, introduced more subtle (I hoped) plotlines and some humor, and finally, in 2005, I broke through with a satisfactory ending. Essentially, that's the version you are about to encounter with *The Ballad of Johnny Bell*, though, with the help of Phillip Howerton at Cornerpost, I've made a thousand minor changes, mostly in style. He corrected some of my Ozarks references, too. He knows everything.

With that 2005 version, I tried to interest agents—and finally did land a new agent in 2008. He shopped around another novel, and said he'd send out what by then I was calling *Goat Boy of the Ozarks*, after he'd placed that other novel. But he was an old, old man, older even than I am now. On a cold March day, he took a bad fall on the Philadelphia ice, and afterwards he closed down his agency.

In 2011, in despair, I self-published *Goat Boy*. (That title came about because the editors of my short story collection from 1990 liked *The Walnut King* better than whatever title I had used. "The Walnut King," an excerpt from the novel, was the first story in the collection.) *Goat Boy of the Ozarks* refers to the satirical, or perhaps farcical, play within the novel, but the title never quite worked. Some people thought it referred to bestiality; others thought I was trying to imitate John Barth.

We've all heard stories in which the self-published novel makes the writer famous and rich (Andy Weir's *The Martian* is usually cited), but while self-publishing is not exactly vanity publishing, you're unlikely to sell many copies. Certainly, I didn't. Not least, you're up against thousands and thousands of competitors, all using social media in pretty much the same way. But *Goat Boy* made some little progress, nonetheless, impressing Ozarks scholars such as Brooks Blevins and Steve Wiegenstein. I owe this lovely new edition of my very old, very young book to their encouragement, and to the fine stewardship of Phillip Howerton at Cornerpost—as well as to his wife and partner, Victoria, who gave the new book its gentle title.

It is, in the end, a gentle, nostalgic novel, and it's often pretty funny. It's my favorite novel, though how literary or timeless it is I'm not qualified to say. It's awfully gratifying the novel has finally found a home—just about forty miles from where it's set.

John Mort
April 26, 2022

It is better to be a young June-bug than an old
bird of paradise.

Mark Twain
Pudd'nhead Wilson's Calendar

Chapter One
The Least of These

A woman hovered above him, bathing his forehead with a washcloth.

She'd been there all along. Was he a prisoner? Yes, an outlaw with a price on his head, and guards stood outside the door. Perhaps he'd lost his memory, as in one of those old novels George Bell left in the shed. It would turn out that he was a rich man's son or some lost prince.

For a while it seemed as though weights pressed on his eyelids. Then fuzzy light poked through, and he could see. The woman sat back, hardly more than one hundred pounds of her. She had short black hair, a face white as a carp's belly, and her black eyes darted about as if she were guilty of something.

"Praise the Lord," she said.

Off to his right were a little boy and girl. They seemed like one person, but sometimes they became two. Their energy worried him. "He's awake! He's awake!"

"It's a miracle," the woman said, crying a little.

The suddenness of their voices frightened him, and he wanted to run, but his legs were weak and clammy under the blankets. He wore a flannel shirt and nothing else, and he wondered what had happened to his own clothing. There: atop a dresser, clean and folded.

"You slept right around the clock," said the woman.

He nodded but couldn't find his voice. Outside, the wind howled, and through the glass he saw snow swirling under the soffits. Tears came to his eyes, and he didn't understand why. It was like a sad movie where his eyes began watering despite his instructions to himself not to be a sap.

The two kids hung on the doorknob, twisting about, prancing like cats. An older girl, in yellow slacks and an oversized tee shirt, fluttered by behind them, casting one quick glance in his direction. Her eyes were upsetting somehow, almost mournful. She must be the washcloth woman's daughter. Their dark eyes were the same.

Now he remembered the woman, and the girl, as they'd peeled away his frozen clothing and rubbed his legs. When they tucked blankets around him, he thought they were demons wrapping him in a shroud and kicked hard. There was a man, too—a big man who held him down with his icy hands. He fought the man. Perhaps he bit him.

"Everett says he thinks he knows you. Seen you totin' a gunnysack full a walnuts down Highway E. But we wasn't sure who—"

He got out two words: "Johnny Bell."

"You can speak. Well, Johnny, I'm Lucy Ogletree, and these are my twins, Ronnie and Rosie. We was comin' home from service—dear Lord, it was *Christmas*—and there you was on the road." She smiled as if unsure. "You're sick, you don't have to talk now."

But he wasn't sick anymore, and what had happened began to grow clear. He saw himself plunging down the white hill. "Yes, ma'am. I just run and run and then my legs gave out."

"He's a big strong boy, I said to Everett, or he couldn't a stood the weather. Suzanne, that's my oldest daughter, she was worried about frostbite." Lucy grabbed his hand and stroked the ends of his fingers. "They was kinda swollen and she wanted to send for the doctor, but we prayed, and they never turned black. I 'magine you run away from home."

Johnny choked. "Ole George Bell, he—"

Lucy nodded. "That's awright, that's awright. Take these."

Johnny swallowed aspirins with a gulp of milk. He made a face.

"Goat's milk," Lucy said, smiling. "Suzanne takes care of 'em."

Rosie and Ronnie leaped up and down. Ronnie called out loudly, "Suzanne *lu-uves* you."

"Ronnie, you shut up," came a voice from down the hall.

Lucy said, "You two run upstairs."

"I didn't say nothin', it was him," said Rosie.

"Don't talk back." Lucy advanced on the twins, who stood their ground, squirming, but then she slapped Ronnie on the cheek. The boy stared at her defiantly, but Rosie began to cry. "What did we do?"

She shoved them into the hall and Johnny was grateful. An area of the room no longer had to be watched. Lucy pulled her chair next to the bed and picked up a handkerchief and bottle of olive oil. "Bend your head," she said.

"Ma'am?" He eyed the olive oil warily. It explained why his hair was so greasy: she'd been anointing him in his sleep.

"The Lord will heal you," she said, and a light came into her eyes he hadn't seen before.

Johnny had never understood how he knew, without looking, that there was another presence in the room. It was a kind of spiritual feeling. This was not the presence of the Lord, however, with which he had a slight familiarity. It was Lucy's husband, Everett. Suzanne had run out to the broiler house, bringing her father the news of Johnny's miraculous awakening.

Everett was a short, thick man with a shock of black hair that flopped off the crown of his head like a rooster's comb, and no sideburns. The haircut made Everett look ridiculous, but he was serious, too, and angry. It was almost as though he felt inclined to knock your head off for thinking he looked ridiculous.

He pulled up a folding chair and bent near like a dentist, staring down on Johnny with pale gray eyes. He smelled of ammonia and sour mash. He sat back, his inspection completed, and brought a fist down into his palm. "Johnny Bell," he said. "Guess you been a pretty sick boy."

"We was gonna pray," Lucy protested, holding high her bottle of olive oil.

Everett ignored her. "Somethin' in the headlights—goat, deer—and I swerved. That animal saved your life."

"It was the work a the Lord," Lucy said.

Everett smiled and didn't look quite so mean. "You was completely outta your head when I picked you up. And you kicked like an ole billy."

"Yes, sir."

"Now, we ain't clear on who you are. Suzanne, she come out to me there in the broiler house, she says, 'Daddy, he's an orphan.' That so?"

"I reckon."

"What you mean, 'I reckon?' Near as I can figure, you lived up over the bluff somewheres, maybe in that ole abandoned place?"

"Yes, sir."

"You didn't live there *alone*."

"George Bell . . . my grandfather . . . it was his place from a long time ago. The old homeplace. We came from Brownsville, Texas."

Everett settled back. "Long way from Texas to Missouri."

"Yes, sir." Under the blankets Johnny pinched one leg. It helped him to hold back his tears.

"Too soon," Lucy said, putting a hand on her husband's arm. "He's been through an awful trial, Everett, and I don't believe he's well."

Everett grew quiet. At last he said, "We'll work this thing out, Johnny. I called Sheriff Harpster. He's a good man. A veteran."

"Yes, sir."

Suzanne came in with his supper on a tray, and Johnny fought back tears yet again. Only his grandmother had ever brought him food like that, and anyhow a grown man would have cried, offered such a meal. There was home-made bread and a bowl of chicken soup. Potato salad! Lime pickles! And more goat's milk, but Johnny believed he could get used to it. He would have thanked Suzanne for the food, but she never met his eyes. She kept yanking at her hair.

Lucy's voice rose in prayer, and Johnny thought of all those churches in Oklahoma and Arkansas, where there was always some old woman playing the piano. People ran up and down the aisles and spoke in tongues. *Bippity bippity bippity,* the people said. *Kohala ma shigima chi.*

"Jesus brought you in outta the storm and saw fit to let you live," Lucy said. "He has a work planned for you like all of us. Say, 'Help me, Lord.'"

Johnny bowed his head and here came that olive oil again. "Help me, Lord," he said, and he could not have argued the point. He needed help.

Next morning Johnny sat on the kitchen steps, which were on the south side of the house in a spot of sun. The gravel in the driveway glistened with melting snow, and every now and then a heavy icicle broke off the broiler house. A red throw rug flapped on the clothesline and reflected like a flag in the windshield of Everett's big flatbed truck. Blackbirds fought over a piece of ground where chicken feed had spilled, and a tomcat stalked the blackbirds, his tail held high like some mighty predator's.

Now and again there was a banging from the broiler house where Everett worked, but Johnny didn't want to visit with him. The man had stomped through the house in early morning, cursing the chicken business. No one dared speak.

Around ten a dark blue Lincoln drew up, and Reverend Larkin waved. He owned the feed mill where Johnny had sold walnuts in the fall. Larkin franchised Everett and Lucy's broilers—and everyone else's. He'd known George Bell in long-ago days.

Johnny pulled up his collar and hurried around the corner of the house, trying to act natural. Reverend Larkin had been kind, but at the moment Johnny couldn't abide being told how sad the reverend was about George Bell's death and bowing his head in a moment of remembrance.

Larkin parked outside the feed room by Everett's Caterpillar tractor and walked into the broiler house, his back pitched at an angle to offset his gut. He wore a brown suit coat and a straw hat. It was warmer today, and perhaps Larkin had put on the hat in the cheery hope of spring, but it made him look like a carnie.

As he opened the door, a broiler the catchers had missed squawked and flew past him. It was the bird's first taste of freedom, but it had no use for it. It huddled in a clump of rags under the Caterpillar, shuddering from the cold.

Then the sheriff drove up in a big Plymouth with high tail fins. The car was black and looked fast. He stared hard at Johnny and nodded.

Before the sheriff could enter the broiler house, Everett and Reverend Larkin came out. Johnny glanced at the men anxiously and then stepped into the yard, pretending interest in a chewed-up tennis ball. He bounced it off the propane tank, ran out for a catch, and threw again.

Everett and the reverend argued. The sheriff hung back, cupped his hands around a match as he lit a cigarette, and watched them with brown eyes that bulged a little. He grinned, but Johnny didn't assume he was amused. Policemen scared him.

"Lotta risk," Reverend Larkin said, grabbing his hat with a gust of wind. "As it was, your meat averaged three point one per bird—"

Everett fingered a check. "That's good."

"It's excellent, Brother Everett. Twenty thousand birds went out Friday night, and that was best in the Co-op. Reason I decided to bring out the check. To offer congratulations for a job well done."

"But then—"

"Your meat was good. But what hurt you—I mean, besides what hurt all of us: bottom dollar prices; wish we'd get somebody in a high office who'd take the plight of the family farmer to heart—what really hurt you was your feed conversion. More than fifty-one per hundred. Some wastage there, the figures don't lie, Brother Everett. As it was, you did fine, but I don't need to tell you, that's a high rate. Mornin', Sheriff."

"Charley."

He didn't call him "Reverend," Johnny noticed, but Larkin gave the sheriff a wink all the same and brought forth a lame joke like preachers were supposed to do. "Law out here! You got a still up on that bluff, Brother Everett?"

"Corn mash and chicken shit," Everett said.

The sheriff laughed, but then they all went silent and looked at Johnny.

The reverend stepped near, almost as though he meant to kiss Johnny, and put his hands on his shoulders man-to-man. "I'm so sorry for your troubles," he said, and Johnny knew he was, but squirmed from his reach.

Everett was surprised. "You know our—"

"Yes, yes," Larkin said, dropping into his concerned preacher's voice. "Matthew 25:40, even unto the least of these, Brother Everett. I appreciate what you and Sister Lucy have done here."

Everett grunted. "Wouldn't be good for anything at all, couldn't help in a time like that."

It was like he had the St. Vitus Dance, except that instead of twitching his nose and making strange noises, Johnny broke into tears. He hated himself. He would go through life crying every time he saw a newborn baby or dead possum on the road. He ran a few steps, then stopped in the driveway, and turned about, not knowing what to do. The *least* of these, he thought. I'm the least of these.

"Sad business," Everett went on, studying Johnny, and no longer angry. He nodded toward the house. "We could all sit in the kitchen, Sheriff. There's some coffee left from breakfast."

"You two go ahead," the sheriff said. "I'll talk to this young man first."

The sheriff led Johnny through the broiler house to the far end, turned over two buckets, and they sat where the sun streamed in. Johnny waited for the man to speak, but he merely grinned, lit a cigarette, and blew smoke. George Bell and Johnny had had some troubles with the law, and Johnny was frightened he'd be hauled off to jail. He couldn't sit still and stepped to the broad implement door facing south.

He could see a long way, and so much space calmed him. He'd walked all over the land, scrounging for walnuts and easy firewood. There were two short valleys, the eastern of which had been in corn, and the western—rough, rocky land—good only for goat pasture. Dividing the valleys was a bluff covered with oaks and cedars twisting up out of a jumble of limestone that had been peeling away back when the Osage Indians owned it.

On the ridge behind the bluff lay George Bell's place. It wasn't a week ago, Johnny thought, that he sat by the kitchen range, his feet propped on the oven door, and read *Tarzan of the Apes.*

"You a tennis player?"

He'd almost forgotten the sheriff still sat there. "What?"

"Saw you with that tennis ball. Sometimes, I play tennis with Bob Taney, he's the algebra teacher. Have you had algebra?"

"No, sir."

"You'd be what, maybe seventeen?"

"I'll be sixteen February 2."

"You're big. Sophomore?"

He'd missed a lot of school and was only in the ninth grade, give or take. "Yes, sir."

"Bob was sayin' how Red Buck needs a tennis team. The girls go for tennis players, he said. Almost magical."

"They like football players," Johnny said. Brownsville flashed in his mind, and cheerleaders in the hall.

"No doubt about that. Name's Joel Harpster, by the way."

They shook hands, but Johnny still couldn't think of anything to say. The sheriff made a production of lighting yet another cigarette, reminding Johnny of George Bell doing the same thing, and in much the same way. The old man was mostly wrinkles, though, and tobacco had made his voice raspy.

"Chicken house stinks, don't it?" the sheriff said at last.

"Yes, sir."

"Not like pigs, though."

"No, sir."

"No correlation there between the strength of the manure, however. Pig shit is weak. Chicken shit gives you big red tomatoes."

"Yes, sir."

"That all you can say? Yes, sir? No, sir?"

"No, sir."

"What's your opinion of Everett and Charley Larkin?"

"They don't get along."

He motioned to the rafters. "What's your opinion of Everett as a farmer?"

"Seems like he did awright with his chickens."

"Good as you can do with somebody else's chickens. His heart's not in it. He's always wantin' to traipse off somewhere and make big money with his bulldozer. Big ideas, big money, that's Everett, only don't you tell him I said so. What you think of Charley Larkin?"

A week or so later, the point of Harpster's questions would sink in. The sheriff had already talked both to Everett and the reverend and was conducting his version of a child custody interview on behalf of Joshua County. The least of these needed a roof over his head.

"George Bell knew Reverend Larkin way back," Johnny said at last. "What he thought was that it ain't such a good idea to mix business and religion."

"Not to mention politics." Harpster laughed. He snuffed out his cigarette and stretched his arms high. "Which I won't. I realize you're from Texas, but where do you think your home is, Johnny Bell?"

Johnny studied his shoes. "I don't know."

"I walked back to your place. What a terrible thing to see."

Johnny couldn't lift his eyes.

"You want a cigarette?"

"Maybe I—"

"Don't mean to corrupt a minor, but just this once." Harpster lit two Pall Malls and handed one over. "The brand nobody wanted over in Vietnam," he said. "I got to smokin' 'em because they were always available."

The Pall Mall stuck to Johnny's lips. When he tried to pull it away, it slid from his fingers and went out in a little puddle of snow water. He looked up in agony. "My granddad—"

The sheriff nodded. "Your grandfather was George Bell."

"Yes, sir."

"Sorry. Never saw such a thing. But this is my job; I've got to do it."

"Yes, sir." Outside, a herd of goats pulled at the grass where the snow had melted. The billy stared at him with his yellow eyes and an old man's white beard. Johnny put his fingers through the chicken wire and pulled in a long breath of cold air. "George Bell and me," he said. "We was livin' down in Texas with my Grandma. And then she died."

Chapter Two
Walking to Missouri

What's a farmer do when he's cast upon the world? George Bell slapped up dry wall for many years, until his knuckles were swollen and his back went out. He worked as a maintenance man for a California community college. He nailed on roofs, shored up sagging porches, mowed yards, and hauled trash. Sometimes, he junked out several lawn mowers, made a new one, and sold it.

His wife, Mary, always seemed to find work as a maid, or in school cafeterias. No matter how poor the soil, she'd scratch out a kitchen garden and put up tomato juice, sweet corn, and green beans.

George drank some, but was seldom in an argument, worked hard, and saved his money for the most part. But he hated regular jobs, and he hated cities. Sooner or later, when the lights of prosperity gleamed on a far shore, George would abandon ship.

He'd load everything Mary and he owned into the Studebaker truck and drive back to Missouri, where he'd invest their savings in some rundown farm. He'd buy a few cattle, plant some milo, and build fences. He was born in the Missouri Ozarks, and no other place would do.

You'd have thought that one of those farms would have turned a profit. Mary could have worked in town for the little cash they needed, and they could have fulfilled her dream of a "permanent home." But a drought followed George: the ponds went dry, no one could make hay, and the livestock had to be slaughtered. If the weather cooperated, then half the town got laid off when the shoe factory moved to Mexico. George and Mary would sell out at auction, load up the Studebaker truck again, and travel back to the city.

Besides Missouri, they lived in Florida, California, and Tennessee, none of which Johnny remembered very well. Then there was Texas.

About the time Kennedy was elected, Mary threatened to leave George Bell if he didn't find her a permanent home. Possibly it was an empty threat, since, unsatisfactory as he was, George Bell was all she had. But he, too, was weary of traveling, of seeing every fine place from the kitchen, the loading dock, and the motel parking lot. They stopped at a vegetable stand, counted their cash, and studied the map. They were in Brownsville. They might have gone farther, but ahead of them was the border, alien and frightening, and Missouri lay half a continent behind them.

"If a man don't have any money, he should at least have the sense to live in a warm climate," George Bell announced proudly, like an explorer in one of Johnny's schoolbooks.

Both George and Mary were drawing Social Security by then, and both had arthritis and half a dozen other ailments, so somewhere warm and dry suited them. They wouldn't fit into Latino culture, but they didn't fit anywhere.

They rented a shotgun house with an acre of land, grapefruit trees, and plenty of shade from live oaks. The house set down between the Port of Brownsville, where the boats came in full of bananas and pineapples, and the town dump. The dump had strategic value. "I allus been able to fix things," George Bell explained.

George Bell had his dump, and Mary had her permanent home, and life was good for several years. Johnny liked the school well enough, though three-quarters of the students were Mexicans who spoke Spanish most of the time and didn't speak to him at all. He had one friend, another misfit named David Bareiro. David was a short, plump kid embarrassed by eczema, and perhaps Johnny was his protector, though they weren't bothered much. Neither had anything anyone wanted.

David was a doctor's son, and his family lived downtown in an old rock house, behind tall, whitewashed walls that David's father claimed absorbed the heat. Johnny stood under the trellis, dodging bees from the bougainvillea until David emerged, his mother's high-pitched dos and don'ts, *en español,* nipping at his heels. They bicycled out to the Boca Chica Loop, where the army had camped in the Mexican War, and smoked cigarettes. They looked for buried treasure like they were littler kids than they were.

Sometimes, they went down among the boats, where it seemed there was always a big, grinning deckhand from Honduras or Panama, who threw them a bunch of bananas. They tied bananas on their carriers and took them to Mary, who made banana cream pie. They sat under the grapefruit tree, eating the pie and drinking iced tea, planning their next adventure. Then—the previous spring, about ten months ago—Mary died.

George Bell explained that Mary had lived a long life, and that it was time for her to go. He brought out the "family Bible," read something about flowers being cut down and men being born of troubled women, and insisted Johnny accompany him to the Baptist Church.

The church was hot, the preacher was a bore, and Johnny began to doze. Suddenly, accompanied by a tinkly piano, the old man hopped up and went forward. Strangers prayed over him, and he sobbed openly. He announced that he was a failure in life, was full of grief, and that he needed Jesus for strength to carry on.

He'd been washed clean, and that was a good thing because he wasn't long for this earth. He saw his life in a different way now. He meant to set Johnny up so that he'd never have to suffer or go without like Mary had. George Bell had the bluest eyes of anyone Johnny had ever known. They glowed with the presence of the Lord.

Hardly a week later, a Social Security check arrived, and George Bell drove over to Matamoros for a tour of the cantinas. He came home cradling a bottle, and sang, "You Are My Sunshine" all day. He played Hank Williams songs on scratchy records he'd found at the dump. He played Lefty Frizzell. He played Jimmie Rodgers, danced down the hall, and splendidly fell. He played the Weavers singing "Irene, Good Night," and cried. "Mary liked that song," he said.

Johnny missed his grandmother but didn't understand all the carrying-on. He worried about what next to eat. Mary used to issue him thirty-five cents for his school lunch, but he could get by on potato chips and save the rest for the movies. Never mind the potato chips; he had no lunch at all. He lined up for commodities like Mary taught him and ate government cheese and raisins most of the month. Sometimes, he caught fish under the bridges. He could have shot George Bell, the old goat, for drinking up supper.

"Mary was a *kind* woman," George Bell said, looking at Johnny with his bleary blue eyes. "I loved her with all my heart."

Johnny considered this. Mary wasn't particularly kind, though she wasn't cruel. She was abrupt, and practical. As for the love that filled his dear old grandfather's heart, perhaps, but then the question would have been how large his heart was.

"Always take care of your teeth," Mary used to say, and she'd smile to show hers, which she claimed were originals minus one. But neither she nor George Bell trusted doctors, and by the time Mary went to see one it was too late. This, too, was practical, because Mary *knew* it was too late. She reasoned that if she'd seen a doctor earlier, he'd only have doped her up, and strung her along, and took her little wad of money.

She died of hardening of the arteries, and high blood pressure, and finally, a stroke. But both Johnny and the old man knew that the true verdict was that she was worn out. And that she'd lost interest. In George Bell, certainly, but even in Johnny.

When he was little and had a cold, she'd make him breathe in Vicks over the stove, and then tuck him in, and bring him celery soup. But she had no insight into the life of a teenager. "You just think you got problems, Johnny Bell," she said.

Pimples sprouted like turnip seeds on his face, and he was convinced that his nose was abnormally large, but Mary had no sympathy. "You have a warm bed and enough to eat," she said. "That's all that matters."

Toward the end Mary didn't pretend anymore that her life with George Bell had been a good one, or even that he had done the best he could by her. Johnny came down the hallway quietly once, and caught her staring at George Bell, asleep in his ratty old chair. There was a look of contempt on her face so pure it made Johnny think of murder.

She took no solace from religion, and so there weren't any old cronies from Sunday School at her funeral. There was George Bell, David Bareiro, Johnny, and the funeral director. With her cheeks rouged, Johnny hardly recognized her.

"You take a mule," George Bell said. He lay on the mildewed couch on the screened-in porch, where they caught a breeze from the Gulf under the oak trees, and you could find your breath. He sipped his whiskey, which he drank openly now, and waved a hand to keep off flies. They'd all gathered when the rain began and stayed when it stopped.

He wore bib overalls like he always did. Not his good pair, and they hadn't been washed since Mary died. "Used to have a team," he went on.

"Mules," Johnny said automatically, having heard this story before. He waited for his commodity potatoes to boil.

"It was 1933. Hail, you couldn't get a job nowheres, but they put up an announcement at the courthouse, didn't make no difference if you was a Democrat or a Republican, they needed summer crews to mow grass. Men lined up around the square and they all needed work more 'an I did. But for some reason they hired me."

"How you met Grandma," Johnny said.

"Mowed a hunert miles, between West Plains and Springfield on U. S. 60. Maude and Isabel, good ole gals."

Johnny spread commodity butter on the potatoes. He didn't offer to share. "Your mules?"

"They knew just where to stop! They'd plod along all day, then pick things up an hour from Plunge Crick. Couldn't hold 'em back. Stake 'em down, give 'em some oats, they was happy. Find a woman like that."

"You did," Johnny said.

The old man didn't hear. He held his glass to the light and shook his head sadly. "The country was wild then."

"The country was wild then," Johnny said, in a Mickey Mouse voice.

"Hardly any cars—"

"No candy bars—"

"—and if you *had* one you couldn't afford gasoline. I'd get under the cottonwoods and cook up some crappie and sun perch, and smoke a pipe, and fall asleep lookin' at the moon. Didn't know how good I had it.

"One day I was workin' down near Sumac Springs, the road was cut outta the bluff there, and you had to watch you didn't get too near the edge. I looked up and there she was on the fence, little bitty thing. Great big eyes. She'd never been outta Josha-way County and I told her I'd take her to California."

"You never went to California."

"Yes, we did, Johnny Bell." His blue eyes grew moist. "Only not right then, a course, not at that precise moment."

Next day Johnny caught twenty pan-sized mullets with a net. It was enough to fire up the smoker, but George Bell was too drunk and dreamy, anymore, to do such useful work, and Johnny couldn't find any wood but palm fronds. He gave half the mullets to a neighbor and fried the rest. He ate the mullet with the last of his potatoes and didn't know when he'd eat next.

"You got any money?" he asked.

George Bell fished in a breast pocket and produced a wrinkled five with tobacco crumbs all over it. It was a fortune, worth a pound of hamburger, ten pounds of potatoes, some bread, maybe even some cheese.

"That all?"

The old man blew smoke and sighed. He unfolded a newspaper clipping for *Tarzan the Magnificent*. First the money, then a movie? Something's up, Johnny thought.

"This Gordon Scott, he ain't the real Tarzan," George Bell said. "Johnny Weissmuller was the real Tarzan. He could swim along faster than a woman runnin' on the shore."

"He was good, awright," Johnny said. "Only he got *old*."

"Yes," the old man said, his blue eyes sad. "They made him into Jungle Jim."

They hadn't seen a movie together since Johnny was thirteen, when his grandfather, to save twenty cents, had told the clerk that Johnny was only eleven. Johnny was already five foot ten, three inches taller than George Bell. They'd hardly reached their seats when a high school boy who worked there came down the aisle and asked them to leave. Roger, his name was. He was a gringo like Johnny, but also a football player. Once Johnny saw him in the hall kissing a cheerleader named Rita. Johnny stared at the shame and waste of it all. So beautiful a girl, so mistaken.

George Bell stood on principle, refusing to pay for two adults, but he hadn't been able to persuade Johnny to go to the movies again. Still, it was hard to resist Tarzan, and he was playing in the fancy old theater downtown, where they weren't branded men.

Better still, Johnny held onto his five for another day, because the old man bought him a fine enchilada lunch, with lime *paletas* for dessert. With full bellies, they sat in the front row because of how nearsighted George Bell was. It was Friday afternoon, and they were alone in the theater, except for some ancient Mexican women wearing veils and long gloves. About halfway through, during a love scene, George Bell said, "What would be your opinion 'bout headin' for Missouri?"

Here it was, Johnny thought. He should have held out for more than a five. "Another worthless farm—"

"Naw, naw. I'm too old to work like that again, Johnny Bell. I'm talkin' 'bout the home place—where your mama was born. What would be your opinion 'bout goin' home?"

Not *my* home, in Johnny's opinion. He pictured a white house, deep in the woods with a great red moon shining down. His mother, a little girl, lay in bed, the shadows of pine branches moving across her sheets. If she stayed awake long enough, she'd see the deer come to her window, to lap at the block of salt a much younger George Bell, her father, had put out for his cows.

A pretty picture, but it belonged to his mother. Rather, his grandmother, describing what a good girl his mother had been. She died when he was four. A tornado bore down on the pasture and she was struck with a tree limb, but they found Johnny unharmed, crying in the sunshine. There weren't any witnesses, but Mary always claimed that his mother, Kathleen, had given her life for her child's. She'd gone straight to Heaven, saintly and pure. This happened near Red Buck, Missouri, on the place George Bell called home.

Johnny didn't remember the tornado, and he didn't remember his mother, for that matter, though now and then he dreamed of her, a pretty woman off in the distance. Sometimes, her lips moved, but he could never make out her words.

His father's name was Joe Daws, and George and Mary didn't like to talk about him. There weren't any photographs.

All Johnny had ever been told was that Joe was a hero in the Korean War, and before that an evangelist around "home." He meant to marry Kathleen but the navy drafted him. He didn't become a sailor but a navigator on bombers. He was blown up over the Sea of Japan and so the casket they buried in Red Buck didn't have anything in it.

But there you were: they'd find nothing in Missouri but dead people. The ones who weren't dead were ignorant, and poor, and didn't have enough to eat.

Johnny tried to sound pitiful. Occasionally, the tactic had worked with his grandmother. "I won't ever finish school."

"You ain't been to school since Mary died," George Bell said. "And they got schools in Missouri, Johnny Bell."

Johnny watched the movie for a while. Life was much simpler in the jungle. When you were hungry, you plucked a banana. Wrestling an alligator looked troublesome, but it didn't come up all that often. Generally speaking, the most complicated thing Tarzan had to do was to rescue beautiful women. They were always dropping by because of the safaris. "You know I have trouble makin' friends."

"People in Red Buck knew your daddy well, with his preachin'. Your mama, why she was a popular girl. You'll be acquainted 'fore you know it."

That night Johnny studied the map: bold red lines for highways between cities, crooked blue ones going to forgotten places, of which Missouri seemed to have more than its share. In *Tarzan of the Apes*, the Frenchman D'Arnot showed Tarzan the map of where they must go to reach France and the beautiful Jane Porter. Tarzan stretched his fingers across North Africa and the Mediterranean and said, "Not so far." Johnny knew more about geography than that, but Missouri seemed as far away as France.

The way George Bell put it, going home was for Johnny's benefit, but Johnny couldn't comprehend this. In Brownsville they had a grapefruit tree and a fig tree in the front yard, and once Johnny had grown a pineapple. He could wander up and down the ocean, picking up sponges and cocoanuts and other useful things. When he could afford a rifle, he planned to head up the Rio Grande and shoot turkeys, and deer, and Catalina goats, and maybe later he'd wander down into Mexico. But Missouri was a cold place full of hillbillies, and he had no future there.

He'd refuse to leave. He'd hide on Padre Island until George Bell had gone. He'd go around shirtless and barefooted, in one of those straw hats that was all splinters. He'd net mullet and dig clams and take the tourists exploring. One day, he'd meet a sad-eyed Mexican girl, and they'd live by the sea forever.

"That Studebaker truck'll never make it," he said. "It's got a burnt intake valve and it's blowin' oil like fog."

"Exhaust valve," George Bell said. "Which ain't as bad. But you're right. That truck might not make it."

"Well?" Johnny had him now. "What'll we do then?"

The old man smiled. "Walk."

Along the coast they grew pecans and tangerines, and the land was clear and flat, and once in a while it rained. But if you headed north, you were soon in dry country, where nothing grew but prickly pear and mesquite. If you were fool enough to keep traveling, before long you'd reach a range of low black mountains, deserted except for coyotes and javelinas and maybe a jackrabbit or two.

The Studebaker truck hovered near death. First, the water pump went out, then a fan belt, then a radiator hose, then a master cylinder so that they drove without brakes for half a day. Unless you counted armadillos, Johnny thought, there was nothing to brake *for*.

Then all the ball bearings fell out of the U-joint and they stopped. Because he didn't trust Johnny with his money—or perhaps, to return—George Bell hitch-hiked some sixty miles to Uvalde, leaving Johnny by yet another of those dry rivers. This one, the Frio, had some pools. Frio meant "cold" in Spanish, but Johnny had never visited such a hot place.

They'd brought potatoes, canned soup, and dried beans from Brownsville, so he had food enough. He rose at dawn and made coffee. Through the morning he lay low under the mesquites, reading his Tarzan story. Sometimes, he called to the roadrunners and fearless grackles that scrounged the camp, but they ignored him.

Mid-afternoon, with the grasshoppers jumping all around him in the brittle grass, and keeping an eye out for rattlers, he hiked down to the riverbed. It stretched a quarter-mile wide, nothing but round stones that the sun had bleached white. The stones were hot. Sweat poured off him and immediately evaporated. The sun shone so brightly he couldn't see, and he closed his eyes for twenty steps, then opened them to get his bearings.

At last he reached the pool where he drew water every day. He stripped naked, dove for the cool center, and gasped for breath. The cold water filled him with joy and he laughed. His laughter echoed under the big arch of the highway bridge and made him feel lonely, as if he'd been cast in a *Twilight Zone* episode in the aftermath of a nuclear war, and he was the only man left on earth. He swam for an hour, then sat on the white rocks and fished, using grasshoppers for bait. Toward evening the perch bit eagerly.

When the mosquitoes dive-bombed him, he ran back across the stones, which looked like a million little moons in the night-time. He stoked up his fire to fry fish, and warmed a can of beans, and wished for Mary's iced tea. By then the air had cooled, and since he didn't have a radio, or light to read by, he wrapped himself in George Bell's blanket, looked up at the moon, and let the owls and whippoorwills sing him to sleep. During the night, deer passed through, and one time a dozen wild hogs. They pushed against the truck and snorted and squealed until he feared for his life, but at last they meandered away.

Sometimes, a goat visited as he was eating, drawing near the tail gate like a friendly neighbor. The old billy she belonged to stood under the mesquites, lifting his head in the air, snorting. The other does ran into the brush and back again, but Johnny's doe kept looking at him with her soulful eyes. In a few days she let him pet her. He quartered two withered apples for her and after that fed her potatoes.

"I wish you could speak English," he said. "It's kinda crazy around here."

"Bra—aaat," she said.

"Or Spanish," he said. "*¿Cómo estás?*"

He was down to four potatoes when a tanker truck stopped and released George Bell. They spent the afternoon hammering on the U-joint and attaching the drive shaft again.

"It'll be winter before we get to Missouri," Johnny said.

"Hand me that ratchet wrench." George Bell paused to wipe the sweat from his eyes. It must have been 120 degrees under the Studebaker. "Winter!"

"It'll be cold, and we ain't got no money, or anyhow I don't, and there ain't much to eat. Weren't you the one said that if a man don't have any money, he should live where it's warm? I mean, we could go next spring if you still wanted to."

"Might not live that long, Johnny Bell. Shove on that drive shaft."

The thing clunked into place.

"You think I care 'bout this trip," he said, panting, blinking sweat away as he tightened bolts. "But my life is over. It'll be *your* place, Johnny Bell. Your inheritance."

In the morning they headed north again, and Johnny could see for a hundred miles: sagebrush, prickly pear, and acres of bleached sand, with now and then a caved-in house and a broken windmill. All the people must have been hiding.

At last they started to see trees again, and pasture, but they avoided San Angelo and Abilene because George Bell didn't like driving in cities. A policeman might stop them for one of the busted things on the truck, and say, "Sir, have you been drinkin'?" even as he reached for his handcuffs. They steered by the stars, stopping in towns that had all but blown away during the Great Depression.

Johnny kept score, whether the church or the saloon was the last to go: saloons ran a little ahead. The old man disappeared for a while, leaving Johnny to scrounge in the treeless city park with its broken swings and benches, or wander inside the gas station. It seemed the identical, snuff-dipping old woman kept moving along ahead of them. Everywhere, she stood guard over her dusty Zagnuts.

The sun baked Johnny's brains until he forgot where he was from, where they were going, who he was. He heard the tires slapping through the asphalt sticky from the sun, and thought he'd melt. His saintly mother was in Heaven but her son had descended to hell.

Johnny drove for a while, and nearly fell asleep, and then the old man drove, and did fall asleep. He ran onto the shoulder and Johnny grabbed the wheel and turned the truck onto the highway again. They were hardly doing thirty but it alarmed them, because a great gully yawned below, and no one ever would have found them.

Then one day Johnny woke and low, green hills crowded in, so that he could no longer see to the end of the world. Cottonwoods bent in the wind, high above the creeks, and willows clung to sand bars. Cattle stood in the shallow, red water. That's all you needed for life, Johnny thought: water. "Where are we?"

"South of Lawton. That was the Red River we crossed."

Oklahoma, he thought. Your first stop outside of hell.

They camped that night down in a wash a hundred feet from a red dirt highway, by a silent lake. The water was full of alkali, George Bell explained, and hardly anything grew around it. Frogs croaked weakly but no fish jumped. This part of Oklahoma was green but nearly as deserted as Texas. When dark came Johnny climbed a sand dune and couldn't see even one light in the distance.

But the heat had gone. His fingers and ears tingled with cold, and he could see his breath in the air. Everything was bright and spooky in the moonlight. This was the lone prayer-*ree,* he thought, and as if he needed proof, coyotes across the lake made a woeful serenade. Behind him, in the woebegone hills, their girlfriends yipped in answer.

George Bell hovered near the fire, drinking his doctored coffee and smoking, rubbing one leg. Johnny heated lima beans and ate them slowly with crackers, thinking of smoked mullet, and potatoes, and orange marmalade.

"Well, Missouri," George Bell said at last. It was as though Johnny was supposed to ask questions, but he couldn't muster any interest in that place where you had to show them.

George Bell climbed into the truck bed. He began to snore and Johnny thought he was pickled for the night, but then he sat up and called, "Mary!" Laboriously, he crawled from the truck and went up the road to urinate, his shadow limping along a hundred feet ahead. "Lord God Almighty," he shouted out. He threw his bottle, and it skittered toward the lake. When he returned, his eyes glowed like tiny blue fires. He crawled onto the truck again and poured a splash of whiskey, downed it, lit a cigarette. He broke into a fit of sneezes, threw the cigarette away, and pulled up his blankets.

Finally, there was silence on the prairie.

Johnny built up the fire with sagebrush and sat reading *Tarzan of the Apes.* He had reached the part where Tarzan learned the truth about his identity, forcing him to give up his beloved Jane. It seemed to Johnny that Tarzan was out on the prairie somewhere, heroic, of course, but also lonely. "It ain't so," Johnny would tell him, if he staggered into their camp. "Your mother wasn't an ape!"

Cold, Johnny crawled onto the truck seat, arranged a pillow over the door handle, and wrapped his feet in a blanket. He sat up to a yip and screaming: the coyotes had moved to the nearby sand dune and were looking over the camp. Their crazy yowling trailed off.

The old man woke again. "Where's that bottle?"

"Grandpa—"

"There." He coughed and took another nip. "Cures colds."

"You shouldn't drink so much."

"Cain't afford to eat." He sighed, and his tone changed. "We get to Missouri, I'll get saved."

"Again!"

"Down deep I allus been a religious man. Mary, she'd didn't hold with it, and there was no finer woman on this earth. But you know what the Bible says about bein' unevenly yoked."

"Huh?"

"Go to sleep, Johnny Bell. You'll need your strength for Arkansas."

They sailed eastward. Johnny's driving had improved until he'd grown more skilled than the old man, but the sky and land seemed the same on the horizon, and he couldn't stay awake. He pinched himself and stuck his head into the wind. Every once in a while, George Bell drew a cup of water from their thermos, threw it on Johnny's face, and giggled when Johnny jerked upright.

The old man opened pork and beans and praised them as if they were chocolate-covered almonds. "Beans are one a the great bargains in life," he said. "Great Northern beans, black-eyed peas. Learned that in the Depression."

"Learned that in the Depression," Johnny said, in his Mickey Mouse voice.

The engine began to run hot, and they stopped in a wind-swept town full of Indians lined up to see Elvis Presley in *Blue Hawaii*. George Bell said they were Cherokees who had arrived here from the Trail of Tears even before he was born. They came all the way from Georgia when the federal government forced them off their farms. Some came up the Arkansas River, and some walked through Missouri. Many died on the way because they didn't even have beans to eat.

"How could they just force 'em off their land like that?"

"They was Injuns," George Bell said.

Behind the wheel again, Johnny ate some crackers and a piece of cheese that had nearly spoiled from the sun, and the old man smoked, and sipped from his bottle, and fell asleep.

Some girls passed in a fancy new Ford. The one on the passenger's side had blonde hair and blue eyes; she gave the truck a withering glance and said something to the girl driving. That one gunned the motor and swerved sharply, causing dust to rise like brown snow. Johnny had to ease off on the gas so he could see.

Past Tahlequah, the exhaust valve hissed like an angry goose. Hills rose up everywhere and Johnny couldn't maintain their speed. He kept downshifting to second, then reaching third again on flat land. George Bell frowned, as if this were a driving lesson and Johnny was doing something stupid, but then he bit his lip and looked ahead. The engine shuddered and Johnny hit the clutch, crunched into first, rolled backward on the slope. He revved high and eased out the clutch again. The truck crawled to the crest, lisping, firing on five.

George Bell sat up straight.

Going downhill the engine ran smoothly again, and the heat gauge backed off. It was wonderful country, after all those dusty miles. Far below, a crooked blue river flowed, and the hills, the trees, stretched as far as Johnny could see.

"Welcome to Arkansas," said the old man, his blue eyes wide. "Better get up some speed."

Down in the valley, by a field of corn long past its time for harvest, the road hugged the river, and Johnny coaxed the old Studebaker up to sixty. He figured to gain enough momentum for the next hill, but the road curved into a bumpy iron bridge, and he had to downshift to second again. He accelerated and the engine sounded all right, and they climbed around hairpins going on forever. Then there was a bang and he could feel the engine compression seeping away like a last breath. He downshifted to first. He shoved in the clutch, revved high.

"Stomp on it!" said the old man.

The engine died and they rolled backward. The truck veered toward the shoulder, with treetops just under them, then a sheer bluff, and a pool far below. He hit the brake. He shifted to neutral and stepped on the starter. The engine fired, rattled, gasped. Johnny shot it gas and the truck bucked forward a few feet. The engine died again and the truck slipped backward.

"Love a God, Johnny! We—"

He cut the wheel sharply and they veered into a landing where all manner of trash had been thrown. The truck's rear end heaved up and fell hard on a rock shelf.

"Birdbrain kid! If you'd a let me—"

"I never drove in hills before."

"Just remember who done this, big boy. Get out. You . . . get out."

Johnny walked to the bluff. He could hear George Bell grinding the starter but the engine wouldn't fire. The battery stuttered and died.

A tractor tire lay in the grass. Johnny rolled it off the bluff and it went bouncing, bouncing through the rubble below, through the grass, high into flight and then down into the cedars that clung to the hillside. The old man came up and they watched as the tire splashed into the pool. Blackbirds rose like smoke and a red-tailed hawk sailed elegantly over the pasture.

"I'm sorry about that Studebaker truck," Johnny said. "Maybe if we got another battery—"

"It's done." George Bell bent far forward and spat off the bluff. "*Never* had no luck in Arkansas."

*   *   *

George Bell could walk for hours, but with no warning he'd crumple. He sat cursing, rubbing his leg. "Give me your hand, Johnny," he'd say at last, and shakily rise, and grab his old suitcase full of booze—and silver dollars, for all Johnny knew. Finally, the old man reached his pace again, like the dead truck, coming up slowly through the gears.

It seemed to make little difference to him whether they walked or rode, whether they made five miles a day or forty. Drinking was what mattered. Too much and he'd sleep the morning away, but the right amount wound him up somehow, and he could outlast Johnny.

Johnny staggered along with his duffel bag, thinking of the mashed potatoes Mary used to make, and the tapioca pudding, and the macaroni with commodity cheese. Even some of that dried milk would taste good. He'd eat it right out of the box.

Often, they had no breakfast but coffee and maybe a slice of bread. After several frosts, persimmons were tasty, and wormy apples leaned over fences, but little remained in the vegetable gardens. Sometimes, Johnny begged a dollar from the old man, and ate hamburgers when they passed through a town, or bought a few cans of life-giving beans. He ducked into general stores and, if no one looked his way, grabbed a sack of potato chips. He sold pop bottles, and in ten miles of walking he'd have a dozen, but they grew hard to carry. One day when they camped below a city dump, he pawed through busted washing machines and electric fans and vacuum cleaners, yanking out copper wire. He sold twenty pounds at a scrap yard by the railroad tracks and made enough for a feast.

He ate hot dogs, canned spaghetti, and potatoes, and half a loaf of bread remained for fried Spam sandwiches in the morning. He lay back bloated, sipped coffee, and read *Tarzan and the City of Gold*, which he'd found in a box at the dump. This time Tarzan stole the gold from Opar with the help of his loyal Waziri tribesmen, and almost fell in love with the high priestess, La. It should never have happened, but Tarzan had been hit on the head, and lost his memory of Jane Porter.

Even Tarzan couldn't take Johnny's mind off the cold. He built a fire, but winter crouched in the woods now, and the open fire only half warmed him.

"Grandpa," he murmured. Johnny whipped at his arms and jumped up and down. "George Bell!" But the old man was out for the night, whatever warmth he needed drawn from his bottle. Like a baby, sucking on his damn bottle. Perhaps, if he never woke up, Johnny wouldn't care. He plunged into the woods. He dropped into a gully and grove of cedars; the glowing red eyes of deer fastened on him. They coughed and pawed the earth like demons. Tarzan would have jumped on the back of the nearest buck, slit his throat with Lord Greystoke's hunting knife, and eaten the meat raw. But Johnny didn't have a knife and he was scared. He bolted, ran until the cedars caught him, stung him, threw him down.

A light winked through the brush. Johnny climbed to his feet and burst from the cedars onto the stubbles and shattered stalks of a cornfield. The light shone dully from a dozen long chicken houses.

He stepped inside the first and knelt in the dimness. Below, in the pit where droppings fell, a rat stopped in a patch of moonlight, sat up like a prairie dog. Johnny crept onto the catwalk, whatever sound he made masked by the shuddering of the ventilators and the low moan—one great, sleepy whine—of thousands of caged birds.

The catwalk stretched out like a narrow wooden road. An occasional egg rolled from a cage onto a conveyor belt on its long journey toward the light. Johnny followed the belt, crouching. The eggs rolled onto a carpeted table.

A man stood guard, and Johnny jerked into the shadows. But no: the man had fallen asleep in his broken armchair, his feet over a crate, an army blanket pulled to his chest. Fire glowed around the door of a barrel stove, and Johnny crept up to stand near, and turn round and round. A little television fluttered as President Johnson made a speech. Johnny slipped behind the chair, studying the sleeping man's quivering nostrils. Quickly, he filled a bucket with eggs. A chicken sneezed.

"Boy! What?" The man stood. He was big—going to fat, and going bald. "What the hail. You stealin'?"

"I just—"

"Go on." The man plopped back in his chair. "What would I care? Go on. If they think I'm gonna stick around here, way things is, they're full a shit. Good God, *take* 'em. *Steal.*"

"I'll put 'em back." Johnny glanced toward the front door. The man was slow on his feet and maybe he could slip past him. "I'm sorry, sir."

"*Sir!* Where you from?"

"Texas. That ole Studebaker truck give out and we ain't got no money. We're tryin' to get to Missouri."

"Freeze your balls off." The man pointed at the television. "Don't you worry. Won't be no poor people with that genius we got now. 'Mah fellow Americans.' You think *you* got troubles."

"I was kinda hungry, and I—"

"Wife left me, whatcha think about that?"

"I—"

"Better or fuckin' worse, ain't it? Well, she understood the better part. I ain't no rich man, is it my fault?" The big man glared. "I never *stole*. I worked my ass off here, them birds. She wants to drive around in a God damn Cadillac, no skin off my ass. Death do you part, I thought that was the *deal.*"

Johnny stepped toward the door.

"You leavin'? You don't wanna talk to me? You leavin'?"

"Got to, sir."

"Take them eggs. If you'd just *ast* me, good Lord, you coulda took a crate. Know how many chickens we got here? Thirty-four thousand, and every one a them ole biddies lays an egg a day, or we turn her into soup. Lotta eggs, huh?"

"Yes, sir, it sure is." Johnny stood at the door. "Real sorry about your trouble."

The man settled back and pulled up his blanket. "That asshole."

"Sir?"

"Gettin' them boys killed; they oughtta shoot him."

One cold day in the lowlands, a flatbed Dodge pulled in front of them and slowly gained speed. They'd had a ride for twenty miles, and Johnny was hoping for another, but the man and wife looked straight ahead, as though the thin old man, and the thin boy, didn't exist.

On the bed were bales of hay, a chain, bolt cutters, and a girl Johnny's age. She was pretty, though she had a dirty face, and her clothes were as worn as his. Her eyes bore down on him like he'd betrayed her. It was as if she cried out, "Release me!" and Johnny wanted to. He'd take her away like Tarzan had Jane, and they'd live happily ever after in their Ozarks tree house. He ran down the highway, waving. The girl looked about frantically and pulled at her hair. At last, she laughed. He bent at the knees, panting, as the truck wound away and the old man drew slowly even.

His leg was worse, and Johnny was sorry for him, sometimes. Then the absurdity of being out in the cold, walking to Missouri when they could have lived the high life in Brownsville, overcame him.

He turned angrily, the girl's sad eyes making him brave: "Why don't you ever talk to me?"

"What—?" The old man looked blearily at Johnny.

"Say you know I'm *here*. Tell me why we're doin' this crazy thing."

"Wolf's at the door, Johnny." George Bell's blue eyes became as clear as the water off Padre Island, and he nodded emphatically. "I'm gonna be dead soon, and if we was in Texas, what would you have? Nobody gonna tell you what to do on your own place. You'll be set up for life!"

Toward evening, the wind rose and they settled under a bridge, one long arch that said "1936." There were humps of sand, deep water churning around the roots of sycamores, and stately lineside bass all but motionless despite the current.

"How come you to leave that old farm?" Johnny asked. "If it was so wonderful?"

"Drought." His eyes were almost closed. He sucked in smoke and let it go with a long low gurgle. "They talk about the Dust Bowl, but it was pretty near as bad in the Fifties. Clouded over like it was gonna rain, but it never. Trees died—big ole oak trees! Cows would try an' eat them dry leaves. I seen the fire come through the woods, down low. Hit a field a oats and leapt across it like an electric arc. Then come along burnin' slow. Like one a them Ole Testament plagues."

"Did it rain frogs?"

"Never rained at all. So . . . We lit out for California with all the damn Okies. I got on as a maintenance man and we done awright.'"

"I think I'd like it in California."

"Better 'an Texas?"

"That's home. I'm goin' back someday."

The old man was quiet for a time. "It was allus warm there," he said at last, like he was drawing a moral. "I'm gonna miss them pink grapefruit."

They left Jonesboro, where there were pilgrims and paper turkeys in the store windows, and climbed for miles. The mountain stood at the edge of that howling wilderness called the Ozarks. It was late afternoon, cold, with snow flurries, when George Bell dropped to the pavement.

Johnny ran to him and pulled him to the shoulder. "Grandpa—"

"Get a certain age, they oughtta just shoot you. Kindest thing! Sick all the time, food don't taste no good." He sat, rubbing his leg. His eyes burned blue. Feel it. It's like *ice,* Johnny. Ain't that like ice?"

"We should go home."

George Bell stared up the road. "I 'member this hill. They's an S-curve on up there. I had a '32 Chevy with mechanical brakes. We come down all tanked up, and Billy, Billy Jarboe, 'member him? He hit a patch a ice. Well—"

"You can't make it, Grandpa. It's gonna snow. And, and—you can't walk. You won't eat, you drink that awful stuff—"

"Come in on your mother's tit, go out on whiskey. That's probably in the Bible." He laughed, and then, pushing against an oak, brought himself to his feet. "We'll get a ride, Johnny: be there tonight. Sit by the fire and fart." He reached into his coat. "Take my knife down to that clump a hedge trees and cut me a walkin' stick."

"Texas, Grandpa. We could catch the bus!"

"Go on."

As darkness covered the mountain, and they stumbled toward the crest, a Chevy truck came screaming, orange lights flashing. It swerved and roared past; sparks flew up the straight exhausts by the cab. George Bell, leaning on his stick, shuffled onto the shoulder as the thing shrieked back, the two shadows within hollering and waving.

A window rolled down. "Cold night," the driver said.

"Yes, sir," Johnny said.

"Well, ain't he polite," the other man said. "Give that boy a drink."

"Let him be, Carl. He's a good kid."

"Any action up here on this mountain, boy? Where's your sister?"

"It's just me and my gran'dad. I don't know what you mean, action."

The driver revved his engine. "Boy don't know what you mean, Carl."

"Ain't nothin' technical about it. Hail, ain't no action in the whole state a Arkansas. You jackass, why'd we come down here?"

"No action to home. You said, down in Jonesboro—"

"The hail with what I said. Son, you need a ride?"

"Yes, sir. We're tryin' to get to Red Buck, Missouri, and my granddad—"

"From Missouri! Well, hop in, hotshot, we're headed for Ft. Wood. Gonna be soldier boys."

"I don't know what we'd a done if—"

"Christian duty, get people outta Arkansas."

Without a word, George Bell crawled into the bed and burrowed into a mound of hay and dried manure. Johnny hovered near, not knowing what to do, as the truck rolled down the mountain, clawed its way up another. In the cab a bottle passed between the silhouettes, and the truck veered off the shoulder, then sharply left, over the faded yellow line.

The stock rack jangled and the bed swayed like a boat. The wind shrilled. Johnny's hair flew back and water ran from his eyes, but he was a brave man in a noble tale, Tarzan enduring every hardship to save a friend. Then he, too, sank in the hay, his cheeks frozen, and covered his head with a tarp.

Could he still move his toes? If only, when they arrived, Mary awaited, her supper warm.

After a long time, he poked his head into the terrible wind and saw that George Bell had stood. The old man rapped on the glass. How did he know where they were? Even in the darkness, he remembered every creek and hill.

The truck stood rumbling on the grade, its headlights making cones that swirled with snow. Johnny helped the old man to the pavement, crammed his hands inside his coat, and leaped up and down. Off the road, the wind gushed from under a railroad viaduct.

"Boys take care," the driver said, sucking on his cigarette.

"Much obliged," said George Bell. "Don't get yourselves killed over there."

They stumbled under the viaduct and then the old man collapsed in a patch of weeds. "Better work up a fire," he said, his voice no more than a whisper. "Need a fire."

"Is this Missouri? Where's the house?"

"Make a fire, Johnny. I gotta warm up."

He found pieces of railroad ties, dragged them down into a big pile, and broke off an armful of weeds for tinder. His matches kept going out in his frozen fingers, but at last the flame took. He pulled the old man near and covered him with a blanket from out of his suitcase. The old man said nothing.

He discovered bent galvanized sheeting in the gully, straightened it the best he could, and propped it up to cut the wind. He sat shivering while the flames rose, and he thought of the beans in his bag and how wonderful they would taste, and at last he fell asleep.

Chapter Three
Tennis, Anyone?

They taxied the square and parked in front of the Howdy Doody Café, and exactly then, as though they'd been announced, the creamery whistle blew for noon.

The sign for the café—with a puppet on it hoisting a cup of coffee—squeaked in the wind. Tiny pellets of ice bounced off the hood, mixing with the steam that rose from the cooling engine. Sheriff Harpster hadn't spoken on the drive except to answer a call from Deputy Wells about a cross dog out in the county somewhere.

"Don't shoot him, Cecil," he said. "Sizemore thinks more of his dogs than his kids." Then he looked over at Johnny with a grin so wide it seemed forced. "How about a cheeseburger?"

"I don't have any money."

Harpster snorted. "I'll send the bill to Charley Larkin."

The café smelled of grease and cigarettes, but the apple pies on the counter looked appetizing. Johnny found a table and looked about miserably, but soon enough he understood that no one was interested in him. A soft-spoken man had a question about moving a house, and the sheriff told him who to call to get the power lines lifted along his route. Another fellow, meaner looking, wanted to know if a certain bridge over the Piney River would be overhauled like he'd heard, and who would be awarded the contract.

Harpster frowned. "That's still up in the air."

"Sure would like to make a bid."

The sheriff nodded. "I bet you would."

The man dropped his head and retreated.

Shirlene, the waitress, brought their food, and Johnny dug in while she flirted with the sheriff, straightening his collar even though it seemed perfectly straight already. Harpster wasn't pleased with her attentions, though to Johnny she seemed nice. Older women were hard for him to fathom.

"Who's this handsome young man?"

"Name's Johnny Bell," Johnny said, trying to mimic Harpster's aloofness.

Shirlene laughed. "Do you like Johnny Cash, Mr. Bell?"

"Sure."

"He's gonna be in Springfield only I don't have no way to get there."

"That's a shame," Johnny said, eying the sheriff.

Harpster frowned—or no, it wasn't a frown. He looked tough, the way he always looked when he wasn't making the big grin. Was his grin a fake?

Shirlene brought over some ketchup and straightened the salt and pepper shakers and filled their water glasses, and looked at Johnny again as if to say, what's *wrong* with him? Harpster still didn't react, and at last she shuffled off.

The sheriff looked hard at Johnny and got down to business. "Everett has a grown son."

"I ain't met him yet."

"Max is in Vietnam. My point is, Everett could use an extra hand out there, which would be you. I grew up on little places like that. You are *never* done."

Work was all right, Johnny thought, but he wasn't sure how much of Everett's moodiness he could take. "I been thinkin' about joinin' the navy."

Harpster nodded. "Like your father."

"You knew him?"

"Before my time. I remember the revival meetin's, and him preachin'. Big tent down on the fairgrounds. I was in, what, the fourth grade. He was drafted, same as me."

"You were in Vietnam?"

"They had me in Lebanon—I mean the country, not the town—and then I was at Ft. Carson for a while. I was set to get out only it didn't seem like I'd ever done anything, so like a damn fool I volunteered for Vietnam. It is fucked up beyond all recognition, Johnny." He laughed. "Finish school. If you don't wanna stay with the Ogletrees, there's another option."

A crowd of judges and commissioners and lawyers filed in from the courthouse, and several said hello and wished the sheriff well in the upcoming election. Others walked by like he didn't exist, though they were smiling at *someone,* as if practicing a smile. A smiling courthouse woman said hello, and this time the sheriff was interested, and hurried after her before she could reach the restroom. She nodded and smiled some more.

Shirlene tried to fuss over the bill, but the sheriff laid down his money, stepped back to light a cigarette, and glanced at his watch. Somehow the top button of Shirlene's blouse had come undone, and when she bent forward with the sheriff's change, Johnny could see her breasts, or almost.

"You think about Johnny Cash," she whispered.

"I will," Harpster said.

"I know you like him," she said. "I seen you play 'Ring of Fire' on the jukebox."

Harpster grunted and failed to observe Shirlene's blouse. Why was the courthouse woman desirable when Shirlene isn't? Once they were outside, Johnny said, "I think Shirlene likes you."

Harpster flipped his cigarette away. "Put it this way, son: Red Buck's a small town. Would you rather have a girlfriend or a good place for lunch?"

As they turned onto U. S. 60, Deputy Wells reported that he'd had to shoot the dog after all.

"What did I tell you, Cecil? Excuse my radio procedure, but are you fucking deaf?" The sheriff pulled the handset back like he meant to throw it, then thought better of it and slammed the thing into its socket.

"That stupid hillbilly," he said. "You know how many Sizemores there are?"

"I—"

"About twenty-five. Twenty-five Democratic votes that suddenly went Republican." Briefly, the sheriff's face reddened, but then he buried his anger somewhere, and gave Johnny about half of the glorious grin. He pointed out the shoe factory and the creamery, the football field down the hill from the high school, and the park. And then he stopped at the tennis courts, pulled two rackets from the trunk, and proceeded to bat balls over the net.

The sky went gray and it started to snow, not heavily but with some ice in it and the kind of wind that makes you long for dinnertime. Johnny's ears and fingers stung and he thought that playing tennis while snow fell was crazy. A fleeting depression, erratic as the sleet, slid through him. But he grabbed a racket, hit some solid volleys, and even returned one of the sheriff's serves.

Then he ran after a ball he could see was going to hit near the line, slipped on an ice patch, and fell. He lay laughing until the sheriff came over and gave him a hand.

When in the car again, he stole glances at the sheriff, not knowing what to expect: the good guy, the bad guy, or just the guy. They drove north, turning at a fire tower on what looked to be the highest hill in miles. Without speaking, the sheriff poured Johnny a cup of coffee from a thermos and waved him out of the car. As Johnny stumbled away, he heard Harpster chewing out Deputy Wells for making it necessary for the "county" to apologize.

Johnny climbed the slick steps to the first landing of the tower, where a gate blocked his ascent. Still, he could see all of Red Buck, looking bucolic covered in snow. Helplessly, his eyes traced the railroad westward, and spotted the viaduct where he and George Bell had spent a miserable night. He couldn't see the lane into the trees, but made out an indentation where the house had been. He didn't cry. He simply stared and shivered.

They headed back toward the Ogletree farm, the sheriff smoking silently, steering the big car with one finger. The snow fell steadily. Once the car skidded slightly and Harpster slowed. They passed the spot where Everett had yanked Johnny from the drift, and Johnny looked up the ridge line, but couldn't see through the trees.

"There's a car in that old shed a yours," Harpster said, as they turned down the Ogletree lane.

"It was my dad's. A Ford."

"Old flathead eight. It's a '36, I think. Big 16-inch wire wheels. *Might* run—I mean, it's been out of the weather." He came slowly to a stop in the Ogletree driveway. The tires made a sound like when you shift positions on a plastic seat.

"Foster care's for shit," Harpster said.

Johnny didn't know how to react.

"I can speak to it. Old man was never there; then my mom died. One ole boy, he took it to me with an iron bar, and I laid him out. They blamed it on me."

Johnny looked up, holding his tears.

"With Max gone, Everett's in need of a hand. He figures his chickens and goats will get taken care of for the price a feedin' you. But then there's Charley Larkin.

"His motivation is sentimental. He thinks you are your father. He's an upright citizen, no question—"

"Runnin' for sheriff, too."

Harpster grunted. "Let's not hold *that* against him. Nor his gimcrack religion. I'd be the first to say he's a good man."

Snow puffed along between the goat barn and the house and shot out from the drifts on the broiler house roof. Johnny didn't want to leave the warm car. He wanted to eat another cheeseburger and play more tennis with the friendly sheriff, rather than deal with the nasty one who worried about dead dogs and Republicans.

"I'll stay with the Ogletrees," he said, though he could as easily have chosen the preacher. So far, at the Ogletrees, he liked the food.

"Everett it is, then, and we'll be expectin' you to attend school, Mr. Bell."

"Yes, sir."

"And to come in to see me." He smiled crookedly—not exactly the same thing as his grin. Maybe it was real. "Law enforcement is a lonely business."

"Yes, sir," Johnny said. "I guess a person can be popular but still lonely."

He'd heard his grandmother say this, too, but as soon as he'd said it, he wasn't sure it was true. He fumbled for the door. A wave of loneliness passed over him.

The sheriff put the Plymouth in gear again, edged forward, then rolled down his window. "Why did that old man come back here, Johnny? With winter so near?"

"He was sick. He was a lot sicker than I knew. And he said we didn't have nothin' down in Texas, but here—"

"Damndest thing I ever saw. I think—" He shook his head. "I think he was so tanked up he didn't even feel it."

Chapter Four
Hellfire

Up in a pine, like a bird that doesn't know winter has come, a small windmill rattled.

"Kathleen nailed that up there."

Johnny was pleased the windmill had survived, but it was a little girl's toy, and wouldn't put food in his stomach. Still, he tried to picture a warm and happy day with crickets chirping, robins twittering, and his mother calling down from the tree.

"Daddy! Look what I did!"

Wind pushed the toy faster, carrying away his summer fantasy. That old house won't stop the wind, he thought. A lot of the windowpanes were busted out. The screens, orange from rust, had curled up as if someone had taken a can opener to them. The tin roof, also orange, was probably full of holes.

George Bell stomped across the porch, shaking the snow from his boots. "Nice in the summer," he said. "Mary used to sit out here and snap beans." Then his boot broke through a rotten board, and he needed his stick to pull himself upright. He cursed, tore at the plywood covering the door, and disappeared inside. If he hadn't been so cold, Johnny would have laughed.

To make his blood work, he wandered around back and began pulling fallen limbs from the snow. He thought he might find an axe in the sprawling machine shed but couldn't open the door. Even so, he had a high pile of wood and was fumbling with his matches when the old man yelled.

A big wood range stood in the kitchen. George Bell had filled the firebox and found a jug of something that might once have been kerosene. Smoke backed up and clung to the ceiling, and then the flame began to draw.

"Nothin' else, we can sleep in the kitchen." The old man looked mournful. "It never was much of a house. Not a straight line in it. That green oak, you nail it up and I guaran-damn-tee she'll bow."

"We could go home—"

"This *is* home!" George Bell brought a fist down on the dinette table. "Just lackin' any comforts. Come on," he said, and led Johnny into a room that was empty except for three beer bottles by the broken-out window. A brown shock of Johnson grass poked through the rotten flooring. "Kathleen's room. Mebbe you'll wanna sleep here."

Without a bed? There was no moon, no block of salt for the deer. No pine trees whining in the wind. There were trees of another sort—heavy, tall, and bare.

"Walnuts." George Bell patted Johnny on the back, startling him. The old man seldom touched him, except when he was smaller and more of a nuisance, and periodically required a cuffing. Now, slimmed down from life on the road but strong, Johnny hulked over his grandfather, who seemed almost feeble. His touch was distressing.

"Most people, they'd plant fruit trees, hard maples by the house. Dad and me set out them walnuts when I was your age. Takes forty, fifty years to make a log. It's been—it's been—sixty-one years."

"Sell the nuts?"

"Sure. But it's the wood, Johnny, the timber. You can dig up the roots, even, they got a pretty grain called burl they use for gun stocks."

"Enough money to go home on?"

The old man sighed. "Enough to live. To give you a start."

"Let's cut 'em," Johnny said.

Now the fire was roaring, and they returned to the kitchen and hovered near the stove. "When I die and ascend to Heaven," the old man said, lifting his arms, and fluttering his hands as if they were wings. "Do what you want."

The galvanized machine shed had stood the years better than the house, but George Bell's key wouldn't work and Johnny came in through a window, busting it out with the fire poker. Groping in the darkness, he found a hammer and screwdriver, and drove the pins from the entry door. The big implement door remained solid, except for one rotten board, and it rolled free once he'd doused the track in oil and dug out around the bottom.

He found worn-out garden tools, small engine parts, V-belts and flat belts, and various greasy things you'd use on a tractor, such as turnbuckles and lengths of chain and long, heavy bolts. There were plenty of steel buckets—banged up, but they didn't leak. Mice had accounted for the baskets, but a crate or two could be repaired. No point in counting all the cans of paint, transmission oil, and pesticide that had lost their labels, and frozen and thawed so many times Johnny could only guess what was inside. He found a chain hoist, a buck saw, shovels, picks, a posthole digger, and several axes.

And the Ford that had belonged to his dad.

The tires were flat. So much dust and bird shit had congealed that he couldn't see through the windows. When he opened the door, he smelled decay—death, almost. Still, the car wasn't so dirty a man couldn't clean it up.

Hanging on to the hedge stick, the old man lowered himself to a potato crate. "Kathleen allus said, 'My car, my *car,* Daddy—that's the only thing I have of Joe's.'"

"Was it runnin'?"

"I am not a Ford man nor do I like a V-8, but it ran awright. We was short on funds and you couldn't haul nothin' in it, so we left it. Meanin' to come back, like I say, only the drought hung on, and when we finally did arrive, well, you know—Kathleen died in that storm. After that, this place—" His voice trailed off.

"Could we make it run?"

He shrugged. "You can allus make 'em run, Johnny. Depends on how much money you wanna spend—if you wanna replace every part, and in this case, might be hard to *find* parts. It was gettin' to be an old car even for Joe Daws."

George and Mary had stuffed the best of what they couldn't haul into the Ford: curtains Mary had sewn; a cutting board and some butcher knives; saucepans, and a set of dishes; a Coleman lantern; Mason jars, in boxes that had never been opened; blankets wrapped in oilcloth; and books. There were novels by James Oliver Curwood, Harold Bell Wright, and Peter B. Kyne, but best of all was a high school annual from Littleton, Colorado.

Johnny saw his father, at last, in a crew cut, holding a basketball. He stared at the picture for an hour, looked in a mirror, looked again at the picture. Like Tarzan, he had a father.

He cut a piece of hardboard for the broken pane in his mother's window, and stuffed rags through holes in the siding. He swept the floor, laid plywood over the Johnson grass, and made a pallet to sleep on. If he kept a constant fire in the kitchen, and otherwise stayed under the blankets, he remained warm.

He lay leafing through the only thing he'd found of his mother's: a copy of *In His Steps*. On the flyleaf was the red imprint of a mouth where his mother had practiced her lipstick. Beside the mouth was, "To Kathleen from Joe."

The story was about a preacher in Topeka who was too busy to help a passing stranger. The stranger tried to find work but he looked like a bum, and everyone turned him down. At last, starving, he showed up in church service, where he delivered a lecture about helping the down-and-out. "Is that what you mean by following in His steps?" he said and fell over dead.

The preacher knew he'd done wrong. He didn't want to kill any more starving men, so he began asking "What would

Jesus do?" before every major decision, and encouraging his flock to do the same. Pretty soon, the entire country was asking itself what Jesus would do.

As the moon rose, Johnny lay studying the dead kiss. He closed his eyes and imagined muggy summer nights in the bottoms, great wailing and joyful cries under the revival tent, and a Ford V-8 humming over the hills.

The old man paced the kitchen, throwing his hands in the air, raving. As if he disturbed them, shadows leapt when he passed. "Didn't wanna come, Mary," he said. "Too much grief here, you know that. I done it for him, he's all we got, Mary."

What would Jesus do about the old man's booze? Would he pour it on the fire? George Bell drank for years, but when Mary was alive, he did it on the sly, and perhaps that held down his consumption. Now, he drank so much he lived on it, sucking down carbohydrates and his daily vitamins.

Johnny heard the oven door plop down and a chair scudding over the linoleum: The old man had propped up his wounded leg. There was a little splash as he poured more whiskey.

What would Jesus do?

"Man has his needs, even the Bible says. Better to marry than burn, it says."

Johnny stared at the great red moon, just as his mother had. A different wind blew, but he heard her windmill. He plunged his toes under the same blankets she had. Perhaps she heard the old man raving, too, when he was still young: "You'd just lay there and cry. Sweetheart, you would. What's a man gonna do?"

George Bell had burned all the wood, but just outside, Johnny found a broken kitchen chair; he fed it to the coals and bent near. He made coffee but had no food. He doubted the old man would return with much other than whiskey.

He'd leaned a ladder against the house so his grand-father could inspect the chimney. Now he climbed high to survey his heritage of barren walnut trees. He couldn't count them all, nor could he calculate their worth, but went for gloves and began gathering nuts. It was cold work picking them from the half-frozen ground, but after several hours he'd made a high pile. He hulled them with a hickory mallet, then filled two coal scuttles and headed for Red Buck. By the sun, half a day remained.

Down the tracks a quarter mile the rocky, hilly ground leveled into fields, with corn and pasture on the north, then rows of broiler houses such as he'd seen across Arkansas. A mile farther, on the highest hill around, stood the water tower and the high school. He remembered Brownsville, worrying about his old clothes and not being accepted by the Mexican boys in their toreador pants. All of that seemed like easy work now.

What would Jesus do?

He neared a great, sagging building plastered over with Funk's and Ralston Purina signs, with pipes stretching to vats in the sky, and big trucks parked behind an open scales. He picked his way through the ruts and dirty snow in the parking lot, then set his buckets near a man who threw sacks of crushed oyster shells into the cab of a feed truck.

"You take nuts here?"

The man grinned. He reached into his back pocket for snuff and poked a wad by his teeth. "Ain't no nuthouse in Joshaway County, boy."

Johnny was too hungry to laugh. "I mean, do you buy walnuts? I got a lot of 'em."

"You the Walnut King? I been lookin' for him. Sure, come on back to the scales." The man's accent was so strong he was difficult to understand. He must be a hillbilly, Johnny thought.

He followed the man down an aisle between pallets stacked high with bags of feed and fertilizer. Everything smelled of sour corn, gasoline, and lime, and the air was about half dust. The man poured Johnny's walnuts into a hopper and moved the brackets until the arm had balanced. "Name's Virgil Showalter."

"Johnny Bell."

"Why ain't you in school, Mr. Bell?"

"We just moved in, and I—"

"Ain't kin to George and Mary Bell?"

"My grandad."

Virgil's head jerked up, and he stared so steadily that Johnny had to turn his eyes. "They pulled up stakes 'bout the time I bought my place. That girl died, it dealt 'em a blow. Your mama?"

"Yes, sir."

"You ain't got no juice up there!"

"Sir?"

"'Lectricity. Is these here walnuts a serious matter? Hail, bring me all you got." Virgil eyed the scale and spat again. "Rat here's 'bout seventy-five cents. You could sell some a them trees, Mr. King a the Nuts. I do woodworkin'; might be in the market myself. Y'all sittin' on a gold mine there."

He was a friendly fellow and Johnny didn't mean to be rude, but he'd spotted a row of vending machines in the office and could have screamed, he was so hungry. He waved a glove at Mr. Virgil Showalter and stepped into an aisle crammed with hardware and animal medicine. He walked across an oak floor so old that it dipped where people had walked back when the place had been an actual grist mill. He tried not to look at the chocolate bars and barbecued potato chips.

In the center of the storeroom stood a potbellied stove, and Johnny took off his gloves and wriggled his fingers until pain shot through them. He'd have pulled off his shoes and warmed his frozen toes if the feed mill weren't such a public place.

A plump fellow in a tie stood behind the cash register, talking to a farmer. They kept jabbering as if Johnny were no more than one of those sparrows hopping around in the feed, so he walked over to the cash register. Finally, the man in the tie said, "Help you?"

"I got seventy-five cents comin' for walnuts." Johnny looked down at his shoes and fingered the zipper on his filthy coat.

The man gave him a hard look but moved toward the cash register, talking all the while. "Peabody, what do you think a this Arkansas outfit? They gonna run the world?"

The farmer shrugged. "Got it down to a science, I guess. Ask me, it ain't farmin' no more; it's factory work."

"Know anyone goin' over to 'em, Peabody?"

"Sure don't, Reverend."

The man in the tie shook his head. "Takes feed to make meat. Better feed you got, less it's gonna take, no gettin' around it. They grind up chicken feathers and call that feed; I just won't do it." He handed Johnny three quarters without looking at him and smiled at Peabody almost sadly. "We allus been competitive here."

"It's close margins, and that's why they're feedin' back feathers."

"They take the blood, the manure, and feed it to cattle."

"Hadn't heard *that*. I thought we done killed all the Nazis."

Johnny ran for the vending machines. He bought a Nehi grape soda, two Hershey bars and a package of garlic potato chips. He broke open the potato chips and saw that the men were staring at him. "You want me to eat outside?"

"Oh, no," the man in the tie said. "What's your name, son?"

"Johnny Bell."

"Mama Kathleen!"

"Yes, sir."

"Oh, goodness . . . I was saved at your daddy's meetin'. I was standin' there, I was thinkin' . . . there's somethin' *about* that boy. You *look* like him. Remember him, Peabody? Joe Daws?"

"Too far back for me, Reverend."

"He could pack 'em in. And George! Johnny Bell, did George come back?"

"We just got here. Ain't even had time to buy groceries."

"Mary?"

"She died."

"Aw. I'm so sorry to hear that." For a moment, Johnny thought the man was going to cry. "I—well, I—I'm a son of a pup! Come home with me, Johnny. Have supper."

"I can't."

"Tomorrow evenin', then. Bring ole George. Will you tell him, son? Charley Larkin, he'll know. Lost sheep, oh dear *Lord.* Luke. Chapter fifteen. Verse fifteen." Larkin opened the door to his office, where a big picture of Jesus looked down. He pulled a flat of eggs from a cooler. "Take these."

"I—"

"I'm your friend, Johnny," Larkin said, holding out the eggs. "Take 'em. I'm your friend."

In the morning, when Johnny crawled out of his blankets, he found George Bell sitting forlornly by the stove. He wore a baggy suit he'd dug from a trunk in the shed, along with a crumpled hat like gangsters in movies wore. Maybe once the suit had fit, but the old man had lost a lot of weight. With a clean shave, he looked as fragile as an egg. "Don't laugh at me, Johnny."

"You goin' to see Mr. Larkin?"

George looked away. "I prayed through, Johnny. I know I made some terrible mistakes in life. I was proud. I didn't treat Mary right, nor you. But Jesus, He died on the cross even for me."

"Grandpa, we have friends here."

"Yeah," George Bell said. "Friends everywhere you look."

When he'd gone Johnny went outside to saw more wood. The sky was nearly as dark as night. Toward noon, wind shrieked over the ridge and spat snow. He built a rick of wood against the house and hurried inside to warm his hands. He was worried about his grandfather, if he'd be able to make it back. He put the beef, potatoes, and carrots the old man had bought into a pot. Saved, or forever lost, the two of them could eat a hot meal as the snow flew.

In mid-afternoon George Bell limped to the back door. He poured coffee, then unscrewed his whiskey. "What's this shit?" he said, pointing to the pot.

"Stew! You bought it. "

"Whatever you say." He drank from the bottle, then poured the rest of it into his coffee. He threw in three cubes of sugar and took a long swallow, his nostrils flaring, his blue eyes dancing. "You'd starve to death, had to depend on me."

"How was church? Did Reverend Larkin know you?"

"I didn't recognize him, he's put on so much weight. Visitin' them lonely widows, I spose, and havin' that second piece a pie. Not to mention political gatherin's, can you imagine? He's runnin' for sheriff!"

"Did you get saved again?"

"'You better get to a doctor, George,' he says. 'You don't look so good.' Well, Bareiro told me *that.*"

"Dr. Bareiro? You never—"

His blue eyes glowed. "Charley's very interested in you. Wondered how you'd been raised. Whether—he *would* put it this way—whether the Lord was a presence in your life. He said you look like your daddy."

"Do I?"

"Mary thought so. Oh, Lord, Johnny, don't you turn into another preacher." He began to shout. "Fifty to the square mile as it is! Ole Charley, well, he was a good man, I wouldn't claim no different—only he was a fool. One time, I had to light the pilot on his water heater, that's how damn dumb he was. But he knew how to smile, allus said the right thing. And somehow, he's made money. He's what you'd call an administrator. Drives all over the county ministerin' and 'ministratin.'

"I'm seventy-four years old, and I don't understand it, how a man as dumb as that could prosper, when I couldn't hardly feed my family. It breaks different for some of us, like in a card game. Oh, I drank. Maybe I ran around a little. But some people is born way down, and by the time they figure out just how far down, it's too damn late."

"Maybe Reverend Larkin walked in Jesus' steps."

"He changed money in the temple, that's what he done." The old man sighed and riffled through the Bible like it was a paperback Western. "I worked like a dog."

"You should go to a doctor, Grandpa. Reverend Larkin's right. He's your friend, he—"

George Bell threw the Bible. It hit the chimney and fell to the stove, and Johnny batted at it, and it dropped to the floor. He hugged it close. It was the family Bible.

"I suspicioned it, Johnny, I knew it all along. I just couldn't take it. There ain't no Jordan River, no milk and honey. Ain't nothin' at all on t'other side. Ain't no t'other side!"

He laughed. Then he turned white as though he'd vomit. "No sweet Jesus holdin' out his nail-scarred hands. *God?* That's just another word for *bizness.*"

Toward dawn Johnny found the old man slumped in a corner of the kitchen. He felt the wounded leg, and truly it had frozen. He's *dead,* Johnny thought. Then the old man coughed and reached out for his whiskey, never opening his eyes, and Johnny stumbled out the door, thinking, a doctor. I've got to find a doctor.

He ran beneath the walnuts, blinded by the snow, sliding on the slick leaves. He climbed onto the railroad tracks and lay for a moment, panting. Then he heaved to his feet and turned toward the feed mill. Reverend Larkin would find a doctor.

A train whistled around the bend. The track had been cut through a bluff here, and he climbed the frozen bank, and waited above, his back and buttocks stinging with cold where he'd slid in the snow. Gondolas of coal passed beneath him, and he pictured himself leaping down, crawling toward a covered car. Somehow he'd find his way back to Texas.

Tarzan could do it, Johnny thought, but I'd break my leg. And Tarzan never had to deal with sick old men who cursed God. *Wei-ay-ayn!* went the whistle, and the cars clacked by: *chicketakoot, chicketakoot.* A gray-haired black man stood on the caboose steps, slowly raised his eyes, and frowned. Johnny stepped back, brushed the snow from his hair, and the train rounded a curve.

He stalked through the snow to the front door of the feed mill, then remembered that today was Sunday. Not only that, it was Christmas. Families everywhere were having a big meal, kids were playing with their presents, but to George and Johnny Bell today might as well have been the ninth of May.

Not that Christmas ever had amounted to much. Mary bought him underwear, possibly a sack of rock candy, but to her the holiday was merely a day off. Johnny laughed. Because of the baby Jesus he wouldn't be able to find a doctor unless there were an emergency. Perhaps the old man's sickness qualified, but Johnny didn't even know where to locate a phone. He was wet from the snow and darkness neared.

The problems of the Bell Family would have to wait until morning. He'd get out of these clothes, and eat some stew, and crawl under the covers while the old man raved. In the morning he'd talk to Larkin, and whether or not George Bell wanted it, bring help.

He struck across a corn field. Snow came down in fistfuls, no wind in it, silent. He wished he had another place to spend the night. He wished that he'd never see George Bell again.

Down in a frozen creek bed, with the hedge trees and red cedars crowding over his head, it was as though there were no other world. He sat on a big rock, cold through and through, but enjoying the pure silence even as he shivered. He might die here and no one would know. The creek would wash away his flesh, his bones would sink into the mud, and as with his father there would be nothing left to gather up and mourn. What did it matter, anyhow? Why fret over a person as they died if you never noticed them in life?

Something crashed up the hill.

He ran. He reached the summit and stood to catch his breath where the trunks of the walnut trees rose in the dark air. He ran from one tree to the next, following a glow on their bark, trying to see through the snow. He stood still, trying to suppress his panting. He heard the fire crackling. He ran along the flat ground of the ridge, the walnut trunks shining more and more red as he passed.

Flames engulfed the wall by his mother's bedroom and darted around the rotten eaves. A two-by-four came scuttling from the attic; there was a *pop! pop! pop!* from tar in the old wood.

Johnny made a run for the back step, pulled at the door, but an evil black smoke surrounded him, and then the heat knocked him back. He ran his fingers over his face and discovered he'd burned away his eyebrows and singed his hair. He scrambled toward the shed and banged into the rusted lawn chair. George Bell sat there.

"Grandpa, the house!"

Johnny threw his arms around the old man's legs. In

the snow lay a bottle of vodka, three-quarters empty. Why vodka? He never drank vodka. "Grandpa—"

He didn't understand why the old man had come out here to drink, when he could sit by the stove. He'd dozed, the fire had got away from him, he'd had to leave. Weak as he was, he couldn't walk—crawl—any farther.

No. He'd set the fire. And sat here on the banks of his River Jordan, drinking himself, and freezing himself, into oblivion.

What do I do? Johnny thought. What do I do?

He didn't care, Johnny thought, walking round and round the burning house. A piece of tin shifted up, and flames, orange and blue, poured across the roof. Johnny's shoes slopped through the melted snow. He wanted to die, Johnny thought. He forgot all about me because he was so sad, but we came so far. We came all this way, and he burned the house!

The roof swayed, buckled downward, and collapsed. Firelight flickered over the old man's dead face and Johnny couldn't bear to look, but he had to. He'd never seen such a face. It wasn't happy but not sad, either, not horrified. That face knew something. Had just found it out.

"Oh," Johnny said. "Oh."

He ran again through the walnuts, downhill, wildly toward the creek. He plunged through the ice and wet one leg to the thigh. He ran across the corn field, then lost his way. He ran through another woods and heard hogs snorting and banging into their feeders. He burst onto the farm-to-market road and fell.

He lay shivering and crying, but after a while he closed his eyes, and felt warm all over. He thought of his grandmother and her warm supper, and of his father's picture in the annual. Somewhere above him, flashing red and blue out of the blackness, he saw the map of Missouri, with yellow splotches for cities, and tiny black dots for places such as

Red Buck. He'd lost the map somewhere, on the road from Texas.

Chapter Five
Your Damn Tears

Through the first days of the year, he scooped manure in the goat barn—easy enough, because all he had to do was find the concrete floor beneath, and shove. Adding excitement were the rats, which made tunnels in the manure, and nested in pockets of straw. When he turned over a wide, dry layer of manure a rat crouched for an instant, surprised. If his reflexes were quicker, Johnny killed it with his shovel.

Once he found a nest of babies—blind, pink, with skin so transparent he saw their hearts pumping. He scooped them up on the shovel, threw them outside, and stared at them writhing in the snow. They made him want to cry. He cautioned himself that in this hard world you had to be tough and couldn't worry over something so useless as baby rats. Then he stared off dreamily.

Suzanne broke his reverie. "I brought you some hot chocolate," she said, and stepped gingerly over the rats. She sat on the high milk stool.

The stool was in a patch of sun, and she turned her head at different angles, until at last Johnny deduced that she'd done something with her hair, though he couldn't remember how it had looked before. "Thanks," he said, dropping his head low, studying a pattern of roses on the cup.

"You get to stay with us, Johnny. Are you glad?"

He nodded. He had plenty to eat and a warm place to sleep, the principal ingredients for a satisfied life.

"How are your fingers?"

"Huh?"

"They were all swollen when Daddy brought you in out of the snow. I got lukewarm water and bathed and bathed them."

"And my toes?"

She looked away. "Those, too. Mama wouldn't call the doctor—"

Lucy had poured olive oil on him, and mumbled about Jesus, while Suzanne might have saved his foot. "You were my nurse."

She sighed. "Someday, I'll be a nurse." She leaned near, her voice tender like Mary's had been when he was sick. "Are you . . . okay?"

She wasn't talking about his toes now. She meant how was he holding up after the death of George Bell, and he appreciated her asking, but wasn't sure. He was sorry for the old man's suffering but he'd been freed of something, too, and some days he was glad his grandfather was gone. Or so he told himself. The old man had left a big hole and it was hard to figure what went there. "I'm awright."

"You have to go to school. Until you're sixteen, that's the law. Then you can drop out. Was school a lot of fun down in Texas?"

He shrugged. Life in Texas seemed remote. But lately, shoveling manure, he'd concluded that it was important to earn a high school diploma. Otherwise, he would not succeed in life. "How come you have to drop out?"

"Mama says it's in the Bible."

"How you should drop out when you're sixteen?"

"Like the Amish do."

"How you gonna be a nurse if you don't graduate from high school?"

"I don't know, Johnny." A fleeting terror lit her eyes, and Johnny understood she wasn't as confident as she tried to be. She held her head at still another angle and tossed her hair again. "I'm sposed to show you how to take care of the goats."

They herded in Bonnie and Pauline, two of the gentlest does, and milked them while they lapped at corn mash. Everett gave them chicken feed because he already had it, and it occurred to Johnny that this might be one reason his feed conversion with the broilers was high. That and so many rats.

"How many milkin' goats are there?" he asked.

"Nine. There used to be a lot more only Max, that's my brother, let them all go wild."

"They're just out in the woods?"

"Some of them died. There. Noth*ing* to it, right?" She liked to emphasize her *ings*. Perhaps it proved she wasn't a hillbilly like her father.

Suzanne was clearly delighted to rid herself of a chore, but running the milker wasn't hard. She showed Johnny grain in a barrel and hay in the small loft. The other goats butted at the door, and Johnny let in a doe named Pearl.

"You need to strain the milk through these things," Suzanne said, holding up cotton pads.

He strained Bonnie and Pauline's milk, then threw them hay. The Timothy hay smelled sweet. The two goats chewed thoughtfully and perhaps even gratefully, looking at Johnny with their yellow eyes—smiling, almost.

Suzanne clapped her hands. "They're happy, see?"

"Friendly as beagles."

He thought she was nice once you talked to her a little, not much different from another boy. And she'd saved his toes, so he forgave her dumping the goats on him. Compared to chickens, they'd make good company. He blurted it out: "You wanna go to the Poultry Festival?"

She stood in the doorway, laughing. "It's not until June, Johnny."

"Wanna go?"

"Sure," she said, bringing a hand to her hair again. Then she dropped her eyes like he'd seen women do in movies and walked toward the house. She didn't look back, as if she knew he expected her to. He kept watching, and near the house she jumped, and broke into a run.

When the truck brought the baby chicks, Everett was still on the road, lining up bulldozer jobs for spring. The rest of the family joined in to stretch chicken wire around the brooder stoves, and fill watering jugs, and pour corn mash onto cardboard trays for the chicks to scratch in.

The chicks stayed directly under the brooders through the first days. One night the temperature fell to two above, and Johnny hovered near them, watching that they didn't huddle so closely that they smothered. Still, there were two hundred dead in the morning, which he carried out to the edge of the woods and dumped. Crows, hunched in the bare oaks, pounced on the chicks before he was halfway back to the house.

Still more manure awaited him in the broiler house—he had to get the place clean before the chicks expanded into chickens. Since he didn't know how to drive the tractor, he used a fork and wheelbarrow. It was mindless work and sometimes, without realizing it, he talked to George Bell.

"I thought you was gonna get saved," he said, shaking the fork angrily. "I heard you talkin' to Jesus, then you said he didn't even exist. You don't make sense!"

In ten days, the chicks doubled in size and sprouted pin feathers. He took down their wire pens, and perhaps a thousand of them gathered and ran from one end of the house to the other. Running en masse, they seemed like liquid sunshine, pouring in and out of shadows.

Thursday afternoon the sky filled with clouds and a nasty wind blew in from Oklahoma. He closed every door in the broiler house and crawled under a brooder stove with *Tarzan and the Lost Empire*. Lying in the fresh shavings, staring at the blue flame, he fell asleep, and when he woke the chicks clung to him like a fuzzy yellow carpet, and pecked at the buttons of his shirt. He set each one carefully aside and went back to sleep. He dreamed about George Bell, riding a buck with his hunting knife high—then he was Tarzan with blood on his teeth. Something struck him in the ribs.

"Comftable?"

Johnny sat up too quickly, half-afraid Everett would hit him, and struck his head on the lip of the brooder. "I got all done, and I—"

"How come them goats ain't milked? They got a reglar time: six every night."

Johnny stood, rubbing his head. "Six? Suzanne—"

"That girl don't know. Don't watch her, she'll dump in the milk without strainin' it. You milk nannies reglar and keep the barn clean, their milk is sweet to drink. Max nor Suzanne, neither one, could understand a basic thing like that. And stanchions. You don't milk a goat in no stall like a cow. You—"

"Put 'em high, on a stand. And when you're done you disinfect the stand."

Everett stared. "Naw."

"Otherwise, that goat stink will build up, and pretty soon your milk is sour." He favored Everett with his broadest smile. "Lucy gave me some books from the Department of Agriculture."

"Right."

"Goats ain't sa-cep-tible to tuberculosis, particularly, like a cow, but they can't stand no drafty nor wet place, either. They'll take the cold but not the damp. 'Specially not a bred-up dairy goat like these Anglo-Nubians you got here. After you milk each nanny, you got to wash your hands, and it's a good idea to wipe off their tits, too."

"Ah huh. Let's get over to the barn."

Since Suzanne's instruction, Johnny had scooped out the rest of the manure and dumped it on the vegetable garden. He scraped, scrubbed, and disinfected the concrete floor, then threw clean straw bedding, banishing the rats at least for a while. He whitewashed the slab oak siding and boarded over two slits that had opened up over the years around the windows. He built a small milking platform and suspended a drum of disinfectant above it. Finally, before the platform, he placed a table and two bowls: one filled with disinfectant, the other with water. He even found an old towel and hung it on a nail.

Everett nodded. "Kinda fussy, but good. Bring 'em in, Johnny. We'll milk."

When they were done and Lucy still hadn't called, they carried the milk to the cooler in the broiler house. "Take out a load a manure 'fore supper," Everett said.

Everett opened the double-doors and backed in the trailer, cutting it precisely around the chicken wire, missing a post by less than an inch.

"I see you moved out the wire," Everett said. He handed Johnny the scoop shovel, taking the fork for himself.

"Yes, sir. They grow so fast, and I like to watch 'em run."

He laughed. "Never cared much for chickens, but a baby anything's wonderful. When they come in?"

"Right after New Year's."

"Trust Charley Larkin to bring 'em while I'm gone." Everett set to with the fork, and they worked motion for motion for a while, in a sort of contest as they waited for Lucy to call. The crisp evening air cooled their sweat and dissipated the smell of ammonia from the manure. Finally, Everett grunted and threw his fork onto the wagon.

"Take her out, Johnny."

"I never drove a tractor, sir."

"Time you learned. Little Ford like this, easy as automatic transmission."

Johnny wasn't so sure, but climbed over the hitch. "What do I do?"

"You got your clutch, your throttle, and your brake," Everett said, pointing. "Brakes aren't much good, but you ain't goin' fast. Push in the clutch . . . fine. Slide her around to first . . . well, that's high. You cain't shift while you're movin', now, like in a car." Everett pushed the stick around, saying, "High, low; high, low. Second. Neutral. Reverse. Okay: fire away. All you have to do is—"

Johnny had watched farmers coming and going at the feed mill, so he knew how the starter worked, but he held it down too long. The engine fired immediately but the starter made a terrible noise.

"Let off!" Everett shouted, and Johnny jerked his foot back.

Everett's cheeks rippled with the effort to hold in his anger. "Bad on the starter. If I gotta replace the Bendix, take me all mornin', and it ain't for free. Awright, awright: you're in first. Let out on the clutch, real slow . . . "

Johnny released the clutch halfway.

"Now the throttle. Not much. Just like automatic—"

Johnny pulled the throttle far out, released the clutch the rest of the way, and the tractor leaped forward. This rattled him and his foot slid off the clutch pedal. The tractor bucked like the Studebaker truck had before it died and the trailer hunched forward, then yanked back again on the tow bar. The chicks rose in alarm, scattering, and because he was watching them, he barely missed the support post. "Push in the clutch!" Everett yelled.

Somehow, he couldn't. Meaning to steer free of trouble, he pulled sharply left, but then the trailer veered right, binding the hitch. The drop pin lifted and fell back into the tow bar again with a jangly squawk. He was scared he'd crash through the wire, and because he was concentrating so hard, he forgot to brake. The wall drew near, and he threw his hands over his face.

"Pull back the gas!" Everett yelled. "You dumb . . . brake! Brake it! *Brake!*"

He did, but not before the front wheels veered off a bucket and slammed into the wall. A crack appeared in the mortar between two cement blocks and steam hissed from the radiator. The engine died. The tractor rolled back

Everett ran up. "How come you didn't use the brake? Ain't you got no brains?"

He slumped on the iron seat. It was cold in the broiler house and he was back in Arkansas, with George Bell yelling at him. Everett raised a hand as if to strike him, and he wanted to die.

"Know what that'll cost? Who you think's gonna pay for it?"

He put a hand on the big tire and flipped to the ground like Tarzan. He crouched for an instant, but before Everett could say another word he vaulted into the twilight. He ran all the way to Highway E.

He'd fallen into a trance. It was like one of those flying dreams, where he soared above Oklahoma and Texas and went out of sight of land over the Gulf of Mexico. Dear God, how he wished he could fly. Fly, fly away.

Pretty soon he heard his feet pounding the road, his lungs gasping in the cold air, and had to stop because his side hurt so badly.

He'd left behind his coat and gloves and stocking hat. He wondered if a man could survive out here all night when it was no more than twenty degrees. His bones ached like they had on the road. He reached into his pockets for matches but didn't have any, though he had thirty-seven cents, which would buy some candy bars if he could make it to the bus station.

One of Charley Larkin's feed trucks came chugging up the grade. When it was at its slowest, he jumped onto the landing attached to the back. He rode for two miles, freezing down to his soul, all the way to U. S. 60. He hit the ground when the truck pulled into the feed mill and ran another half mile.

By this time he'd calmed down and didn't care whether Everett Ogletree lived or died. All he wanted was to be warm.

He screamed aloud and some old fellow in a Cadillac honked at him. The bus station was open but instead he crashed through the police station door.

Sheriff Harpster was at his desk, reading, but Johnny hardly saw him. He charged toward the oil stove by the wall. He resisted the urge to hug it. In a while the sheriff came over and handed him a cup of coffee, and then he held out a blue jacket like policeman wore. He yawned. "It was the sheriff's."

"You're the sheriff." And this was his jail. There were cells down a dark hall, and somebody snoring, and somebody groaning in pain.

"Will be if I'm elected. The coat was Sheriff Lord's—he died in October. He wouldn't mind if you had it." He yawned again and motioned to a chess board. "Sit down, hotshot."

He'd played chess in Brownsville, in study hall with David. But he wasn't as skilled as the sheriff, and all he could think of was Everett's anger. Soon most of his pieces were on the sheriff's side of the board, but Harpster didn't appear to notice. He smoked Pall Malls, answered two phone calls, and went into the jail for a while to talk to the groaning man.

"What you expect, you get so shitfaced?" he said.

Johnny couldn't make out the groaning man's reply.

"I am *not* callin' a doctor. It's a waste of tax money."

The man mumbled.

"Awright, if it'll shut you up, I'll get you a pan. You miss, and you're cleanin' it up."

And then Harpster sat smoking again, seemingly calm. "Everett kick you out?"

"I—"

"The county went to considerable trouble to get you in a situation. I would appreciate some cooperation."

Him and his county, Johnny thought. "I didn't do nothin'."

Harpster's voice grew kinder. "He hit you?"

"He was yellin' at me 'cause I messed up his tractor, only I told him I couldn't drive it."

"Yeah." Harpster snuffed out his cigarette. "There's lots of kids to feed out there, and the chicken business is headed south. The man's on edge. Have you cooled down?"

"I like to froze out there!"

"Well, now you have a coat. Maybe next time you just sit there and let Everett rave. It won't last forever, and meanwhile, you're gettin' fed. They *are* feedin' you?"

Johnny nodded. "Feedin' me good."

"Then button your lip. The county can't be expected to hold your hand all the time and wipe away your damn tears. The man saved your life, am I wrong or am I right?"

"You're right."

"I can't hear you."

Asshole, Johnny thought. "You're right!"

"Follow me, I got somethin' to show you."

He led Johnny down the hall between the cells. Johnny stole a glance sideways, and smelled vomit, but the groaning man had fallen asleep. Another fellow hulked back in the darkness; Johnny saw his burning eyes.

Rough as his tone was, Johnny thought Harpster meant to deliver a lecture how this jail was where he'd end up if he didn't mend his ways. But the sheriff marched past the cells, turned a key, and flipped on a bank of fluorescent lights. They entered a room not much larger than Everett's goat barn, with a desk, two tables, some chairs—and half a dozen aisles of books. It was the Red Buck Public Library.

Harpster propped up his feet and made another call while Johnny wandered among the novels. In the *B*s he found *Tarzan and the Golden Lion, Tarzan and the Ant Men, Tarzan the Untamed,* and *The Beasts of Tarzan.*

"Even Red Buck," the sheriff said. "Even poor, benighted little Red Buck has a public library."

"Thank you."

"How I make it through the nights." Harpster opened a drawer and pulled out an ink pad and stamp. "I read about the ancient Greeks, or Australia, or the Civil War. Some big battles right here in Missouri."

"They didn't know which side they were on."

"Right. The Bald Knobbers, so called because they met on cleared-off hilltops—you should read about them, Johnny Bell. Good guys and bad guys, not fifty miles from here. Outlaws!"

"Did you ever go to college?"

The sheriff stamped Johnny's books, leaving the cards for the librarian to find in the morning. He glanced at his watch. "I took a couple of courses, but it was a long drive, and I didn't know what I was lookin' for. I mean, other than pussy. Then the deputy job came along." He reached for a cigarette, glanced around at the books, and put it back. "And now maybe a chance to be sheriff."

"I want to go to college," Johnny said.

Harpster nodded absently. One instant he was angry, the next, hardly in the room with you. They walked back toward the jail, and abruptly Harpster turned toward the stacks, and lifted his hands high. "As sheriff, I will bring library services to every citizen. We'll buy a bookmobile!" He laughed and then jerked backward as if surprised Johnny remained in the room. "Whud you say?"

"I said I was readin' a book when all that business with Everett started."

The sheriff flipped out the lights. "You shoulda thrown it at him."

Johnny slipped into the goat barn, where he'd made a pallet of blankets and where he kept his worldly possessions—a toothbrush, his radio, and an alarm clock. He also owned a flashlight with a new set of batteries, so he could read *Jungle Tales of Tarzan* under the covers.

Somehow the Ogletrees had seen him, because the yard light flickered on, and Lucy yelled she was about to throw his supper to the cats. The goats rustled at the barn door, looking in on him with their pleading eyes. We love you, those eyes said, even if nobody else does.

The lights in the barn came on. "Get to the house, boy, and eat your supper," Everett said. "No sense in this."

He crawled from his blankets and trailed behind, feeling silly. Lucy brought a plate of fried potatoes out of the oven.

Everett did his best to smile. "You want some ketchup?"

"No, sir."

Everett placed two dollars by Johnny's plate. "Sheriff called. He—well, I just wanted to say, you done a good job with them goats. Baby chicks, too—Luce was tellin' me how you got 'em through that cold snap."

"He done it all by himself, Everett," Lucy said.

Everett patted the table as if he were playing drums. "Call that money wages. If we was to turn a profit on them goats, far as I'm concerned half of it's yours."

"We want you to be happy here," Lucy said.

Johnny felt like crying but restrained himself. No one would wipe away his damn tears.

"I got a little too noisy there," Everett said. "We had— oh, in some ways—a tough year. The Lord will send trials, but like the gospel song says, further along, we'll know all about it. And this is the new year, right?"

"Right," Johnny said, between mouthfuls.

"I thought you'd busted that radiator, but I can solder along the top there. Teach you how."

"I wanna learn."

Everett nodded shortly. It almost seemed as though he was angry again, but abruptness was his nature, Johnny saw. He'd misunderstood the man.

"What say we go huntin' Sunday afternoon? Sposed to snow again, and that's good for rabbits. You can use that ole .22. If you promise not to shoot me."

Johnny worked hard to keep his voice from trembling. "I promise."

Chapter Six
The High Priestess of Opar

An ice storm blew through Saturday night, hammering the roof and scratching the windowpanes, but in the morning the sun, breaking through the clouds in long, slanting beams, made all the world sparkle. Tree limbs hung like silvery spider's legs, and every blade of grass was a tube of light.

Johnny liked the sound his boots made, crunching the ice across the pasture. Carrying the Marlin .22, he felt strong and purposeful.

They followed the creek, then climbed the bluff along a goat trail, hanging onto trees in the slickest places. Everett pointed to piles of droppings, themselves encased with ice. "Plenty a rabbits. 'Bout all this country's good for."

They stood atop the bluff like kings looking down on creation. Everything was a blinding white. The shining, icy railroad tracks pierced the glittering town. Sunlit power lines struck to the north like streaks of fire.

They stopped where a bulldozer had pushed up a high pile of brush. "Virgil Showalter wanted me to build a pond up here," Everett said. "Went through all kinds a contortions to bring in the Cat—passed through your grandfather's land. Your land, I guess. I thought it all belonged to the state."

More than one hundred acres, Johnny had learned, though it was high ground, cut up with hills and sharp ravines, so rocky and thorny you could hardly bludgeon through. Even in pioneer times, no one tried to farm it. Still, if he owned land, could you call him a nobody? If you owned land, somebody else could be the least of these.

"Turned out there wasn't enough clay to make a seal. Just rocks. I'll hold your rifle, Johnny, and you climb up there and tromp around some."

He meant the brush pile, and Johnny understood why, but ice coated every branch and finding a foothold proved difficult. Twigs snapped at his touch. Finally, balancing, he spread his legs between two uprooted hickories.

"Jump up and down."

Hanging onto hickory limbs, he bent his knees and managed to push.

"Harder!" Everett commanded, and Johnny leapt up and came down with all his weight, skinning his leg on a slick limb. But something rustled and burst through. Everett's shotgun roared like the voice of God in the cold air, crackling far over the valley below. Johnny lifted his head in time to see a cottontail go tumbling.

"There was two," Everett said. "I was poppin' in another shell when the second one ran. Any more in there?"

Johnny was cold and felt sorry for the rabbit. "Naw."

"Bet there is. They burrow down where a fox cain't get to 'em. Let's change places." Johnny crawled out and picked up the rifle while Everett climbed laboriously and set his feet. "You can use the shotgun," he said. "Just don't blow my head off."

Johnny held the shotgun lightly with his middle finger poised by the breech, and his index finger pointed along the barrel, as in a photograph he'd seen of Pancho Villa. Everett came crashing down, and quickly two cottontails ran together along the bluff's edge and turned sharply uphill. Johnny drew a bead ahead of the slower rabbit and squeezed the trigger, but as he fired there was a shift of color in the background, and he lifted the barrel high.

"Cain't you hold onto that gun?"

"I saw a goat."

"Oh." Everett sat on a limb, then began disentangling himself from the brush. "Wouldn't wanna dress out no goat today."

"It was real shaggy, like—"

"Gone wild." Everett threw Johnny a box of matches. "What say we go down to them sawed-off stumps and build a fire?"

Johnny gathered twigs and leaves. The fire sizzled and popped with melting ice, then finally took. He sat back, proud of himself.

Everett swung the rabbit round and round. When its head twisted off, he ran his pocketknife under the loose fur along the backbone. He pulled the fur either way down to the feet and then cut them off. "Here," he said, and Johnny held the back legs apart while he slit the skin of the belly up to the twisted neck. In the frigid air, the entrails pulsed and steamed.

Everett speared the rabbit and pulled two rocks near the fire, and as the burning wood made a bed of coals, he moved the meat near. They sat by the fire, looking down on the farmhouses below. Cattle lingered near to barns to be milked. This might be Sunday, but they never had the day off.

"How it is in Alaska," Everett said. "Only the land's rich up there. You can go out and shoot a bear, 'stead of a little cottontail."

Johnny chewed on a twig. "Me and George Bell ate coon once."

"Reckon we've all ate coon. Long as you don't have to eat possum, good Lord." Everett frowned. "That goat, Johnny . . . doe or buck?"

"Doe."

"Wonder if we could catch her. I think she run into that ravine."

Johnny knew the story but wanted Everett's version. "They get loose?"

"Oh, it was Max." Everett stared across the valley. Clouds had overcome the sun again, and the air seemed colder. "He let 'em go. I was so busy right then, wasn't hardly ever home. Lucy was sick. You know, she gets . . . *sick,* Johnny.

"Winter come, and they'd got back in there and had younguns, and when finally I talked to Max about it, he said he was 'sperimentin'.' Some 'speriment!

"Up from your place they's two-three other 'bandoned farms, then it all turns state forest; you might as well chase after deer. Registered animals like that. Excuse my language, it's damn shame." He sighed. "Goats was my idea. Thought maybe we could find a way to be independent on the farm. Maybe even get off that rented land and buy our own place."

"Max is in Vietnam?"

"I think he's through the worst of it now. We pray to God he is." Everett turned the rabbit over and its juices splattered on the coals. "Don't ever take up farmin', Johnny."

"How come?"

"You'll starve to death! I tell ya, we're all at the mercy a these big companies—they take the politicians out to dinner, and set the prices. The poultry bizness. It's crooked and it's cut-throat, but there ain't no margin with corn, neither. Say you get everything balanced and looks like you might turn a profit, nickel a bushel, say. Then it don't rain and the grasshoppers breed. Or you get flooded. What happens if you're laid up? Charley Larkin gonna come and help? He'll just wring his hands and look up toward the purty blue sky.

"So off goes Everett Ogletree on his bulldozer. That machine's a sewin' machine in my hands. But I got overhead and I don't hire out cheap. I expect to be paid."

"You think that rabbit's done?"

Everett handed Johnny the hind legs in his greasy handkerchief, snapping off the forelegs for himself and propping the rest by the coals again. He chewed thoughtfully. "Here's the thing, Max. I mean, Johnny. If I was a young man, and knew then what I know now, I'd roll that Cat up on the International and head for Alaska. Go to Juneau, or Sitka. I hear you thinkin', 'cause it's the only thing people has ever heard about Alaska, it's cold. Well, it ain't around Sitka! They get them warm winds just like in Seattle. They raise cabbages weigh eighty pounds."

"What you gonna do with an eighty-pound cabbage?"

Everett laughed. "Good point. What I'm sayin' is, Alaska is the last frontier. The land a opportunity."

"You been there?"

"Durin' the war, sure. Worked on the Alaska Highway."

"This rabbit's good," Johnny said.

Everett didn't seem to hear. He jumped up and began kicking in the fire. "Let's catch that little doe, Johnny."

"She'll run like—"

"No, no." Everett pulled his belt off, and motioned for Johnny to do the same. "I got an idea."

Everett disappeared downhill where the ravine widened, and Johnny followed the ridge line, crossing the ruined barbed wire fence marking his land. Soon he heard a familiar sound. He couldn't place it for a moment. Then he saw his mother's windmill and stood with his arms gone limp, confused.

He pulled himself forward from tree to tree, but every step was a fearful thing. Finally, he reached the clear place by the shed, and could see the plain of ashes where the house had been, and a remnant of the chimney, slick with ice. He almost expected to confront George Bell, frozen in his chair—but no, Sheriff Harpster had taken care of all that.

As if from miles away, he heard Everett shouting, and stumbled to position himself along a deer trace, at the head of the ravine where the rocks broke apart.

Here she came.

He knew better than to grab her leg, because she'd kick his teeth out. He came down on her like Tarzan, quiet and strong, slipping one arm around her neck. Before she knew what happened he had the belt over her head.

She ran, dragging him over the rocks and banging him into walnut trees. She ran straight against the shed, then round the corner and into the ashes. He tugged on her hard, and she sat back like a dog. She looked at him pitifully, not truly wild. The rarest thing in a goat, she had blue eyes. He sat next to her, not afraid she'd bite now, and stroked her fur, which was full of twigs and beggar's lice. After a while, she stopped trembling.

The pallet where he slept had been about two feet away, and there stood the kitchen range, next to which George Bell drank himself to death. One of its legs had come off, and it slumped to the side, but it looked usable. Everything else was gone, though now Johnny understood that there hadn't *been* much else.

He led the doe out of the ashes. She strained at the belt, her blue eyes fearful. "We'll take you back to the nice warm barn," he told her. "Plenty of sweet hay. We won't eat you, OK?"

Everett came up at last, panting. "You got her!"

Johnny nodded. His legs were wobbly.

"Thought she was gonna run toward me for a minute." Then, as if for the first time, he looked around. "This is your place."

Johnny couldn't speak.

"I'm sorry—I just didn't think."

"That's all right."

They picked their way down the bluff, Everett carrying the guns and Johnny coaxing along the doe, both of them cold now, snow whisking around them. After a while Everett said, "Never seen such big walnut trees."

"Yeah." Johnny picked up the goat, because on open ground the belt halter didn't work well, and she kept trying to lie down. He believed she hadn't found enough to eat in the wild and wasn't strong. He shut her in the barn with the other goats and gave her some hay. "La," he said. "That's your name. Think of yourself as the high priestess of Opar."

"Bra—aaat," La said. Her blue eyes were calmer now, though she trembled when Johnny touched her.

He trembled, too. He went into the feed room and drew himself under his blankets and cried, and saw again that frozen face, staring into the truth. Not drunk enough, he thought. Not drunk enough that it didn't hurt.

Chapter Seven
Green Shoes

Johnny wore a pair of Max's jeans that were an inch short but otherwise fit well, and a long-sleeved flannel shirt that Lucy had patched at the elbows. Presentable, but Suzanne giggled when he pulled on the green gym shoes he'd bought at Art's Army Surplus. He pointed to his only other shoes, the chore boots caked with manure.

"Here comes the hillbilly corps," Suzanne muttered.

She'd arranged his schedule so to be nearly identical to hers, but even in his confusion Johnny wondered how he would pass eleventh grade. Suzanne told Mr. Kowalski, the principal, that Johnny was a junior like herself, when he had yet to graduate from the ninth grade. Then she laid it on about Johnny's trials in the woods, how he'd witnessed his grandfather's death, nearly frozen in the Christmas storm, and been at death's door for days.

"I read about that in the paper," Mr. Kowalski said, turning to Johnny with soulful eyes. "I'm sorry, son."

Stepping off the bus, Johnny the Junior took a deep breath, and asked himself what Tarzan would do. What, for that matter, would Jesus do? Nothing fazed those two, and he couldn't let them down. He brought up his head and instructed himself to be calm. But kids were everywhere: shouting, elbowing through, swimming their way down a hall so long Johnny couldn't see the end.

"Just act natural," Suzanne said. "They don't even see you." She grabbed his hand and they bobbed and weaved their way toward the "boiler room," directly across from the gym. "After P. E. you go there," she said. "Ask for Mrs. Koontz; she's your advisor."

His terror subsided. None of it mattered, as it turned out: General Suzanne's careful plan of attack, his imposter's academic status, his hillbilly wardrobe, or even what Jesus would do. It didn't matter how the kids looked at him, because he saw a vision.

She backed away from her locker, a dark-haired girl with flashing dark eyes, the brightest splash of color in a blur of girls taking off their winter coats and straightening their sweaters and checking their hair in mirrors. It seemed as though she did not begin her motion until certain he was watching. Then she pushed shut her locker and turned, so that her short skirt swished about her thighs. She turned her back to him, didn't meet his eyes, but he knew she'd seen him.

"Johnny, we'll be late," Suzanne said, tugging at him. As if he were blind, she guided him toward a flight of stairs.

The vision turned, threw Johnny a quick, dazzling smile and moved on.

"That's Janie Epstein," Suzanne said, staring up at him angrily. "She's a—a cheerleader!"

He staggered through a swinging door as if his life were a detective story and the tough-talking dame had shot him in the gut.

Amid lockers and benches and dripping shower heads, down a long, narrow room with forest green paint peeling off its white predecessor, twenty-five boys bounced balls, guffawed at dirty jokes, and snapped towels just short of naked white asses. At least three arguments rose quickly almost to blows, and abruptly died. You could gag on the stench: medicine, disinfectant, sweat, methane bleeding off the sewer, urine. Like Brownsville, Johnny thought.

A big boy pinned a pudgy kid against the lockers and held a beaker from the biology lab to the kid's lips. The beaker was half-full of a yellow liquid, and the kid sweated and writhed. Johnny had seen it all before with his friend

David. A puny kid could excel in classes, but bullies would nail him in the locker room.

He felt a pang of loneliness, as if the pudgy boy were David. "That's my locker," he called out, and waited for the big boy to back off.

The room grew quiet.

"Huh?" said the big boy.

"I need to get dressed out for gym class, and that's my locker."

"They ain't assigned, you—" But the big boy wasn't any larger than Johnny, and he stopped to ponder. The distraction was enough for the pudgy kid to twist away.

"It's just tea," the big boy said, and poured the yellow stuff onto the floor, and some of the boys laughed. Others eyed Johnny to see if he had any other tricks, but then Coach Henry, a short man with a loud voice, began blowing his whistle and shouting insults. "Let's go, girls," he said. "And don't you talk back at me."

The pudgy boy passed by. "I'm Dick Frawley," he said, as if apologizing. "Thanks."

"Who's that big guy?"

"Bobby Sills. Coach's pet." He sighed. "I *hate* P. E."

Out in the gym, they fell in line for push-ups and jumping jacks, and then most of the boys paired up with their buddies and went to different sides for volleyball. Johnny was last choice along with Dick.

"I guess we'll take Green Shoes," the captain of the orange team said.

But Johnny was a good volleyball player and the orange team won because of his spikes. He felt a rush of confidence until three boys broke off by themselves as if they were the Kingston Trio. They sang "Green is the color of my true love's shoes" and "Green shoes, how I love ya, how I love ya."

After volleyball, Coach Henry made everyone climb the rope that rose to the ceiling. Johnny's muscles were hard from life on the road and from Everett's endless chores. He was the only one to reach the top, up by the skylight where two sparrows eyed him nervously.

"All right, Green Shoes!" Coach Henry said.

They all sat Indian style to see a demonstration from the wrestling team. Two strong boys in blue shorts and tight little helmets faced off like bull calves under a sign reading "Beat Mountain Vale." One was Bobby Sills, and the other was Gary Tyrell. Coach Henry circled, blowing his whistle for no apparent reason. Soon the coach declared Gary victorious, though both boys were still standing, and it seemed to Johnny they'd made the same moves. Coach Henry said, "OK, Green Shoes, you give it a try."

"I don't know—"

"He's chicken."

"Give him *yella* shoes."

Even with their name-calling, he didn't want to do it. He'd had some scuffles with Mexican kids before they learned to let him be, but he knew nothing about this hillbilly fighting. Johnny walked slowly to the mat, imagining himself as Tarzan when he bested wicked old Tublat, but glancing at the clock, hoping the bell would save him. Here he was on his first day— his first hour—of school, facing off against Red Buck's champion wrestler.

Who did not turn out to be Bobby, but Gary. Bobby played referee, circling around them as they bent forward and hunched up their shoulders.

"Get your arms down, Green Shoes," Bobby said, and pulled Johnny's arms to his sides. "It's wrasslin', not boxin'."

"Right," Johnny said, shaking him off, and eyeballing Gary. Coach Henry blew his whistle, and Gary reached out quickly with a leg, and Johnny fell to his knees. He bounced up again and held his fists high.

"Arms down, Green Shoes," Bobby said. "I ain't tellin' ya again."

Johnny didn't understand. He could take this boy if they'd let him fight.

"Get him, Gary!"

Gary threw him again, but this time Johnny twisted and placed a hand around the boy's neck and pulled him along. He wasn't sure then what happened. Gary kept trying to pin Johnny's arms, and Johnny kept trying to get up, and he grew angry and desperate.

"Pull off his green shoes."

"Pull off his shorts."

He thought it was Bobby Sills talking. They wanted to strip him naked and shame him.

"He's not flat," Coach Henry put in. "Get him flat."

Johnny didn't know what this meant. Again he tried to rise, but Gary pushed him down. "You bastard," Gary said. "Stop it!"

Somehow Johnny half-sat and worked his arms free. He snapped at the air like Tarzan—he'd have bit off Gary's nose if he'd leaned close enough. Then he went after Gary as if he were Satan. He no longer knew where he was. He didn't hear Coach Henry shouting.

Gary backed away, holding his arms before his face, and Coach Henry and Bobby Sills grabbed onto Johnny, restraining him until he stopped thrashing.

"Mad man," Bobby Sills said. "Jerk!"

No one spoke in the locker room. Johnny looked in the mirror and saw that he was bleeding on his cheek and daubed at the cut with a paper towel. When he finally headed for the shower, the boys stepped aside, as if he were Moses and they were the Red Sea.

He knocked and no one answered. He opened the boiler room door and blinked, not from the bright lights, but because the inside was dark as a cave. Finally, by the far wall, he saw a woman sleeping on a couch. "Mrs. Koontz?" he whispered.

She wore a short skirt with suns and moons on it, as if she were one of those flower children from San Francisco. In her sleep the skirt had climbed her thighs. He considered tapping her on the knee but it seemed too forward. Should he go outside and knock again?

The phone rang. Mrs. Koontz sat up stiff as a zombie and reached over the end of the couch, knocking to the floor a stack of safe driving pamphlets from a tire company in Ohio.

"Right, right, he just caught me at the door," she said. She pulled at her long hair and hung up. She lit a cigarette. "You must be Johnny."

"Yes, ma'am."

"I'm Mrs. Koontz. Running a little late this morning." She laughed—a low, gentle laugh. "Mr. Kowalski tells me you're the boy who . . . well, the transfer."

Suzanne had written him a speech. "We moved up here in the fall and we were really busy, and I never came in to register. I'm a junior."

"Sure." She rose, threw back her arms in a stretch, and Johnny saw her belly button. He estimated he'd seen close to fifty percent of her by now.

She poured herself some coffee that looked as if it might have been made before Christmas. "Sorry, Johnny. Some trouble . . . sleeping." She slurped the coffee like George Bell used to go after whiskey. "You're staying with Suzanne's family? Her parents don't come in for conferences, but she tells me they want her to drop out. Why?"

"I don't understand it, either, ma'am. I think Everett— I mean, Mr. Ogletree—thinks it says in the Bible you should drop out of school at a certain point, like the Amish."

"Suzanne's not Amish."

"No, ma'am. Suzanne really likes school. The Ogletrees think the schools teach about evolution and how one way a thinkin' is as good as another, and pretty soon the devil takes you over, and you forget to live a moral life."

Mrs. Koontz let out a long plume of smoke. "Don't you *hate* that?"

"Just hillbilly talk, seems to me."

"I get so sick of them. What about you, Johnny? Are you a reader?"

Johnny wished he could have one of her cigarettes. "I like to read Tarzan stories."

"That's fine. Maybe we can broaden your horizons a little." She dropped a cube of sugar into her coffee, then set down the cup, put out her cigarette only half-smoked, and lit another. A portion of a sweet roll remained on a plate, and she nibbled at it.

"I'm *trying,* but I just can't get going." She sighed. "Ever feel like that, Johnny?"

"Lots of times, ma'am. This mornin', even. I haven't had the best of days already, and I contemplated goin' home."

"Good word, isn't it?" She sighed. "Been doing quite a lot of contemplation myself lately. What does it all mean? I ask myself. Let's sit here a moment longer, okay, Johnny?"

"And figure out what it all means?"

She laughed again. "Go on, sit down. Are you scared?"

He sat on the edge of the couch. "They ganged up on me in P. E. but they didn't get away with it, and I'm awright now. I get scared sometimes, but then I just take a big breath, and bull my way through."

"Wow." She stared at him so long he was embarrassed. "I'm sure you'll do fine, Johnny," she said at last. "In my class, anyhow." She smashed another half-smoked cigarette. There was a cracked mirror by the door, and as she combed at the snarls in her hair, he slipped the stubs into his shirt pocket.

"Are we ready?"

"Ready and able, ma'am."

Off they went as if into battle, she the fine lady, he the knight, up those same battered steps, through the now deserted cafeteria, and across an open place where sleet fell.

An old man in overalls shuffled past, throwing rock salt. He eyed Mrs. Koontz and gave Johnny a wink.

Suddenly, Johnny looked at Mrs. Koontz a different way. Perhaps she wasn't a lady such as you'd find in a story, not someone to defend or rescue. He could fathom why the janitor lusted after her, but still her hair was tangled, and lint dangled from her sweater, and what might be cat hair. She was sad, he thought, which surprised him, and made him trust her.

A hush fell on the classroom as they entered. Kids ran for their seats and grabbed their books, and there was a moment of silence before the talking resumed, about one-quarter the original volume. Mrs. Koontz clasped Johnny's arm and leaned so near that he could smell the tobacco on her breath, and her perfume. She stared as though in their walk to class she had at last figured out what it all meant and intended to tell him. Finally, she let him go.

He looked over the faces but everything blurred. Terror welled, but then he saw a hand waving over in the corner by some boxes and stacks of textbooks. It was Suzanne Ogletree from his previous existence. He went up the aisle with his eyes low and settled near a sick-looking rubber tree in the very back.

"What happened to your face?"

"I ran into the floor."

She handed a book across the aisle. "Read," she said.

"All you have to do is read?"

"She calls it 'Individualized Instruction.' She's going through a divorce and she doesn't even try anymore."

The class calmed down and everyone was reading or pretending to. The book Suzanne handed him was *Pride and Prejudice,* by Jane Austen. The cover said the book portrayed the dance of courtship and how people strove to get along in life. He read fifteen pages and the characters still hadn't left the house.

There was a commotion up front as a big kid lunged forward. He stomped his feet, scooted his chair, and coughed. The class tittered and Mrs. Koontz threw them an evil look.

It was Gary the Wrestler, only now he was scrubbed up and wore a jacket with a big "C" on it. Johnny hadn't seen him because he'd been so flustered coming in, and then had hidden behind the rubber plant. Johnny now studied him in profile. His book was a baseball story and sounded interesting, but clearly Gary hadn't read it. He kept saying, "I don't know" and "If you say so."

Suzanne whispered, "He never studies. His dad owns the Chevrolet garage and he's on the basketball team."

"The wrastlin' team, too. Does the 'C' stand for Chevy?"

"Cougars," she said, as if she was either going to laugh, or hit him. "*Read.*"

Gary pushed back his chair with a screech and slouched toward the class again, making a face that said, "This is *so* stupid." The class tittered again, not because Gary was funny, Johnny thought, but because he was a basketball star and heir to a fortune in Chevies.

Then a girl with thick dark hair slipped to the desk, smiling brightly. She turned the chair so that she half-faced the class.

"You've seen *her*," Suzanne said.

Johnny stared. Jane spoke distinctly, but low enough her voice didn't carry, except as music, perhaps, that you hear off in the distance. She seemed to enjoy talking about her book. She made sad Mrs. Koontz laugh. She was an angel!

Suzanne slammed her book shut. "Let's go to the library."

"What?"

"To get a book for you. You don't seem to like *that* one."

They marched to the desk for passes. He glanced at the cover of Jane's book: *To Kill a Mockingbird.* He'd read it, too, down in Brownsville. They had something in common, and he stared hard at her, waiting in agony until she brought up her eyes.

Finally, she did. But she gave no sign she recognized him and seemed irritated that she had been interrupted in her discourse by a mere commoner. He might have been a chair that had taken it upon itself to walk across the room.

"Johnny?" Mrs. Koontz touched his hand. "Your pass, Johnny."

"Thank you varah much," he said, for no reason at all mimicking Elvis Presley, then turning like a military man to head for his seat again. Several in the class laughed, and a girl smiled and whispered something to him.

"An actor among us," Mrs. Koontz said, and gave him a big smile—while Jane studied her perfect nails.

Suzanne stepped over quickly and guided him toward the hall. Oh yes, the library, he thought. That will be nice. He heard laughter in the distance and realized it wasn't so far away, and then that he'd made a fool of himself before his true love.

Something still worse occurred to him: Jane was Gary Tyrell's girlfriend.

"She's just a flirt. A mean town girl."

He came to earth now and filled with remorse. "She didn't flirt with me."

"She could *never* be interested in you. You're nothing but an old hillbilly, Johnny."

I'm from Texas, he was about to say.

"I'm *mad* at you."

He sighed. Women were a tougher subject even than wrestling. He was happy when they reached the library, and he could escape Suzanne for a moment. They had only one Tarzan book, but he'd been looking for it and figured it would last for a week. The way things were going, he'd be doing well to survive the day.

"*Really* mad," said Suzanne.

Chapter Eight
Softly and Tenderly

Johnny moved a cot into a corner of the goat barn, cleared a shelf for the few items he called his own, and rigged a light so that he could study. Sometimes La pranced over and nuzzled him, but mostly the goats settled down in their bedding and pursued their chief interest: chewing. Even so, they were superior company to most of the people he'd met lately.

Everett returned from up north, took a look at Johnny's appointments, and said, "This ain't necessary."

"Sir?"

"I been meanin' to say. There's a place for you in the attic."

Johnny supposed the attic was Everett's notion of a reward for hard work and good behavior, and no question it was warmer. He had a real bed. He'd enjoy having a table and lamp, as well as shelves for his clothing and growing library. Trouble was, the twins lived in the attic, too.

Suzanne had saved raisin bran box tops and ordered them a set of miniature cars for Christmas. The twins sat at opposite ends of the attic, rolled the cars down the planking, and screamed when there was a collision.

It wouldn't do. Johnny worked like a man, drawing wages even if they were Everett Ogletree's idea of wages. He deserved some respect. Politely, he said, "You guys are too noisy. I'm tryin' to do my homework here."

When they ignored him, he felt he had to be more direct. "I'm gonna tell Lucy what little pests you are."

"That's why we're up here," Rosie said. "Mama thinks we're pests, too."

Ronnie went right to the heart of the matter. "You ain't family," he said. "You ain't doo-doo to my mama."

Doo-doo?

Johnny turned up the volume of his radio, but still could hear the twins banging into the sheeting as they raced around the attic, bouncing balls and generally driving him crazy. Part of him understood that's what they meant to do, and that he should head for the barn and read there. Instead, he yelled, "Sit down!" and, "Shut up!"

"Sit down!" and "Shut up!" came right back at him.

While they were gone to Sunday School, he drew a chalk line from the stairway to the sloped wall. He threw a jump rope, a deck of cards, and Ronnie's cap gun onto the twins' bed. "This is *my* side," he announced, when the twins returned.

They sat on their bed, still scrubbed from church. They looked as sweet as the kids in one of Lucy's magazines. "You stay over there; I'll stay over here. Is that clear enough?"

"Clear," Ronnie said. Rosie sucked her thumb and said nothing.

"And shut up!" he added.

"Shut up!" the twins said, as if they'd practiced it. "Shut up!" they chanted, until Johnny buried his head in his pillow. At last they plummeted downstairs, and he heard crashes and screeches, and cartoon laughter, as they settled down to TV.

When they came up again, he'd prepared. He caught them each by the waist and carried them to the bed. He'd changed strategy, turning himself into a big teddy bear who wanted to wrestle with them and make them laugh, but they fought him as if he were the bogey-man and their lives were in peril. Ronnie, a strong little guy, hit him hard on the nose, then jammed a finger in his eye.

Johnny dropped them on the bed, and said, "Enough! Enough!" still thinking he might become a sort of uncle to them. By then both were bawling, and peace couldn't be made.

"You ole bastid," Ronnie said.

Johnny's hand went up in the air. He *did* think about it, how George Bell and Mary both had boxed him on the ears when he was little, and how much he'd resented it. Oh, but it's justice, a voice said, and he slapped that little devil across the mouth. "Here's what we're gonna do. We'll—"

"Mama!" screamed Rosie. "Mama, help!"

Ronnie narrowed his eyes like a bad man on *Gunsmoke*. "You ole bastid."

Lucy climbed the stairs so quickly Johnny suspected she'd been there at the bottom, listening. Suzanne slipped up quietly, stood with her hands behind her back, and looked at Johnny as if he were bound for the gallows.

Then, dressed for the evening service in his tie and overalls, Everett came stomping.

"He hurt Ronnie," Rosie said.

"Him?" Everett jerked a thumb at Johnny, though there didn't seem to be any other candidates.

Johnny slumped and hung his head low.

"What in the world for?" Lucy said, her voice gone shrill.

"He *hurt* him," Rosie said, just as shrill.

"Let me see," Lucy said, unbuttoning Ronnie's shirt. "Does that hurt, son?"

"Awright," Everett said, before Ronnie could join in the wailing. "Y'all get downstairs."

Lucy pushed Suzanne and the twins before her. On the stairs, she called out, "They ain't hurt, Everett."

Everett didn't acknowledge her. "Stand up," he said to Johnny.

Johnny stood, and Everett knocked him to the floor. "What's wrong? Cain't stand on your own two feet?"

"I didn't—"

"Gonna cry, now? Think I'll let you off easy if you cry?"

Johnny wasn't anywhere near to crying. "I just wanted to—"

"Twins got on your nerves a little, and you took it on yourself to discipline 'em. Yes or no?"

"I guess so, Everett, but I—"

"Stand up."

He stood, and Everett knocked him down. Johnny crouched, spluttered. Everett hadn't drawn blood, but Johnny's face stung all over as if stuck with needles.

"Stand up."

"You'll just knock me down again."

"Stand up."

He stood slowly, rubbing his jaw. If the big ape came at him again, he was going to defend himself. He was taller than Everett though not as thick across the shoulders.

Everett stood with his legs wide apart, his chest trembling, and jabbed a finger.

"Anybody gets beat in this house, *I* do it. Next time you try a stunt like that, I'll whip your sweet ass 'til you *crawl* away. What you gonna do to show you're sorry you hit my boy?"

Johnny shrugged. "Don't know."

"For one, you lost any more wages this month. Number two, you can head for the goat barn again and sleep with the rats. Hear me?"

Johnny fell back on the cot, holding his jaw, as Everett thundered downstairs. There was a great commotion as the family left, and he heard Lucy call his name, but he couldn't do anything but lie still, trying to figure out why life had selected him for a punching bag.

He dreamed that he lay on the driveway, powerless, while Everett bore down on him with his Caterpillar. He woke in darkness and the house was quiet. Sweat poured off him. His mouth tasted salty from blood and he crept downstairs for a drink of water.

Lucy had left a plate of food on the kitchen table, and he took it into the living room and turned on the TV. There were two channels. On the first was a show called *The Many*

Loves of Dobie Gillis he used to watch in Texas. Old Dobie chased a blonde, Thalia, played by Tuesday Weld. Thalia told Dobie right out that she'd only be interested in him if he made a lot of money, and that reminded Johnny of George Bell and how he thought that some people are born poor, never have any luck, and die poor.

Oral Roberts, the preacher in Tulsa who claimed he could heal people, occupied the other channel, and dozens of desperate people struggled to the altar, where they threw away their crutches and coughed up their cancers.

One show made Johnny as sad as the other, but he returned to Dobie. He washed off his plate and wandered through the house, not meaning to spy so much as to find some clue how he could get along in the time he had remaining here. By the fall, when he had some money saved, he'd go on his own. He wasn't doo-doo to this bunch.

He entered Suzanne's room and lay on her bed. He writhed, thinking about Thalia and Jane Epstein. Girls. They'd turn you into a mad dog.

He sat up dazed and looked in Suzanne's mirror across the way. He had pretty much healed from being thrown around in P. E., but now his face sported new bruises from where Everett had hit him. With the hillbilly haircut Lucy gave him, he was a sight to see.

He stepped near and squeezed a pimple. It made a tiny splat and when he tried to wipe it off, it smeared. He felt a stab of guilt for his disrespect of Suzanne, who had saved his toes from frostbite. He knew he had no business in her room and started out the door, but then a demon took hold of him, and he opened her dresser drawers.

She didn't have much. He found some sentimental trash of the kind you held onto when you were a kid: a pretty green rock, a flashlight that didn't work but seemed as if it ought to, some Canadian pennies. Shorts, and jeans, and shirts—all church basement stuff.

She had a picture of Jesus down in her underwear, and another picture of a big stallion she'd cut from the feed mill calendar. Hiding under them was a series of paperbacks about nurses, the same as Mary used to buy in second-hand stores, and ridicule, but kept reading. They were always about some beautiful but underappreciated nurse who meets the doctor of her dreams. Together, they conquered the plague, and then were married because the doctor had at last understood the selfishness of his rich girlfriend, compared to the sensitive nurse.

Under the nurse stories lay a fat paperback with a naked black man on the cover, called *Mandingo,* by Kyle Scott. George Bell had a copy of it in the trailer once. Every page featured a sex scene and Johnny wished he could take the book along. Also, he wanted to ask Suzanne why she kept such a story. That was the trouble with espionage: you could never reveal what you'd learned even when the enemy tortured you.

He thought he heard a footstep. Like a careful burglar, he closed all the drawers, smoothed out Suzanne's bedspread and slipped to the door. No one was there.

He pulled on his chore coat and headed across the pasture, kicking at tufts of frozen grass. He felt sad, but it was a pretty night, with a fingernail moon and stars so close he might have grabbed one. He stopped to listen to the owls, the only bird that sang on cold nights. Not singing, exactly. Just asking who was out there.

Up on the bluff he paused in the starlight, leaning against a walnut tree nearly three feet in diameter. He heard a deer tramping. It made a few quick steps, stopped to listen, and made a few steps more. Johnny slipped into the clearing and yellow eyes flashed at him, then whirled away to the beat of hooves.

Not a deer, but a goat. If he lived up here, he'd catch those wild goats, and . . . well, hard to say. He'd have to build high fences because of how they jumped. And where did you sell the milk? The world hadn't beaten a path to Everett Ogletree's door.

Cheese? Maybe that's how you made money with goats.

He heaved open the shed door, struck a match, and fumbled down the wall for the Coleman lantern. He pumped it up and finally got it lit, propped it on a crate, and yanked on the door to the Ford.

He liked the steering wheel. It was made of hard rubber so old it felt powdery, but his dad—or mom—had mounted a beautiful glass steering knob. The lantern light reflected off it like a fabulous jewel. He imagined spinning the wheel with the knob, pulling onto the open road, and driving all the way to Brownsville.

In the glove compartment he found a frayed map of California, a corroded bolt, and a Prince Albert tin. He didn't remember the tin and pried it open. George Bell must have placed it here on Christmas Eve, because Johnny had sat in the car almost every day before. He'd left the deed to the farm, signed over to Johnny, and the title to the Ford, paper-clipped with two twenties. And a note:

> Joe's car would overheat sometimes so youl need
> to flush it out with Red Seal Lye but it went to
> Tennessee once and back. Your daddy give it to
> Kathleen when he left and I checked on it. You
> have clear title as soon as you sign. This is a good
> place with two springs on it and there are the
> walnuts which are worth real money. So youl be
> all right when you get older. Youl want to finish
> school. Maybe youl end up in the service which
> would be all right too. Only don't get yourself
> killed in that war they cooked up.

He sat for a while, contemplating. Not exactly words to live by, but forty dollars might be enough for tires.

Johnny supposed it was a kind of suicide note, and he couldn't be angry with the old man. If Johnny were as worn-out as his grandfather, and in such pain, maybe he'd want to leave this world behind, too. The sad thing was that the old man never figured out where you went next.

It was almost midnight when he returned, but Lucy was still awake. She sat beneath a lamp with a cup of tea, the radio turned low to "sacred music," as she called it. She nodded to the couch but Johnny sat in the shadows, with quick access to the back door. He feared Everett would emerge and try to beat on him some more, but then he heard him snoring.

Lucy stayed up late lots of times reading her Bible. Perhaps Everett's snoring explained why.

"Did you see your farm, then?"

"Yes, ma'am."

She leaned forward, her eyes bright. "Johnny . . . I want your side a things."

He told her, doing his best to be fair about it, though making sure to rub his jaw as he talked. It had swollen some.

"Oh, he goes too far, too far. And I know Ronnie and Rosie can be a trial. They break my heart, but you know you were wrong. They ain't reached the Age of Accountability."

The Age of Accountability was when you knew the difference between right and wrong. Perhaps he was a little short of that age, too. And when she put it that way, he had to hang his head. I was wrong, he thought.

"You're not a bad boy."

"Don't mean to be, ma'am."

"But all of us—Everett, even Brother Larkin—we're *tried*, Johnny. This earthly life is hard. Day in, day out. I, personally, I just get so weary. And there ain't a one among us who won't yield now and again to the Tempter."

He thought she'd said "temper" at first, but then realized she meant something grander. The Tempter was another name for the Devil. He was the Devil's special agent, a kind of missionary for evil. He was the fellow who'd talked Johnny into hitting Ronnie.

"We all sin and have come short a the glory a God. But Johnny, the Lord has sent a Comforter to be with us in these Last Days."

Lucy and Everett were always talking about the Last Days, which referred to the Book of Revelation and a time when the faithful would be snatched away in the twinkling of an eye. This might happen next year or at noon tomorrow, but you could bet it would be soon. You might be eating bacon and eggs or driving along in your car. You had always to be prepared and sometimes Johnny questioned the necessity of doing chores or taking a bath, if the Rapture was going to wipe everything out.

The Comforter was a good version of the Tempter, and Johnny imagined the two of them off in the background somewhere, haggling over the merits of his soul like a couple of real estate sharpies.

He thought of George Bell torturing himself with these characters and concluding that the whole thing was a hoax. But if it was a hoax, it sure was a big one. If religion was nothing but what some bearded old men thought up back in Bible times, then it didn't matter much what you did. You suffered through life, taking your delights here and there, and then became worm food.

No. Somehow, this mystery of life, this imponderable question swirling inside you, had to have an answer. George Bell hadn't found it, but maybe he was damned from the first. Maybe you really could be . . . *saved*.

Johnny didn't know where the truth lay, but the Ozarks seemed to be full of believers, and he had to live with them. When you were in Rome, do as the Christians do. So rather than debate with Lucy the exact duties of the Comforter— and since he knew how the conversation would proceed in any case—he blurted it right out: "Lucy, I want to be saved."

Her bright eyes took fire again. "Do you know what it means to be saved, Johnny?"

He straightened his back and pounded a fist into his hand as Everett would have.

"My mama left me a little book—I lost it in the fire. It's called *In His Steps.*"

Lucy jerked upright as if he'd stabbed her. "I love that book. Did you know it was based on a true story?"

"Yes, ma'am. You just ask yourself, 'What would Jesus do?'"

"It's so simple! If only people—"

She cried now, and he let loose some tears, too, to make her feel good. "Whatever Jesus tells you," he said, "that's what you do."

"Hallelujah!" Lucy rose to her feet. "You fall to your *knees.*"

The Comforter had possessed her. Did she mean that everyone should fall to their knees, or just Johnny? "Yes, ma'am," he said, and knelt, but she looked toward Heaven now.

"Dear Lord, I know I have sinned!" she cried, and for an instant Everett's snoring stopped. "I cain't bear this life alone."

"Confess my sins," Johnny said, trying to keep her on earth. "That's what I need to do."

"Yes, Johnny," Lucy said softly. "Next Sunday, when Brother Larkin gives the altar call, you can go forward."

She seemed frail and old. Smiling bashfully, she shut off her lamp and the sacred music. Still crying, she put a hand on his arm, whispered "Bless you." Then she slipped away to her bedroom, where the snoring had resumed.

"Brothers, Sisters—" Reverend Larkin looked sober. "You all know the story of Ronald Cruz. I remember Brother Ronald in Vacation Bible School, seems like only last week he was memorizin' Bible verses, a wonderful young man who loved the Lord.

"Well, we've had some sad news, the worst possible news. Just this Friday, two soldiers drove up to the door of our dear Sister Candace. Sergeant Ronald Cruz of the 82nd Infantry was killed by enemy mortar fire." The reverend reached out his hands toward a young woman in a black dress. "Times like these, it can be hard to understand the Lord's will, but we know that Ronnie's in a better place. And Sister Candy, anything we can do, you just say. Anything."

Candy's eyes lifted toward Heaven. Her face seemed pure beyond words. A murmur of sadness passed through the congregation, and dozens cried out in sympathy.

"He was a fine young man."

"He died for his country!"

Johnny wished he could rescue Sister Candace somehow. She buried her head in Sister Showalter's broad shoulder, and sobbed, and Johnny began crying, too.

And then there was Brother Larry Griggs, who wheeled himself into the aisle before the congregation had quite finished sympathizing with the widow. Brother Griggs was wheelchair-bound, and also a war casualty. He'd been shot in some frozen valley north of the 52nd Parallel in the Korean War. That was the one that killed Johnny's father, Joe Daws.

"And pray, oh *pray*, for Brother Griggs," the reverend went on. Griggs nodded shortly, and dropped his head, leonine atop his slack body.

Larkin closed his eyes. "Lord, we know you can heal, we believe by your wounds are we healed, yea, we declare it openly in our Statement of Fundamental Truths. But we must also abide by your will."

Some in the congregation groaned, and two people—Johnny guessed they were Brother Griggs' daughter and wife—rose as if to leave. Griggs lifted a hand and they sat again.

"Brother Griggs is journeying to Tulsa to attend services with the Reverend Oral Roberts, and we pray for him. God bless you, Larry!"

"Amen to that," called out Virgil Showalter, who tended to amen everything. Otherwise, the congregation had gone silent, and Brother Griggs, after sitting in the aisle for a while, staring meaningfully toward Larkin, wheeled his way toward the rear pews.

"Turn with me now to First Corinthians, Chapter One, Verse 27," Larkin said, almost sadly. "'The Lord chose the foolish things of the world to confound the wise.'"

Now, Johnny thought. Time to save me.

But the reverend got off on lemmings, those foolish little animals up in Newfoundland. Perhaps he meant to keep the little kids interested with an animal story, but it didn't work. Rosie put her fingers in her ears, and Ronnie crawled over his dad and headed for the back of the church. So did several of the men, and pretty soon Everett joined them. There was always a group of idlers and naysayers under the sycamores, smoking and chewing and spitting.

Here was the moral: the lemmings seemed foolish as they rushed to the sea, but it turned out that only the weakest lemmings drowned, and what's more they provided food for hawks and wolves. What didn't seem to make any sense at first turned out to be an example of how foolish little animals such as lemmings demonstrated God's wisdom, or nature's balance—pretty much the same thing.

Good story, Johnny thought. And now, let us turn our attention to—

"In closing, I'll tell you the story of a foolish *man*," the reverend said. "This fellow was a college professor at a big university out East. He was full of the kind of knowledge you can find in books. There wasn't anything this fellow didn't know.

"Well, that professor had been invited to speak up in Springfield, and he came into town and had his fancy dinner and went up to his fancy room, where he found the Gideon Bible. That professor was an atheist, I'm sorry to say. And out of pure meanness, he picked up that Bible, and tore it to pieces."

"Dear *Lord!*" cried out Virgil.

Lucy struck an ominous chord on the piano. She wore a long white dress that might have been the one she was married in. Sister Larkin did most of the piano playing, but Lucy had taken a course through the mail and somehow learned a few chords. In tribute to Johnny, she'd rushed her debut.

"And then the strangest thing happened," the reverend went on, half-nodding to Lucy. "The *foolish* thing. A page flew in front of the electric fan, and right out the window."

"Hallelujah!" Virgil called out.

"It turned over and over, and blew up high, and at last settled on the forehead of a poor old wino who'd passed out in a doorway. The wino found a verse on the page–John 3:16, it was—and came to Jesus. And wouldn't you know it, that wino is today one of Springfield's leadin' businessmen!

"I'm sorry to say that the professor, in all his 'wisdom,' went down that broad pathway that leadeth to destruction. I ask you, brothers, sisters, who was wise? Who was a fool?" The reverend paused and stared at Johnny pointedly. "Let us pray."

Johnny dropped his head obediently. Lucy fired up the piano in earnest, holding herself rigidly as if she were afraid of the thing. Sister Larkin began to sing:

> Softly and tenderly Jesus is callin',
> Callin' for you and for me;
> See, on the portals He's waitin' and watchin',
> Watchin' for you and for me.

Johnny looked over his shoulder, and only a few remained. Candy Cruz eyed him through tears. He stepped toward the altar, knelt, and tried to visualize Jesus watching through his portals. "Lord—" he began, and couldn't think of what else to say.

Reverend Larkin came down from the pulpit, touched his head, and Johnny rose.

"Bless this boy, oh Lord," he said, and Johnny was surprised to see his tears. Through all his troubles with Everett, Johnny had forgotten about the reverend. It was appropriate for a pastor to cry when another soul came home, but Johnny sensed something more.

"Come see me, Johnny," the reverend whispered.

Virgil slapped him on the back. He also wanted Johnny to visit with him. "Might have a job for ye, Mr. King a the Nuts," he said.

Anything, Johnny thought, to get away from Everett. "What kinda job?"

Virgil reached for his snuff, but then shoved it back into his pocket, because there was nowhere to spit. "Has to do with our heritage rat here in the Ozarks," he said. "I need a real live hillbilly."

"I'm from Texas."

Candy Cruz held out a limp hand, and Johnny studied her angelic face. He wanted to follow her pretty bare legs— and feed her cows, and fix her car, and put a new roof on her house. One day, he thought, she'd conquer her grief, and he'd be there to rescue her.

Suzanne walked slowly by, her eyes searching everywhere on his face except his eyes, but she didn't speak.

Sister Showalter grabbed his shoulders and wept loudly into his chest even though he had never spoken to her. A parade of white-haired women followed, smelling of Ivory soap and face powder. Lucy came down from the dais and hugged him carefully, but then walked straight up the center aisle and out of the church, her shoulders slumped, her white plastic purse trailing.

Sister Larkin hugged Sister Showalter, and then Virgil, and then Johnny, and asked if Johnny would like to come to dinner.

"Yes," the reverend said, in his hearty voice. "Johnny—"

Then Brother Griggs rolled back into the church and all the way up to the altar. He gave Johnny a nod but was on a mission. "Reverend Larkin, didn't I serve my country?"

"Sure, Larry, but—"

Sister Showalter brought her iron grip down on the veteran's arm. "You need to accept the Lord's will, Brother Griggs!"

"How do *you* know what his will is? Here I have to go clear over to Oklahoma to get help, when—"

"Larry, we prayed," the reverend said. "We tried again and again. I hope Oral Roberts can help you, Brother Larry, but—"

"I got feelin' in my *toes*. I never had that before, more 'an ten years now. What I'm tryin' to say to you, Reverend, it's a sign. God wants me to walk!"

Virgil and several others rescued the reverend, guiding him over by the stove, where they wanted to talk about his candidacy for sheriff.

"This is neither the time nor the place," the reverend said, eying Griggs, but the men went right on, planning an all-night sing-in. One of the fellows was a Moose and said he could make things happen at his lodge.

Muttering, Larry Griggs wheeled his way toward his wife and daughter, and then the church was all but deserted.

As entertaining as a movie, Johnny thought, but when he plumbed inside himself, he didn't feel transformed. He felt like an afterthought. Perhaps some changes would come along tomorrow, but at the moment, it didn't seem his salvation meant much of anything. He went outside and looked around hopefully for Candy. He spied Lucy and Suzanne in the car, not talking. Under the sycamores, men discussed the state of farming. It had never been good and was getting worse. Everett said, "What ya think a this Tyson outfit? Gonna put us all in the poorhouse?"

"Hail, I'm there already."

Everett saw Johnny and frowned, as if the morning had been a chess match and Johnny had made one good move. "Go round up the twins, boy. They're back by the privies somewhere."

Johnny hurried down the stone path between the cedars, and stopped, startled. He saw Candy Cruz far down the hill, walking along the icy Sandy River with a farmer about Everett's age. An uncle, perhaps, or an old friend of the dead soldier's, offering his comforts. The man took Candy's hand and pulled her close. She pushed him away.

He had a wild thought of rushing to Candy's rescue, but then sat on a stump, overwhelmed. Nothing was as it should be this Sunday. The saints weren't interested in his joining them. They weren't even saints.

He heard Rosie giggling. That little angel Ronnie had taken his pants down, and now he peed over the bluff. For such a little guy, he put out a fountain.

"You wanna hold it?" he asked his sister.

"Naw," said Rosie.

"You're scared."

"Naw."

"Let me see yours, then."

"No!"

"You ain't *got* one."

"Time to go, kids," Johnny shouted like the voice of God, and was pleased to see that he frightened them. Ronnie pulled up his pants and scurried after Rosie, his eyes low.

The abiding question became whether the Tempter inspired Johnny, but it was a complicated question. If he needed to follow in the footsteps of Jesus, wasn't it his duty to point out to Lucy what her children were doing? Would Jesus have pissed off the bluff like that, offering up his penis for all the world? Johnny leaned forward from the back seat and whispered in Lucy's ear.

"They ain't reached the Age of Accountability," he added, smiling at Suzanne.

Without a word Lucy turned and slapped both twins hard across the cheeks.

Chapter Nine
Missionary Opportunities

Nodding seriously, Reverend Larkin stepped to the cooler filled with Terramycin, Newcastle vaccine, night crawlers, and a big apple pie. "There's some room for interpretation here, but in our church, when a person is saved, he wants to be baptized. In water and in fire."

The pie danced in the air like the Holy Grail. "Fire?"

"It's what your father had." The reverend smiled. "I've been savin' this for you."

He held out a Bible, with gold letters reading: "Joseph Daws." Johnny leafed through the pages, noting the verses his father had underlined, and his notations in the margins: "First promise of the savior," and "For the sick."

"Thank you," he said, and truly he was grateful. "Makes two things I have of his, the holy Bible and his car."

"That little coupe?" Larkin laughed. "It doesn't run, surely."

"Not right now, but—"

"Joe and I chased all over God's creation in that car."

"On fire for Jesus."

"We were, we were. You can read in that Bible of the fillin' of the spirit—baptism in fire—in the Acts of the Apostles. But Johnny, what Sister Lucy asked me to share with you was some thoughts on the more usual sort of baptism. Water. We always go down to the Sandy for baptismal after Sunday mornin' services, and it's been warm enough here lately to have one."

It had been above freezing, Johnny thought, but the entire matter seemed remote as the reverend cut pieces of pie for each of them. They sat eating the pie, and the work of the Lord was much to Johnny's liking. "I seen some Mexicans bein' baptized once down in Texas."

"Did the pastor plunge 'em under?"

"Yes, sir."

"It's the only way. Now, if we look in Mark, Chapter One, Verse Nine, we see that what Jesus did when he was baptized was to show how the sins of mankind—or just one man—could be washed away. Symbolically, of course."

Johnny lifted his hands high and brought imaginary cymbals crashing together.

The reverend frowned. He pulled a bundle of pamphlets, entitled, "Today's Youth," from a desk drawer, and handed them to Johnny. Johnny didn't react, having reached the understanding that Larkin was a preacher and bound to talk whether or not anyone replied.

"Just think how lucky you are, Johnny."

Johnny nodded, though offhand he couldn't think of even one way.

"You can go to church and get Bible-based instruction. And you can go to the public school or anywhere in your daily walk a life, armed with facts and the Scripture to back 'em up."

He handed Johnny a second stack of pamphlets, "Should You Smoke?"

Johnny panicked. The Reverend knew his secrets.

"These aren't necessarily for you personally, Johnny."

"No, sir."

"Think a them as missionary opportunities. What you'll find in that high school is that there are some wild young people. Maybe they come from broken homes, and they may not have had the opportunity to know Christ. You can go among 'em a witness, Johnny."

He went on talking while Johnny leafed through the Bible. Out fell a photo of his mother, a slim version of Larkin, and a man who was the nearest thing to a stranger. The three posed in front of a bluff where water gushed out. Behind them stood Johnny's car, looking clean and fierce.

"That was at Big Spring," Reverend Larkin said. "Around 1950. You look like him, Johnny. Sometimes, I think you *are* him."

His father wore a fancy gray hat like President Roosevelt might have. Johnny wished the photograph could speak. "He and my mom weren't married."

"They would have been, Johnny. They were engaged—"

"*You* wanted to marry her."

"That's true." The reverend looked sad, and Johnny understood why the old women, the widows and long-sufferers yoked to unbelievers, loved him so. "No man would do for her but Joe, and then ole George got to wandrin' the earth—"

"And here I am."

"Here you are." He smiled. "You should consider the gospel for a career, Johnny."

"Reverend, no. I couldn't talk in front of people."

He waved a hand. "Preachin's not like farmin' or buildin' cabinets, Johnny. The Lord will call you. You pray and you study, and He gives you a sign."

"He gave you a sign?"

"It was a winter like this one." Larkin bowed his head. "I mean a hard winter. We was comin' home from the funeral for Joe. I was so upset, and of course Kathy was upset—"

"You called her Kathy?"

"Surely. Your father, too."

It was a little thing but it sank deep. "I always think of her as Kathleen."

"I was angry that Joe had been taken from us. I came around the curve too fast and skidded on the ice, and we went off the road. The Lord miraculously spared us! Kathleen, she just sat there, cryin', and laughin' like you do when truly your heart is broke.

"I walked up ahead a little and threw myself down, thankin' Jesus and throwin' all my grief upon Him. And it was like Saul of Tarsus, First Corinthians 1, Chapter 15, I saw a light. Paul took the gospel to the far corners of the earth and I'm just a small-town pastor, but from that day on I knew what my life was for."

Johnny didn't know why he asked. "Was my mother a good woman?"

The reverend seemed hurt. "Of course! She was pretty, she had a temper, but good, yes, yes. Full a life."

"I wish I'd known her. My dad, too."

"Yes, I know it's hard for you." Larkin smiled again. "Someday we'll all meet in Heaven."

Before the bell rang, he passed a pamphlet to Jane. "Read it."

Jane's eyes clouded over. "I'm Jewish."

He wasn't perfectly sure what this meant, except that he knew Jews had slain Jesus. Still, they were God's chosen people if only they could accept the truth.

Jane smiled. She had a dazzling smile, but it didn't seem as though she flirted. Dimly, he understood she wasn't under his spell. He'd set something in motion, but she wouldn't tell him. She'd *show* him like a good Missourian.

Even so, they were walking down the hall as if they were friends.

"You're passing these things out all over?" Jane asked.

"Yes, I—"

"It takes a kind of bravery to do that."

He nodded in wonder.

"Coming to the game Friday night?"

He'd need to improve himself if he was going to run around with Jane. He'd need clothes, a car, and to accomplish something. Tennis, perhaps; the algebra teacher wanted to start a team. He smiled dreamily, planning his and Jane's life together as she walked her fingers down his forearm. "Come to the game, John, please."

John!
"I'll sing you a song."

All week Mrs. Koontz talked about propaganda, which Johnny once had thought was something the Russians did, but it seemed there were other kinds. "What sort of propaganda is this?" Mrs. Koontz asked, holding up a *McCall's* magazine ad of an actress trying to sell perfume.

"She's bitchin'," Gary Tyrell called out, and the class laughed. Then it went silent, knowing that sooner or later Mrs. Koontz would give up and provide the answer herself.

Gary was all dolled-up in a suit and tie, meaning he'd play basketball tonight, while Jane wore her cheerleader outfit. She'd invited him to a game where Gary was the star, Johnny thought, but still, she'd invited him. Perhaps it had dawned on her what an oaf her boyfriend was.

"Testimonial," Jane called out.

"Thank you, Jane," Mrs. Koontz said, and asked for other examples of famous people selling things.

"Roger Maris and cigarettes," Johnny said.

"Thank you, Johnny."

"Mickey Mantle and cigarettes," he went on.

"Thank you, Johnny. One baseball example will suffice."

After Jane and John, no one volunteered. Even Suzanne, who always knew the answer, wouldn't speak up. Johnny asked her why once.

"I don't like them look*ing* at me," she said. "With Janie Epstein there, and her big mouth."

Mrs. Koontz gave them an assignment, to come up with ten examples using any of the five propaganda techniques they'd discussed and write a paragraph on each. She stared over the class as if it were a vast sea, and then collapsed in her chair, and put on her glasses, and began to write. It was all over the school that her ex had been back in town. A police matter: he broke into her car, yanked out the radio, and then stole the two rear tires. If ever a person needed Jesus, Johnny thought, gathering his pamphlets.

"Johnny, don't," Suzanne said.

She didn't understand missionary zeal. "I have to spread the word."

"You don't have to be stupid."

Mrs. Koontz didn't see him for a moment, then she took off her glasses. Her eyes were fluttery and red. She studied the pamphlet, finally breaking into a smile. "What *are* the facts, Johnny?"

"Well, ma'am, though St. Paul says in First Timothy Chapter Five that we should take a little wine for the stomach's sake, what he really meant was grape juice."

"And what does Paul say about tobacco?"

"They didn't have tobacco back in Bible times, only Jesus said you shouldn't defile the temple a your body."

"And what kind of propaganda is this, Johnny?"

"It's not—" Suddenly, he wasn't sure what he meant to do. He met Mrs. Koontz's eyes and they'd turned mysterious. He studied the beads around her neck, and a red medallion that said, "Peace."

"Testimonial?"

"That would be if Jesus actually were alive and came out against smoking Camels."

"Plain folks?"

"*Think*, Johnny."

"Glitterin' generalities?"

"Excellent! Not the words of Paul or Jesus, but the way they are placed in the tract. You can use this for one of your examples. Good job!"

Over lunch he stood in front of Noolin Brothers Grocery, but people were disappointed when they found out the pamphlets weren't coupons. A pretty woman shoved two sacks of groceries in his arms, led him two blocks, and gave him a quarter tip.

Well, discouragement often accompanied missionary work. What about all those stalwarts in Borneo, who worked year after year bringing the gospel to heathens, only to be eaten alive? He turned back toward school, but through the window of the barbershop a familiar face grinned from a chair. "Repair job, Ed," Sheriff Harpster said to the barber.

"Don't need no haircut," Johnny said, raising the pamphlets to his face. He hated barbershops even worse than going to the dentist. As the sheriff pointed out, he never went there except to repair the damage inflicted by George Bell or, in this case, Lucy.

The barber sniffed. "Looks like a charity case to me."

"This is Johnny Bell," the sheriff said. "Remember that big fire where that old man died?"

"Sad story," the barber said, and gave Johnny a nod. He was a big man with a big belly who wore a shirt the color of Johnny's tennis shoes that said "Semper Fidelis" on it. The walls were covered with military memorabilia, such as an M-1 rifle and a helmet and a bandolier of ammunition. To one side of these were a rack of antlers and a picture of Ed from the newspaper, holding up his record buck.

Ed liked baseball, too, because autographed pictures of Ken Boyer and Dizzy Dean adorned the wall, as well as a catcher's mitt that had been dipped in bronze.

"How you gettin' along with Everett's goats, Johnny?" the sheriff asked.

"They're registered Nubians."

Harpster shrugged. "Okay, they're registered Nubians. Jesus Christ."

"They're famous," Ed said. "Everett Ogletree's wild goats. I almost shot one once."

"Down in Texas, they hunt goats all along the Rio Grande," Johnny said.

"Rope and tie 'em, too," the sheriff put in. "Ya-hoo! That what you are, Johnny? A goat-roper?"

He dropped his head. He was beginning to despise this man. "No."

"Too bad. I might know of a job for the right sort of goat-roper."

He couldn't hide his interest.

"Just came from the courthouse," Harpster went on. "There's some federal money for fixin' bridges this summer. They'll need crews."

"Yes!"

Ed spun the sheriff around. "Eyebrows?"

"Skip the eyebrows."

"My brother needs a job," Ed said, "and he's a *strong* Democrat. You got more hair growin' outcher your ears than on your head. Females notice things like that, don't think they don't."

"OK, do the ears." The sheriff reached out. "What you carryin', Goat Roper?"

"Oh, it's—" The Tempter, offering him a federal job, nearly caused Johnny to say that the reverend's pamphlets were "nothing." That would have been denying the Lord, like one of the disciples, Johnny couldn't remember which, had. He tried to be brave: "I been doin' the Lord's work."

The sheriff scanned a pamphlet while Ed buzzed his ears. When the clippers stopped, Johnny thought that Harpster would offer more ridicule, but he spoke to Ed as if Johnny weren't there. "Charley Larkin wants to make this a dry county."

"He can dry up hisself."

The sheriff grinned bigger than ever. "Some people might go for it, Ed. Bringin' sobriety and uprightness to public life. Freein' us all from sin. What you think?"

"Allus a certain amount of sin around. Ban liquor and they'll drive to Wright County and run over somebody on the way back. We cain't get nobody to come downtown as it is, without you close the bars."

"He might be thinkin' of our fine high school boys, Ed. Like our little goat-roper here."

"Laws against them drinkin' already."

"Which I have to enforce. Just about nightly."

"Point that out. Your fine record on public drunkenness."

"And maybe how I've always been a good Christian myself. Whatcha think?"

"Pretty hard sell, that last part."

The reverend had never been anything but nice to him. He'd never call anyone a goat-roper. But what Johnny said was, "I think Reverend Larkin's too fat to be sheriff."

He'd never seen the sheriff laugh so hard, and old Ed, not exactly slender himself, had to sit down to regain his composure.

But it was vicious laughter. Johnny slipped out the door and threw the remainder of his pamphlets into a trash barrel, feeling mean, and confused, and all alone. He stopped at the bus station for a pack of cigarettes.

His father marked several verses in his Bible where Jesus cured people of their blindness or cast out evil spirits—miracles. It figured that if you were holding revivals, you needed dramatic stories for the sinners, but Johnny had a hard time seeing them as more than that. He'd have given all he owned—admittedly, not much—to know exactly what his father thought of them, because if you believed in miracles, or didn't, that said much about who you were.

Over popcorn, he asked Lucy, "How come there aren't any miracles in the present day?"

Sweetly, she said, "A rose is a miracle."

"It's beautiful, but it's just . . . there."

"God put it there. It could be a weed, and it's a miracle that it ain't."

"Is anything that's beautiful a miracle?"

She paused. "Yes."

Munching on the popcorn, he thought of Jane Epstein. "A pretty girl is a miracle."

Lucy shook her head. "She may not be pretty underneath."

He thought about this. "Underneath what?"

"Physical beauty is only skin deep. A skinny girl can have a beautiful soul."

Like his green tennis shoes didn't indicate anything about his true self, Johnny thought. "Suzanne has a beautiful soul?"

Lucy laughed. "My Suzanne isn't skinny, Johnny. She's growin' fast."

"Like a weed?"

"Oh, you're just playin' with words." She frowned. "There's miracles 'sides what grows."

He lay back on the cot, arms behind his head. "Like water into wine."

"All the parables. But like Jesus deliverin' you outta the storm, Johnny, and healin' you when you was sick."

Since he hadn't truly been sick, he had difficulty counting this episode as a miracle. The storm, and George Bell's dying, just seemed like a lot of bad luck piled together. Afterwards, his luck turned somewhat better, but how could you think of it as miraculous? If Everett's yanking him from the snow was a miracle, then why hadn't God intervened sooner, avoiding Johnny's frozen toes, or even George Bell's sitting in that chair?

He tried again. "How come Jesus don't heal everybody? How come he didn't heal Brother Griggs?"

"He may be healed in Tulsa."

That would be proof, Johnny thought. "What if he isn't?"

"Then it's not the Lord's will."

If things didn't work out, it was the Lord's will. If they did, it was a miracle. "Don't people die before their time?"

"It may seem like that, but it is allus the Lord's will."

"With my grandfather?"

Lucy frowned.

"He killed himself," Johnny said. "Did the Lord know he was goin' to?"

"You're not thinkin' a the power of Satan. Your grand-father was under Satan's spell."

"Then why did God let the Devil win?"

"Oh, Johnny. You've seen too much. It's just the Lord's will, sometimes, and we cain't understand it while we are here on Earth. It's also a matter a your grandfather's free will. Your grandfather coulda went to Heaven, but he chose the path of iniquity."

He had, of course. That was what going to church that Sunday had been about: one last chance for a sinful man. "He went to Hell," Johnny said. "He's burnin' there right now."

"It's just too cruel to say that, Johnny. The Lord works in mysterious ways. It was a good work a your grandfather to bring you home. Only God can know what tormented the man."

With three minutes to go in the fourth quarter, Red Buck's Cougars executed a series of fast breaks for eight points, and took the lead by four. Sweat poured off the Bulldogs star, a big blond-headed boy named Carson, really all that Mountain Vale had. He sneered and stomped, and ran and passed and caught a pass, and pretty soon bulldozed his team to a two-point lead. But Gary Tyrell kept blocking him, and whistles blew again and again. Gary, really all that the Cougars had, dueled the blond-headed boy for possession all the way down the court, and finally stole the ball. But then he lost control and it rolled out of bounds.

"Away away away away let's take that ball awa—ee—ay," the cheerleaders chanted, after Gary took it away. Every-one clapped to the drumbeat from the band. So much noise rose that some people covered their ears.

Here came that big Bulldog again, out for blood. Gary charged, but then he stopped and simply stood there. The

Bulldog couldn't halt his momentum and knocked Gary down. The crowd moaned but more whistles blew because the big Bulldog had fouled out. It was curtains for Mountain Vale.

It seemed Gary was the underdog, even though he'd outsmarted the blond kid. "Ga-ree! Ga-ree!" Jane screamed, as everyone's hero plowed through boys a head shorter and thirty pounds lighter and racked up twelve quick points.

Jane leaped high with her legs spread. Johnny swayed with the crowd, but all that interested him were Jane's red panties, and her thighs gleaming in the lights. The game receded into the distance. He broke into a sweat as Jane did a cartwheel, and another one, and another one. Each time her little skirt fell, and her legs arched toward Heaven. His idiot penis stood up like a puff adder.

He'd read about penises in a physiology book down in Texas. The book didn't lay out any rules, such how to make the damn thing behave itself because you were in a public place. He hadn't found much help in Tarzan books, either, though he finally understood all that business about the ape man's pounding red blood.

Johnny looked at the lights, closed his eyes, and drifted away on the ocean of noise. He tried to pray, but on the line to Heaven he heard only static.

Gary was good on the basketball court, and he had clothes, and money in his pockets, and a 409 Impala, all because his dad owned the Chevy dealership. That simply meant he was lucky. How could a smart girl like Jane fail to see that?

There was more to it. Jane's man was out there, battling for her. You couldn't get away from it: Gary starred at everything. How, therefore, could she be interested in a goat roper?

Thinking it through and keeping his eyes averted from the Temptress was like holding out fire to wolves. But his pounding red blood calmed, and he felt smarter by a millimeter. The answer? Jane *couldn't* be interested. He should have the sense to avoid someone so shallow and devious.

This would be his policy from now on.

He'd do it.

The horn sounded. Red Buck had won by eighteen points. The Mountain Vale team trudged from the court, heads low, while the Red Buck boys trotted around like state champions. Bobby Sills strutted ahead of them with the school colors, though he was a clumsy player and had never left the bench.

Little kids ran onto the court, hopping with joy. Their parents came down from the stands slowly, laughing, talking about how wisely their tax dollars were spent, and how it would be an early spring. Johnny sat a moment longer, imagining himself to be invisible as Gary trotted over, and kissed Jane, and whispered something in her ear.

"I can't wait," she said, her eyes glowing. So much assurance hung between them, they were so confident of the world they lived in, that Johnny wanted to bawl. You could sort of live without money, but you'd never get the girl. Not the girl named Jane anyhow. Life was exactly like *The Many Loves of Dobie Gillis*. Jane was Tuesday Weld, and Johnny was as out of luck as poor old Dobie.

A bank of lights went dark, and he made his way down the bleachers. He'd be happy on that distant day when school became nothing but bad memories. He walked slowly near the band, keeping a tuba between Jane and himself. On the floor ahead were a heap of pom-poms, and he picked one up and shook it experimentally. Silly stuff.

"Thank you, John," Jane said, taking the pom-pom. "I saw you up there."

"You did?"

Though her face was moist from sweat, she had calmed, and her dark eyes were friendly. He couldn't speak. He stared at the cougar on her sweater and imagined her naked breasts. "You're so beautiful," he murmured.

"You're kinda cute yourself," she said. "Sneaking around."

"I wasn't—" His voice trailed off in a squeak. Love should only be allowed at a distance, he thought. It was nothing but agony when you drew close.

A plump girl, with a clean, flushed face, came up and helped Jane stow away gear. She smiled as if Johnny should introduce himself.

"This is Myra, John," Jane said.

He thought he knew her from Mrs. Koontz's class, but his mouth couldn't form a hello. At last, he made his legs move, and stepped past.

Jane touched his arm with her fingertips. "John, I have a date tonight."

The word seemed foreign, but that was it, he wanted a date with her.

"Myra's free."

He glanced toward Myra, walking toward the far door. "Don't have a car," he said.

"Myra does. She likes you, John."

"Don't want Myra, I want you!" he shouted, causing Myra to turn. He marched after her, and for an instant she must have thought he meant to talk to her, because she stood expectantly. He shook his head, and she lifted hers angrily, and slammed the big door behind her.

Jane ran in front of him. There was a spike of anger in her eyes. "Did you know I was Jewish?"

"I don't really know what Jewish *is,*" he said. "I—I was just witnessin' for Jesus."

"Oh, witness away, John." Jane waved the pom-poms and twirled about in the last of the lights as if she were on stage. "Would you like to hear the song I promised you?"

Sure, he thought. Hammer in the nails.

The game was played on Sunday
In Heaven's own back yard
With Jesus playing fullback

And Moses playing guard.
The stands were filled with angels
And oh how they did yell
When Jesus scored a touchdown
Against those boys from Hell.
> Go with God!
> Go with God!
> Jesus on the one-yard line
> Doin Godalmighty fine
> Go with God!
> Go with God!

If there was more, he didn't hear it, for he'd blundered from the gym, crashing down the dark hall, through the doors, and into the rain. *Rain.* It blended with ice and brought him to his senses more and less. He zipped up his policeman's jacket.

Someone had ridden Max's bicycle while he was inside and bent the handlebars up to a crooked angle. He bent them back and got on, only to find that the chain had snapped. He pushed the bike slowly down the street, growing wetter and wetter, ice in his hair. Three miles to walk.

"Bitch!" he cried, when he'd passed the city limits. She lured him to the game all for that damn song. She'd *practiced* the song. Oh, you couldn't trust anyone, and love didn't exist.

"Bitch!" he screamed to the wind, though mainly he was angry with himself for being such a hillbilly. Here's what a fool, what a God-damned goat-roper, he was: if Jane had pulled up beside him on the dark road, he'd have crawled into her car like a wet puppy. And licked her hand.

An hour later, he threw the bike against the goat barn and crept in, peeling off his shirt, squishing his way through the darkness. He pulled the string to the light. Suzanne lay in the farthest corner of his cot, wet, too, her hair matted to her forehead and hanging in clumps. She was barefooted.

"Johnny—Mama's sick."

Johnny couldn't take it in. "What?"

She cried, and he moved his arms helplessly. Somehow he thought she wanted him to crawl in there with her.

"I'm so cold," she said.

He sat on the cot and tucked his blanket around her shoulders. "Cain't you call a doctor for her?"

"Sick in her *mind*. Ronnie and Rosie were watching TV and kinda giggl*ing*, and Mama went in, and she says, 'There's a nekkid woman on the TV—nekkid!' And I said, 'No, Mama, it's just her outfit, it's white like her skin, this is Lawrence Welk!' Only she says it's Satan, the TV is a devil-box, and I said she was crazy, and she *hit* me, Johnny!"

"Calm down," he whispered. This seemed to comfort her, but he feared the wildness in her eyes. He didn't understand any of these women, Suzanne, Jane, Candy, or Lucy. And he wanted his cot back.

"I'm too old to be hit."

He put an arm around her, and she burrowed into him. The rain came up stronger and beat on the roof. Lightning flashed and the bulb on the pull-chain flickered. She looked up at him like a run-over dog, and he kissed her on the cheek. She twisted around and they kissed on the lips.

"She beat Ronnie and Rosie," Suzanne said, distantly. "Beat 'em awful."

She was not describing the Lucy Johnny knew. The light went out and came on again, and their shadows danced on the wall. He looked down at Suzanne as if from a height. "I'll talk to her."

He threw another blanket around his shoulders and dashed through the rain, stomped his feet to announce his presence, and then marched down the hall. He found Lucy as he had a dozen times, sitting in her housecoat, reading the Bible and listening to sacred music. "Suzanne—"

Lucy smiled gently. "Did you have a nice time at the game, Johnny?"

"Yes, ma'am. But—"

"It's so important for young people to get out. Are you ready for a blessin' this Lord's Day?"

"Yes, ma'am. Suzanne, she said—"

"Past her bedtime, Johnny. We had an argument, just an argument in the family, and she—"

The front door slammed and Suzanne scurried down the hall like some little animal. She ducked into her room and slammed the door. Johnny heard her bedsprings squeak.

Lucy closed her Bible. "Good night, Johnny."

Rain sifted through the screen door and dampened the kitchen linoleum. He needed to crawl under his warm blankets. He needed to fume, calm down, and scheme a way out of this house.

"Night, ma'am," he said.

Chapter Ten
Washed in the Blood

Everett and Johnny came down the hill from the church, stumbled about in the fog, and at last got kindling lighted. They didn't speak. They built the fire high, stood close, and drank coffee until there were coals.

"There's muskrat in this river," Everett said at last, as if delivering moral judgment. Johnny had shown himself to be a Christian soldier, and he knew Everett meant to be friendly, but this was the fellow who'd tried to beat him senseless. "Some in Plunge Creek, too. On my land."

Everett unwrapped the wether. It was old Tublat, whom Johnny had named after Tarzan's irritable ape father. He felt queasy when Everett drove a steel spit through Tublat and wired together his feet. They hung him between cement posts, basted him with barbecue sauce, and fed the coals some dry hickory.

By ten, the sun had boiled away the fog. Swallows flew low over the water, darted up high, and tumbled as though they'd been shot. Then they dove into crevices in the bluff where their nests were.

In the summertime kids climbed the bluff and dove off, dropping twenty feet to the water. But now chunks of ice clogged the shallows, and a foot of snow hung on along the north shore. Wading out there, even to do the Lord's work, seemed insane.

Grease from the goat splattered onto the coals. Everett rose to baste it again and turn it on the spit. Then he stretched out on a table to doze.

Poor old Tublat, Johnny thought. A good goat, all in all, except that he couldn't give milk.

*　　　*　　　*

He glimpsed Suzanne's sweater, coming nearer through the trees, and turned, pretending to busy himself with the blackened chevon.

"Johnny, I'll help you with your car."

He looked out at the swallows as if he'd never seen birds before. "You don't understand cars."

She made a face. "I went to the Ford place and got a book."

She had him there because he needed a manual. She was bright and cheerful, and the gloom of Friday night seemed unreal in Sunday's sunshine. Perhaps he hadn't found her wet and desperate, and hadn't kissed her—and perhaps Lucy hadn't beat her kids. Just yesterday she came out to the barn with a plate of brownies. The twins were beside her, Rosie in a brand-new dress. Ronnie stuffed his face with brownies. He had a bruise on his cheek, but that didn't mean Lucy put it there.

"You got that manual here?"

"In my room," she whispered.

Everett still slept, the state they both preferred for him. They lined up the rest of the tables to form a serving line, and then Johnny waded into the water a little distance to retrieve the volleyball net, which must have blown there in a storm.

Suzanne sat nearby on a rock and dangled her bare feet, but the water felt so cold she quickly pulled them out again. He grabbed an ankle.

"Don't!" she said, kicking free.

Everett snored on. Johnny caught Suzanne's eyes again and the way they glowed made him want to perform great feats for her.

"You don't really like that Jane Epstein, do you?"

He bent to steal a kiss.

She ducked. "Are you scared?"

"What?"

He plopped beside her on the grass and realized that she meant the baptism. "Kind of." He lay back, closed his eyes, and breathed the sweet air.

"When did you start smoking?"

"I quit," he said, sitting up again.

"I saw you behind the barn."

He smoked, sometimes, but life was hard. A person couldn't attain perfection overnight.

"Daddy smokes."

Everett did *not* smoke, Johnny thought. How could he?

"He backslid once, too. Mama told me before Max was born how he used to play poker, drink whiskey even, all the bad things he learned in the army. Then he got saved again. Anyone can backslide, Johnny."

"Suzanne—"

"I'm in-between. I don't go around announcing what a fine Christian I am, but I'm not gonna backslide, either."

"You're a nice girl," he said.

"What's wrong with that?"

None too soon, the first of the families came down the hill, bearing covered dishes and drinks, and he leapt up to tend the meat. Suzanne walked along the water, smiling mysteriously, her hands tucked behind. Johnny opened his father's Bible, seeking knowledge even as his faith ebbed away.

Reverend Larkin wore his straw hat and had traded his tie for a sports shirt, a colorful thing he called his Hawaiian shirt. He helped unpack fried chicken and potato salad and began munching on a drumstick before his wife could shoo him away. "You're just a big ole rat," she said.

Virgil and Sister Showalter launched into a promotional campaign for her stewed tomatoes. "It's Granny Showalter's recipe," Virgil said. "The ole folks, they knowed how to cook a simple thing and make it special."

"They surely did," the reverend said as he tried the tomatoes and smacked his lips appropriately. "Those are *good*," he said, and Sister Showalter beamed. Sister Larkin tried them, too, and wrote down the recipe, and everyone was happy.

Reverend Larkin approached Everett. "Looks mighty savory," he said. "Don't recall eatin' goat meat before."

"Chevon," Everett said.

"Chevon it is."

Lucy came over to stand beside her husband. "It's like venison," she said.

A new fellow named Clyde Fooch set up a charcoal grill and fried crappie in two big, cast-iron skillets. Suzanne wouldn't go near, because Clyde was an ex-convict, but Reverend Larkin had to have some of that crappie.

"Where'd you catch these, Brother Fooch?"

"Elk Crick. By the low-water bridge there. Caught 'em first light."

There were a dozen casseroles, beets and deviled eggs, potato salad, lime pickles made the summer before, spinach salad, Jell-O salad with black walnuts, scalloped potatoes, dandelions cooked with bacon, and barbecued morel mushrooms. These came from Arkansas and were a real treat, the first thing to disappear along with Clyde Fooch's crappie.

For dessert you could have apple pie, blackberry cobbler, sweet potato pie, or carrot cake.

Sister Showalter pointed at Tublat. "What's that?"

"Chevon," Everett growled.

"You cain't tell it from venison," Lucy chimed in quickly.

"I cain't eat goat meat nor onions," Sister Showalter said. "Too strong."

"Not a wether," Everett said.

"What?"

"Meat ain't strong, he was castrated. See, you take a big, fat rubber band, you wrap it around his nuts—"

"Everett!" Lucy said.

Sister Showalter, a substantial woman, looked as if she was trying to determine which word offended her more, castrated or fat.

"Get along with ye, Patty-Cakes," Virgil said, and held out his plate. "I was raised on goat. Howya doin', Evvy?"

"Pretty fair," Everett said.

Reverend Larkin came behind Virgil, and according to his wife, took more chevon, potato salad, and candied sweet potatoes than he could possibly eat.

"It's my duty to sample everything," he said, and everyone laughed.

Everyone but Everett. "Let's line up the babies, so he can kiss 'em."

"Hon, please," said Lucy. "It'll be over soon."

When the line had passed, Everett began wrapping the chevon in tinfoil, and Lucy wiped down the table. Suzanne hadn't put anything on her plate except a sliver of roast beef and some strawberry Jell-O.

"Eat some goat," Lucy told her.

"That's Tublat."

Lucy raised her voice. "Eat some."

Scowling, Suzanne scooped up a few molecules of Tublat and headed to the far end of the park. Johnny couldn't bring himself to eat Tublat, either, but he wanted to wring Patty Showalter's neck for her snooty ways. George Bell was better behaved. Everett put forth his best effort, and people still snubbed him. What about loving your neighbor? Where did the beautiful things that Jesus said matter, if not here?

After considerable argument, and after he'd been promised he'd be allowed to play, Ronnie Ogletree ran up the hill to the church basement to find the volleyball. When he returned no one wanted him, but he made such a fuss that at last he and three other "babies" were assigned to the boys' team.

This would even the odds against the girls, said the girls, which included one young woman, the widow Candy Cruz.

Everyone was sorry for Candy, but even so, the wives of the church had thrown a zone defense around her. She hovered between adults and the teenagers, not belonging to either. And she tipped the balance of a team that was already more skillful. The boys could only compensate with powerful spikes and arguments over rules. Johnny pranced like a goat but seemed to bat everything foul, and watched helplessly as Suzanne leaped high at the net to push the ball in directions he couldn't predict. Once, she stuck out her tongue at him.

She and Candy developed a passing routine as if they'd played together for years. Worse, when Candy and he rotated opposite each other, she gave him a peculiar look, lifting her nose as if he were dirt.

He was near to concluding that she was just another version of Jane when the ball worked loose and rolled between them. They bent down at the same time, and he saw her older woman's breasts, bouncing around under her tee shirt without any bra to keep them honest. She rose slowly, and rather than a scowl, gave him a smile.

Next came a long volley, until they leaped simultaneously. Her little fist came down on his head like a post mall, and he fell. Vaguely aware of laughter, he crawled to the sidelines. Candy neared, smelling of roses, and stroked his face. Her breasts hung like a reward.

"You OK?" she asked sweetly. "I didn't mean to hurt you."

Watching the victorious Candy walk away, he understood he'd been bamboozled. He hoped it happened again.

He recovered enough to join a group of men talking about how far corn planting had advanced, the price of fertilizer, the price of eggs, the amount of rain, Ford versus Chevy versus Dodge versus International trucks.

"It was a real blow to this country when Studebaker went out of business," Johnny put in, experimenting to see if he could talk like a man to other men. They stared at him as if he were the Antichrist, and he wandered onward. He spied Candy again, entering the wooded trail that followed the shore down to the dam. She'd hardly disappeared when the farmer he'd seen her with the day he was saved grabbed a drumstick from the serving tables, grinned innocently at Sisters Larkin and Showalter, and followed.

Look out, Johnny thought. What the farmer didn't see were the dozen pairs of female eyes that focused on him, setting afire his back-trail.

On the shore stood the congregation, clapping and singing.

Shall we gather at the river,
Where bright angel feet have trod,
With its crystal tide forever
Flowing by the throne of God?

The words came to him as if over a long distance. His numb feet sank into the bottom, but at least he wore jeans. One of the girls wore a skirt, her Sunday best, and her bare legs had turned white as bones.

They all moved into the current, with Reverend Larkin motioning impatiently. He was cold, too. "Dear Lord, we come to you on the shores a this peaceful river—" Larkin prayed, and Johnny tried to concentrate on the beautiful words. A peaceful river but also a damned cold one, and the faithful gathered on the shore seemed far away as France. He couldn't make out any of their faces.

"In the name a the Father!" cried the reverend, as one, and two, staggered to shore like sheep emerging from a dip. The girl in the skirt sat in the grass, and yanked at her wet hair, and rubbed her legs. If she'd done it, so could he.

Larkin dropped his great hand on Johnny's head and seemed to hesitate. He smiled sadly. "This young man, Johnny Bell, is new to us, new to the Kingdom of God. We all know of his special trial—"

"Amen!" rose from the congregation. Johnny spied the widow Cruz, but her face was blurred. Down he went, thinking of Candy's breasts even as he drowned in the blood of Jesus.

He'd drawn a long breath, closed his mouth, but the icy water stung his eyes. Blessings drifted down:

> Yes, we'll gather at the river,
> The beautiful, the beautiful river;
> Gather with the saints at the river
> That flows by the throne of God.

He stayed under long enough for his sins to reach the Mississippi. *Raise* me! he thought, and at last "Hallelujah!" rose from the shore. His nose dove toward the sky, and water ran down his icy cheeks. "Praise Jee-sus!" cried the reverend, but Johnny jerked from his sheltering arms and staggered away, his ears sloshing, his feet cold as George Bell. One step, two.

"Amen! Amen!"

He crawled onto the grass, coughed. Virgil handed him a towel and blanket, and said, "God love ya, big fella." He guided Johnny to the fire, where his companions in virtue sat holding hands, and singing.

> Soon we'll reach the shining river,
> Soon our pilgrimage will cease;
> Soon our happy hearts will quiver
> With the melody of peace.

He grew warm then and felt clean. He stood with his back to the fire and laughed with the sheer joy of it all. The girl in the skirt looked up at him with red, trusting eyes, and he hugged her in Christian fellowship. Reverend Larkin hugged them all. Sixty beautiful faces filed past with big smiles. Even Suzanne seemed moved, and hugged Johnny, and cried. Plump ladies whispered their blessings; strong men pounded his back. He sat in a camp chair, slurping hot chocolate, jabbering how the water wasn't really so cold, and oh, how he loved Jesus!

But behind them stood Candy's farmer, cowering before his angry wife. And up the lane, on the hill to the church, Johnny saw the widow Cruz. A dozen angry women urged her onward. Sister Larkin shook a fist. Sister Showalter thrust her face near the beautiful widow's and worked her jaw like an umpire's. In hardly a minute Sister Candy had been banished from the congregation, never again to be seen along the Piney River, gone.

Chapter Eleven
A Boy and His Car

Johnny sat behind the goat barn, soaking up some sun after church. He smoked Pall Malls and read about the 1937 Ford's revolutionary 221-cubic-inch V-8 engine, until La butted him in the crotch. He chased after her and she jumped up on a barrel, tidily packing in all four feet; just as he grabbed for her, she made another leap, and reached the roof. She slipped a little and leaped again to the apex.

He looked up in amazement. "No way you did that."

Catch me up here, her blue eyes said.

"You can't get down," Johnny said. "I bet I have to go after the ladder."

Exactly then, spoiling a perfectly fine Sunday, Everett rolled up the lane off of Highway E. He'd been gone for two weeks and, in Johnny's opinion, the place hummed right along without him. Johnny took La and the others out to feed on clover, and milk production soared.

"The ogre has returned," Johnny called out.

As if she understood, La ran down the ridge and took a leap. Sure she'd break a leg, Johnny made a short run, too, but La plopped into a mound of old hay, and stared at him placidly.

"It's Super Goat!"

"Brrr-att," she said.

Everett crawled up on the truck bed and threw down a bag of seed potatoes, then stood eying the corn field Virgil had planted in his absence. He'd slimmed down some, and his face was brown from sun.

He didn't try to hide his cigarette when Johnny came

near. "Thought you was gonna make garden."

"Lucy said it wasn't worth the trouble."

"Not make garden?" He jumped from the truck and headed for the house, shaking his head at such decadent behavior. "Bring some tools, Johnny; I'll roust out the tribe. *Have* to make garden."

Pretty soon Lucy and the kids came straggling. "You ain't here to take care of it, Everett, and the bugs eat everything," Lucy said.

"Them kids cain't pick potato bugs?"

"Stuff's just as cheap in the store," Suzanne said.

"I like the tomatas," Lucy said. "But I'm tired, Everett, and I just cain't face the cannin' this year. This ain't the Depression we're livin' in. We ain't that poor."

For answer, Everett cranked the roto-tiller and chewed up soil. It was in fair shape already because Virgil had disked it when he planted Larkin's—the Co-op's—corn.

The twins ran behind, picking up stones. Johnny drove two stakes and Lucy stretched string, then he cut several rows with a hoe. Suzanne dropped seeds for spinach, radishes, and kohl rabis.

"I should be study*ing*," she said.

George Bell never wanted the bother of a garden, either, but Mary always insisted. Johnny remembered raising a dozen rattlesnake watermelons planted where the bathtub drained, about a thousand years ago.

"Sweet corn!" Everett said. "That supermarket corn ain't fit to eat."

Lucy rolled her eyes. "Everett, I got supper on."

Before long everyone escaped to the house except Everett and Johnny. Everett dropped cut potato eyes into a bag of sulfur and Johnny spaded holes. Johnny awaited a pronouncement about the size of potatoes in Alaska, but it didn't arrive. Everett lit another cigarette, sighed, and at last turned for the house.

In the kitchen, Suzanne threw her dad a look that did justice to Jane Epstein's malicious techniques. "Your supper's in the oven," she said. "Mama went to bed."

"Luce—"

"She's mad, Daddy."

"I ain't sayin' she has to can. We live out here, maybe the land ain't ours. But it's *sposed* to be a farm."

"She doesn't like string*ing* beans, either. But she's—you're smok*ing* again."

The phone rang and Lucy appeared in her long white gown.

"If it's Charley Larkin, I ain't home," Everett called out.

"Well. Oh, thank the Lord. Hello," Lucy said. "Are you awright, honey?"

"Guess it ain't Reverend Larkin," Johnny put in.

"Ronnie's so bi-ig!" Lucy said. "Your dad's been workin' over toward Springfield."

"Mama," said Suzanne. "Is it—?"

"Oh, well, we need the money."

"Let *me* talk," Everett said.

"It's Max," Suzanne said.

Lucy hung up.

"What!" Everett said.

Lucy's face was flushed. "He's awright."

"Is he com*ing* home?" Suzanne asked.

"Soon. Has to unwind, he says."

"I was that way," Everett said. "He's awright?"

Lucy seemed far away. "Not hurt, he says."

"How come he don't wanna talk to me?"

"In a hurry, that's all. Right there in the processin' place." She stared at Everett for a long time, then turned down the hall again.

Johnny propped the Ford manual against the air filter and pried off the distributor cap to check the points.

"I don't know what they look like," he said.

La gazed down sympathetically from atop the cab. She opened her mouth but didn't bleat. It was more of a yawn, and then she chewed some more.

Points should be at maximum distance apart for gapping.

Men such as Everett and Virgil talked about points as if they were as common as sparrows, making Johnny too embarrassed to ask what they looked like. Points were so common, in fact, that the fellow who wrote the manual hadn't even bothered to provide an illustration. But they were there, had to be.

Proper gap is .014. The points start to open when the lobe of the cam—

Now he found an illustration. He held it directly above the distributor and shone his flashlight. The cam took the shape of an octagon; the lobe was any of the corners. The points were round, rather than pointed. And he made out two sets.

"La! I found them!"

She leaped over the hood and pranced outside.

"Don't go too far," Johnny called.

The points were closed. To adjust them, you screwed out a tiny bolt. He'd liberated a feeler gauge from a heap of old tools in the Ogletree barn, but you couldn't gap the points unless they were apart, the book said so. He pushed Suzanne's fingernail file between them, but they snapped shut again.

To open points, gently crank engine—

No battery. Possibly, he could crank it by hand, like a tractor, but he didn't know how, and didn't have a crank in any case.

—or rock vehicle forward in high gear.

Right! He slid behind the wheel and shifted to what corresponded to high on Everett's tractor: clutch in, over right, up. He stepped to the trunk to lodge his feet flat against the wall, lock his knees, and shove with his back.

The Ford rolled a few feet, and the points opened, but weren't on a lobe. He returned to the trunk and pushed the car forward another foot. The points closed again.

"Dammit," he said, and hurried to the grill, where it was harder to brace himself. Finally, the car hunched backward, and the points opened precisely on the lobe. He filed and gapped them, fitted on the gasket and cap again, and laughed. He went outside and climbed on La like she was a little pony, though he kept his feet on the ground because he didn't want to hurt her. He hadn't felt so fine in months. He laughed and laughed in the deep woods.

"Bra–aat," La said.

It began to rain as he bicycled down Jefferson Street so he rode up under the big awnings at Noolin Brothers, then followed the sidewalks around the square to the library. It was past closing time, and cold, and almost dark.

Just before he reached the police station, Mrs. Koontz came running down the walk with a sack of groceries under one arm, holding a newspaper over her head. He almost called to her but she went straight into the station. He parked the bike, thinking he'd say hello and wasn't it a coincidence she'd come to see the sheriff, too, but she ran right out again.

The sheriff must have stood there in the doorway for an instant, because Johnny smelled his cigarette, but if Harpster said anything, Johnny couldn't hear it. On the street, Mrs. Koontz opened her car door and called out, "Pot roast. Sound good?"

Johnny ran a few steps and waved, but she was already gone. He opened the door and the wind blew him almost to Tulsa. Then he simply stood there, watching as the sheriff turned from his desk, and set down a clipboard.

"That was Mrs. Koontz," he said.

Harpster's eyes jumped. "You were standin' out there?"

"She's my teacher. She's been real nice. I bet you helped

her out when her husband, I mean her ex-husband, was giving her all that trouble. I think it's great that—"

Harpster grabbed a jacket from the hall tree and stepped into the bathroom, not quite closing the door. Johnny didn't understand how someone urinating could sound angry, but it did. He plunked down in a chair feeling the next thing to sick and wished he hadn't come. Where did you go to find a friend? The yellow pages?

The sheriff came out at last, combing his hair. "You," he said, as if he were surprised Johnny still sat there. And something new appeared in his eyes, that look some people had for George Bell and him when they were traveling. Trash, the look said. White trash.

Johnny stepped toward the door. "I–I had a question."

Harpster rolled his eyes. "I should charge a fee."

I could have asked Virgil Showalter, Johnny thought. Maybe he was a friend. "I got a battery only the engine don't turn over."

"I guess you mean that old Ford." The sheriff looked relieved and irritated at the same time. "It's a six-volt, right?"

"Yes, sir. They had some Volkswagen batteries behind Art's Army Surplus."

Staring into the hall mirror, Harpster pulled on his hat and adjusted it carefully. "You bought the battery?"

Johnny hung his head. "I didn't steal it, no, sir."

Harpster peered steadily into the mirror, then came into the office again with a tough guy pose. "My dad had an old one-cylinder tractor once, and it froze up. Rings rusted to the cylinder wall. What you might do—it won't hurt anything—you pull all the plugs and pour kerosene down the wells. Then let her sit a while. You got to realize this is an old, old vehicle."

"I was hopin' you'd come take a look."

He didn't react, except to stop for a moment before the window, and stare into the rainy night. "Why don't you talk to Everett? He knows more than I do about automobiles. Nothin' else, he could give you a pull with his tractor."

"Except that Everett—"

The sheriff held open the door. Rain fell heavily, but Johnny wasn't about to ask for a ride. It was plain enough that he needed one, if Harpster cared to notice. Then Johnny found himself whining. He hated himself for it, but he couldn't understand why the sheriff was so mean. "It won't run no matter what I do."

"Ah huh." The wind whipped at Harpster's face and he yanked on the brim of his hat. "A vehicle can seem personal, but it never is. It's a machine. It's logical. Get everything lined up, it has to run." He glanced at his watch. "And so do I."

Like gunfire, the engine of Everett's International came to life, spluttering in the wet air, backfiring tufts of flame up the long, chrome-plated pipes by the cab. In the fog, Everett's head bobbed in and out of sight.

Lucy materialized from the porch, her hair snarled from sleep. "*Speak* to him."

"Him" could only mean Johnny. They'd found out about the car, Johnny thought. Still, what difference did it make? He almost jumped to the running board to ask Everett if he could borrow his tractor.

Everett revved the engine, then nursed it to a smooth idle. "Don't see the problem."

Lucy made her way through the muddy driveway and disappeared by the opposite truck door. For a moment, Johnny couldn't make out either of them. "Because you won't. They're of an age, Everett. They watch that TV; they get ideas. The Lord—"

"What's the Lord got to do with it?"

"She's your daughter."

"And I trust her, Luce."

"You trust Johnny?"

"He's just a big dumb kid, that's what I think."

Maybe so, Johnny thought, to work for the likes of Everettt Ogletree.

"Should I talk to Brother Larkin?"

"You know my opinion on that subject." He ground the stick and found a gear. "I believe they'll get it figured out, Luce."

"That's what I'm afraid of."

Everett edged the truck forward. "Let me know what you hear from Max."

She turned without answering, clutching her housecoat to her thin chest. Everett grunted, and the International chugged away in the fog.

They waited until there was a teacher's conference at the high school and calculated the rest like a heist. The twins were at the elementary. Lucy had left for her new job, a part-time grill cook at the bus station.

Suzanne emerged wearing cut-off jeans and a pullover and carrying a basket of food. He climbed onto the tractor, and La perched her feet on the fence as if she were praying.

"You can't go," Johnny told her. "We got important things to do today."

She snorted and turned away.

"She has such pretty blue eyes," Suzanne said.

"What?"

"You act like that goat's your girlfriend."

Flashing her brown eyes, she climbed up to sit at the edge of the steel seat, daintily positioning herself not to touch him. The shift came up between her legs. A more sensible farm girl would have ridden on the tow bar, he thought, but he wasn't going to argue with the girl who'd found him a Ford manual.

He had to stop to clip a rusty strand of barbed wire near Virgil's place, and then they chugged through tall weeds, paralleling the railroad, until they crawled down the rocky slope where the viaduct met the wash. He spun up from the gravel and lumbered along the old lane, surprising three turkeys that flopped slowly into the woods. They crossed the bridge George Bell had made half a century before out of railroad ties, startling dozens of cabbage moths that fluttered up, and quickly down again. They reached the walnuts.

"This could be a nice place," Suzanne said. She pointed to the ruins of the house. "What a shame. But maybe—maybe you want your *own* house, Johnny."

He backed the tractor through the implement door and hooked a chain around the Ford's bumper, but work remained. He screwed in his new plugs while Suzanne got behind the wheel and fiddled with the radio, which of course didn't work.

He checked the battery and every other connection. "Go," he said, almost wincing.

She turned the key and there was a terrible clanging noise. "Ow! Is it ruined?"

"It's awright." Not exactly, but the fan blade had rotated slightly, which meant that the cylinders were pumping free. The kerosene treatment had worked. "Go," he said.

This time the starter whirred but didn't seem to engage the flywheel. "Go!"

Now the engine turned over without clanking, but oh-so-slowly, like George Bell climbing steps. "Let me throw a little gas in the carburetor," he said, and propped open the butterfly. "Pump the accelerator."

She turned the key again. The flywheel turned more smoothly, but nothing fired. He flipped off the distributor cap to check the spark between the points. "Go," he said, fighting panic.

She flipped the key again, then came around and poked her nose under the hood. "What's wrong?"

"The spark's yellow."

"What color should it be?"

"Blue."

"How about green? Green's my favorite color."

He wouldn't dignify such ignorance with a reply. "A machine is logical," he said, his eyes sighting through the walnuts. He sighed. "You get your spark, you get fuel, it *has* to run."

"*Has* to run," she said, behind the wheel again, her back straight, her arms horizontal. "What do I do?"

"We're gonna pull it." He placed a foot on the running board and leaned through the window. Her hair brushed his face, and he turned his head and smiled at her sideways. His arms pressed against her thighs as he reached for the gearshift. "This is first," he explained, hearing an echo of Everett in his tone.

"First," she repeated.

"Neutral, second; neutral, third. Okay?"

"Okay."

"Now it's in first. Keep the clutch down and it won't do nothin'. When we get to the bridge, on the straightaway there, I'll raise my hand, and you let out the clutch."

"What if it doesn't start?"

"We'll turn around and try it again. It's gonna seem real balky and maybe shake the car some, tryin' to fire. But if it starts to run, you gotta do two things. It'll wanna chase up and hit the tractor, so you gotta brake. Before you brake, though, you gotta shove in the clutch."

She demonstrated with her feet. "I got it."

"If you don't do that, it'll die, and we'll have to start all over."

"You're a really good mechanic, Johnny."

She looked up at him so sweetly he wanted to kiss her, but he forced himself to concentrate. "If it wants to die, you gotta give it gas, but don't race it. It ain't run in a long time, and that oil has got to circulate."

"Let's go!" Suzanne said, patting the steering wheel.

He ran to the tractor, put it in first, and eased away. The Ford followed faithfully, and he stopped to shift to second. He reached the lane and shifted to high. He rounded the bend and dove into the walnuts doing fifteen. He waited until Suzanne turned the Ford straight, and then he raised an arm. She waved back, and for an instant he wondered if she understood.

Then the chain snapped tight. The front of the Ford leapt up, and he pushed in slightly on the clutch. He didn't want to tear the bumper off.

Rumbumbumbumbum.

"Is it go*ing*?" Suzanne called out the window.

The engine turned over but it hadn't fired. He'd simply dragged the car. He shoved in the clutch and fought a wave of sadness. Nothing leaked. Nothing was blocked. He had spark even if it was yellow. He called back, "You got the choke open or closed?"

"Closed."

That was right, wasn't it? Had he flooded the engine? He ran back to prop a pair of pliers in the carburetor intake. That would keep the butterfly open. Air and gas. Pure logic. Had to run. He jumped onto the tractor again, accelerated gently, raised his hand. The Ford jerked back so forcefully he thought he'd swallowed his teeth. Perhaps they'd need to go back and forth half a dozen times, until they'd knocked the weeds flat, and made a runway.

Rumbumbumbum . . . PAH!

Flame leapt from the carburetor. He ran to douse it somehow, but as he neared the engine, the flame died. The fan belt squawked. He yanked the pliers from the intake as a coughing and *chachachapah!* rose, ragged as a diesel. Smoke rolled. He worked the butterfly and yelled at Suzanne to push in the choke. And there it was: *errruddinnn . . . errrudin nnnnuhnuhnuhna . . .*

He ran to the door. "Thanks, thanks, thanks, thanks," he said, and bent inside the window, and kissed her.

"We did it," she said. "It's runn*ing.*"

"Logical," he said, laughing. *"Had* to run."

*   *   *

He kept looking back at the Ford. He'd never seen it in the sunshine, and the maroon paint shone as if in a car show on the square. The car would be beautiful once he'd washed and polished it, and best of all, it ran under its own power for five hundred feet. He shut off the engine and started it again three times. Miracle of miracles, the spark had turned blue.

Then they sat in a patch of sun by Plunge Creek, under the bridge of railroad ties. Suzanne placed her sweater under her head and bent her pretty legs to the side. He wanted to kiss her some more.

"Johnny, you know what morel mushrooms look like?"

"Sure." He leaned on his elbow a few inches from her face, munching on a ham sandwich she'd made with mustard and dill pickles. The air smelled sweet. Bees hummed among the blooming wild plums.

She pointed up the creek to an outcropping of grass by the roots of a big dead sycamore. Two brownish knobs poked up from the grass. "Are those good?"

"Yes." He remembered the baptism. "But you know that water's cold."

"I just thought Mama might like them."

No question he owed Suzanne a favor. He took off his boots and socks and rolled his jeans to his knees, while Suzanne stepped forward, and wriggled her toes in the warm sand. His bare foot came down on a piece of flint and he teetered, brought a hand down on Suzanne's shoulder to steady himself. The water wasn't far removed from ice. "Jeeeezus," he said, throwing back his head in a howl.

Suzanne took a step into the rotting leaves along the edge, but didn't come any farther. "Ooo," she said.

"We'll come back in August," he said. "It'll be the coolest spot around." As he waded deeper, bubbles of air floated out of his jeans. Toward the center, water rose to his shoulders and he swam several strokes, aching all over. He pulled himself up again by the sycamore and picked a dozen morels. He tossed them across the water to Suzanne, who had retreated to the grass. Braver now, he dove under the surface, then came to shore walking stiff-legged, like Frankenstein.

"Sit here and warm up," Suzanne said, patting the leaves by her side, and he curled up beside her. Still shivering, he plucked clover blossoms and threw them at her. She lay back. "Did I help you, Johnny?"

"You were great." He tried to kiss her but found only her cheek. "I couldn't a done it without you."

"I *wanted* to do it. I have to . . . live my own life." She peeled a strip of sassafras bark and sank her teeth into it. "I like your place. All those big walnuts, they're amaz*ing*. You could make a lot of money, couldn't you? Are you rich, Johnny?"

He grabbed her legs and she kicked at him, laughing. "I'll push you in," she said, leaning back on her palms, and turning her head to spit out the bark. He gathered water in his hands and dashed it onto her sandy feet.

"You're worse than Ronnie," she said.

He fell to his knees, then dropped on top of her, pinning her arms by the trunk of the sassafras.

"Don't! Johnny, let me up."

He knew she didn't mean it. Her breath rushed upon his cheeks and he kissed her, his teeth scraping hers. She tasted like root beer.

He released her hands, rubbed her stomach, and reached beneath the pullover for her breasts. Her bra rose like a castle wall, but his fingers leapt over, and found a cold nipple. Now he ached all over, as if he had the flu.

She balled her hands into fists beneath his chest and pushed. He rose buoyantly, in delirium, and then she raised her feet to his stomach. It didn't seem possible that she was so strong. He fell backward into the stream, and emerged, wheezing, bewildered. He crawled on his hands and knees, sneezing like a dog with worms.

Her legs arched prettily as she slipped on her shoes, and then she stood high above him, on the bridge. He tried to call out but had no words. Slowly, he came to his feet. He didn't feel amorous anymore.

The tractor started. "What?" he shouted, and hurried up the lane, his bare feet finding every sand spur, every shard of flint.

Suzanne rounded the bend and disappeared into the walnuts.

"Hey!" he yelled. "You don't how to drive!"

Chapter Twelve
The Last Days

The whole thing began at the supper table when Rosie said, "Mama, did you know Suzanne and Johnny went off in the woods today?"

Lucy didn't react for a moment. "What?"

"We seen 'em when we come home from school," Ronnie said. "Suzanne was drivin' the tractor."

"How come you was cryin', Suzanne?" Rosie asked. "Did Johnny hit you, too?"

"Oh, Mama!" Suzanne said. "Johnny didn't do anything. We just—"

"We was workin' on my car, that's all," Johnny said. "We needed to pull it with the tractor."

"You shoulda ast," Lucy said.

"Everett woulda just said no."

Her eyes jumped about almost violently, but her voice was calm. "I don't think so, Johnny."

Maybe that was right, Johnny thought. He'd even have taken pride in it. He'd have welcomed an opportunity to show how much he knew, and how generous he was.

Johnny's head sank low.

"He focked her!" Ronnie announced.

Johnny stood, knocking over his water glass. He cheerfully could have brained the kid against a tree, but he forced himself calm, and dabbed at the spilled water. "You don't even know," he said, which surely was true. He himself had known for hardly a year, and then only because of a studious comparison of library books.

Ronnie ran to the doorway. "It's when you get inside a big girl and pee in her," he said, then scurried outdoors before Lucy could catch him. She didn't try. She waved a hand at Rosie, who grabbed two biscuits and chased after her brother.

"Mama—" Suzanne whispered. "You know I didn't— I would never—"

"We'll talk later, sweetheart."

That "sweetheart" spelled trouble, Johnny thought. Suzanne's voice, too, took on a wounded tone, even though she'd already declared his innocence. Johnny knew he couldn't win. He wasn't doo-doo to Lucy.

"*Why*, Johnny?" Lucy asked.

This seemed more of an accusation than a question, but he gave it a try. "I kissed her. She didn't like it, and I ended up in Plunge Crick. We went out there to get the Ford runnin', entire story. What I done wrong was to borrow the tractor without askin', but Everett can be a real asshole to deal with, and it ain't hurt. No *why* to it, Lucy."

"You've broken our trust," she said.

He sensed she'd had her reply ready before he spoke. "You've broken our trust," he said, in his Mickey Mouse voice.

She stared, not comprehending. A wild look slid over her like a coat of paint, and he knew that in a few minutes she'd be on her knees before the Lord.

Next morning, Suzanne weaved down the aisle of the bus, her eyes full of hurt. He didn't pat the seat next to him. He wasn't angry with her for throwing him into the creek, and it was hardly her fault how weird her mother was, but he was sick of the Ogletree family. True, she'd found the Ford book, but he didn't want Suzanne around him anymore.

"Mama and I prayed—"

"Of course you did," he said.

She was startled. "She says not to worry."

"Do I look worried?"

"I mean about Daddy. It was all a misunderstanding,

Mama knows that, only we need to talk about it to Reverend Larkin."

"Him and his focking missionary work."

"Johnny! You're a Christian, don't forget that. But you're still a boy, Mama says—"

"What do *you* say?"

"Johnny, I just don't *know* . . ." She slumped into the seat across the aisle and tried not to cry. Ronnie popped up—and down again, when he met with the look Johnny had for the little cockroach.

At school Suzanne followed him around like La when Johnny had first brought her from the woods. At lunch she tried to steer him across the cafeteria toward their private corner, but he stalked away, and sat across from Jane Epstein. He knew Suzanne wouldn't come near and perhaps he'd anger her. He preferred her angry to weepy.

He had nothing to say to Jane. He'd avoided her since the basketball game. Working on the car, he'd pretty much put her out of his mind.

She was jawboning the editor of the school paper—Johnny's friend from P. E., Dick Frawley. She'd written an editorial in Mrs. Koontz's class about school cliques. She ought to know, Johnny thought, but apparently Mrs. Koontz liked the editorial. Not so Dick Frawley.

Jane's thick hair bounced. Her dark eyes flashed. She wove her slender fingers in the air as if she were playing the flute. She was so damned good-looking she *had* to be right, but she didn't get anywhere with Dick.

What did Dick know that Johnny didn't? Perhaps that Jane had never given him the time of day and was only talking to him now because she needed his one special thing. If he surrendered it, then it wasn't special anymore. His chubby little arms kept right on pumping food into his mouth, and Johnny could see his point. A ham sandwich wouldn't let you down. Jane Epstein, and Suzanne Ogletree, and the entire race of women, were another story.

At last Jane saw Johnny and her eyes lit up. That she'd be glad to see him was the one thing he hadn't expected. She pulled her editorial back. She made those black eyes round, and something on the order of innocent. "You haven't been coming to basketball games."

It was a statement full of irony, which he'd learned about from Mrs. Koontz. She said there wasn't much irony to be found in Tarzan, for instance, and made him read another book, *A Canticle for Liebowitz*. It was about an order of priests, long into the future when the world had been destroyed by nuclear war. The priests thought they were preserving learning as priests had in the dark ages, but really all they were preserving was an order for pastrami from the grocer. Irony had nothing to do with iron or steel. It was the contrast between what the priests thought to be true, and what was really so.

Of course, Jane might have thought he'd enjoyed her song and dance.

He *did* enjoy it. Jane turned him into a fool, and it wasn't even ironic.

"I been workin'," Johnny said at last.

"Did you know that tennis tryouts are tonight?"

"You'll be there?"

"Yes! Yes! *See* you!" she said, squeezing his shoulder, and dashed off. He felt Suzanne's burning eyes but didn't meet them. He ran after Jane and grabbed her hand. Immediately, she pulled away, but he held the illusion long enough for them to round the corner, out of Suzanne's sight.

Many thought tennis was a sissy sport. And Coach Taney wasn't a real coach, but the algebra teacher. When the novitiates began running, about forty strong, they were full of giggles and craziness, as if they were at a picnic. But Taney blew his whistle and clapped his hands and wouldn't allow anyone to *stop* running. After a while, half the crowd had dropped out, and trudged resentfully up the hill.

Since this was the first year for the program, Coach Taney explained, there would be no conference schedule, and thus no letter jackets. Still more of the hopeful marched uphill, fuming at the unfairness of it all.

Coach demonstrated how to serve and how to return a volley with a level swing, how to keep your eye on the ball and still be aware of the center of your strings. He batted a few balls to likely victims and mostly they swung and missed, and fell down, and were doing well if they could hit the ball into the net.

Gary Tyrell, there because of Jane, turned around like a slugger, and hit a home run. Coach jerked a thumb and Gary smirked and said he'd try harder, but the thumb meant Gary was history.

He couldn't believe it. "You can't just—"

"Get off my court, hotshot."

The survivors were impressed. If their coach was willing to eject the school's star athlete, then perhaps the tryout was serious. School letter or not, perhaps it was fair. Gary marched off the court as if he didn't care, but then he hung on the steel fence, watching. He called out to Jane, but she didn't look at him. He marched off and came back after a while riding in Bobby Sills's souped-up '50 Ford. Bobby popped the clutch and laid rubber, and Gary flashed a beer can, and they rounded the corner toward perdition.

"Hey," Coach said, pointing at Johnny. "Daydreamer!"

Coach Taney knew his name. Because of Suzanne, he was a C student in algebra. Johnny figured the "Hey, you," was a test to see if he could be rattled, like the unfortunate Mr. Tyrell. Coach plunked a fat one and Johnny ran a step, crouched, and hit it right for his knees. Coach stumbled, and there might have been a titter among Johnny's growing legion of fans. Then Taney hit one on the opposite side to test Johnny's forehand, and Johnny repeated the shot. "Good," Taney said, and hit one hard straight at Johnny's face. He brought up his racket in self-defense but caught the ball somehow. It could have gone anywhere, but hit the net, hung there, and dribbled over.

"*Very* good," Coach said, and Johnny knew he'd made this hillbilly team. Things might look up in algebra, too.

Next was Dick Frawley, who'd puffed his way through the fourteen opening laps. But Dick had been practicing. Johnny had seen him a time or two in the parking lot behind the bank, hitting balls off the smooth brick wall. His returns weren't fast, but Coach couldn't get anything past him. "OK," he said.

"What?" said Dick.

"You're a keeper."

Jane's friend, Myra, took her turn, and did all right, and went over to sit near Dick in a gallery that had grown rather small. Myra wore her gym clothes, and looked ordinary alongside Jane, who had shown up in a real outfit. Johnny had to allow that Jane wasn't poetry in motion, but she returned most of Coach's volleys, and probably would be number one seed for the girls. "Girls plays the boys, girls play the boys," chanted several of Jane's cheerleader pals, and with a shrug Coach nodded to Jane and Johnny to play for the honor of their sexes.

Jane gave Johnny her sweet profile and bent at the net to show her breasts, but he'd learned his lesson concerning such tactics from the widow Candy Cruz. They settled into a duel. He eased off on his returns when one bounced off her leg, and clearly hurt her. But then she rushed the net and slammed the ball off his nose, causing the girls to raise a cheer. He retaliated with accuracy down the lines, and beat her that way, though somewhere she'd learned how to lob the ball high, so that it looked as though it would land behind the baseline, but at the last moment fall a little inside. He couldn't run fast enough to turn those around. It was the key to winning, he decided. Not just hard, hard, hard, but hard, hard, soft, like a change-up in baseball.

"Shower-time," Coach said at last. "Run! Run!"

As the others took off up the hill, and Jane gathered her gear in her handsome bag, the Coach called him over. "You've played a little, Mr. Bell."

"I been practicin' off the chicken house."

The Coach smiled. "You need to work on your serve. Slow it down, if you can't get it in. Go a little slower on the first one, speed up the second."

"Yes, sir."

Jane trotted after the other girls but dawdled. He caught up and danced all around her, shadow-boxing. "I believe I made the team, Jane."

She laughed ironically.

Everett had been waging a campaign to keep the thermostat low, and the house was cold. The lights were low. There didn't seem to be a soul within miles but Lucy, who sat with her glasses on, her Bible open, her radio holy.

"Johnny—" She paused as if in pain. "Johnny, a parent—a mother—she must be on the lookout every minute of the day. For irregularities, you might say. Now, Suzanne—Everett and I are very proud of her."

He sighed. Lots of conversations had been going on, he deduced, because of the picnic he'd had with Suzanne.

Lucy patted him arm. "Did you speak with Reverend Larkin?"

"Tomorrow."

"That's fine. Are you and Suzanne studyin' together tonight?"

They used to sit together at the kitchen table. Lucy came in to fix herself tea, and later to say good night. She picked up a schoolbook, sometimes, and shook her head at the mystery of it all.

"If we're gonna drop out, what's the point in studyin'?"

She considered this. "Would you rather stay in school, Johnny?"

Of course he would, and could, because he wasn't her flesh and blood and didn't have to go along with her crazy notions. "Only a moron would drop out."

She lowered her eyes and nodded. "The Lord will show the way, Johnny."

He held his tongue.

"Oh—Johnny—nothin' is more beautiful on this earth than the love of a young man and woman for Jesus Christ who died on the cross."

And then she sank to the floor, her eyes on fire. He refused to join her there. He couldn't say if the Lord heard her prayers or not, but in his opinion Lucy had gone loco. "Everett and I neither went through high school. We trusted in God, and he has allus provided. He will provide for *you*, Johnny, and for our precious Suzanne."

"It's just that I don't wanna, you know, throw around sacks a feed all my life. Ma'am."

She didn't hear. "Help this dear boy, Jesus. Bless him and bless my girl in—"

When had he become a "dear boy?" Why did she keep acting as though Suzanne and he were headed off to do missionary work together? He divined what she thought and was astounded.

She reached out her hands like one of those frail people staggering forward at an Oral Roberts meeting, but he jerked away. He clumped through the kitchen, grabbing two biscuits that had escaped the twins. He'd miss Lucy's biscuits, he thought, slamming the door behind him.

"I had five little apple trees," Reverend Larkin said. "And some white pines I bought from the state a Missouri. Last November, a big ole buck got in there and tore those apples up, gettin' at the sweetness under the bark, and in January he took out my pines."

Johnny said nothing. Larkin would eventually get to the point.

"Twice a year, bucks just plain go crazy. They can kill you if you get near 'em. It's the same all across the animal kingdom, it's natural, and a course there's an animal side to we mortals. In young men especially, the blood gets to flowin'. There's no easy answers here, wouldn't suggest otherwise, but we can always take our problems to the Lord. And—"

"Reverend, Lucy's tryin' to get me married. And I ain't but sixteen."

Johnny appreciated that the reverend had no quick answer, tucked in with a Bible verse. The birds and the bees was a tough speech for anyone. Tougher than talking to Clyde Fooch or Everett Ogletree. The reverend cleared his throat. "Maybe she's thinkin' somethin' already transpired?"

Johnny grunted. He'd learned some big words, too, reading Mrs. Koontz's books. "She's *deluded*. Nothin' transpired. I told her half a dozen times. The woman is not right in the head, Reverend."

"She's full a enthusiasm for Jesus." He sucked in a breath. "And she's worried about her daughter. Suzanne comes from a poor family, but she's a pretty little thing. If she ruins her chances at marriage, or if she doesn't find the best man she can, what's she gonna do? Sister Lucy's lookin' out for her, Johnny.

"Everett and Lucy have this idea—I never counseled 'em on this—that too much education, even a high school education, will keep you from servin' the Lord properly. At the same time, they think if Suzanne is finished with school, she's a woman. She can find a job, she can get married—she can have babies. It's an old-timey way a lookin' at things."

"Too old-timey for me. Suzanne wants to be a nurse; she doesn't wanna drop out. I don't, either."

He nodded. "We'll all pray about it, Johnny. I'll try to get out there this week and counsel with Sister Lucy. And Brother Everett, too, if the man will listen to me. Worse comes to worst, you could stay with the sister and me for a while, how's that sound?"

Johnny tried to smile.

"You could work here. Bag feed, do some mechanical work—you'd learn a great deal. Ride around with Virgil. Gonna be a real busy summer takin' birds out."

"Sheriff Harpster said I could have a job helpin' 'em repair a bridge."

"He did. God bless him, but I was hopin'—"

"It's like I'd be independent, see."

"I do see. I guess I'm thinkin' a your father. He rolled in here outta nowhere—"

"Colorado."

"That's right, Greeley, Colorado. We worked on chicken farms, and you know those crews are pretty wild, but he would study the Bible, and talk about a better place, and we got—that is, *he* did—to holdin' revivals. The time was ripe. The hearts a the people were heavy and he had a golden voice."

"Also, he got my mom pregnant."

The reverend nodded.

"Like you think I'm gonna do with Suzanne."

His chin went up, but his eyes were sorrowful. "You should understand, Johnny, that all I want is the best for you."

Johnny was taken aback. And humbled. "I know that, sir."

"Did you know we have a revival comin' in?"

Johnny didn't understand what a revival had to do with Lucy's strange ideas, but he laughed. "Reverend, how you gonna take care a your business, hold a revival, and run for sheriff?"

"People have come forward—the merchants, and some of the farmers—and they want a man with influence in that position. They want a man who loves the Lord, and I do think there's a moral authority goes with the job. People know Joel Harpster from way back, and I'm not speakin' against him, but maybe he doesn't bring that aspect of things to the table."

"The sheriff has to chase around at night, and he should be, he should be—"

"Younger? Well, the department will expand, we'll have more cars, more deputies. That would be my job, shape things up, run it like a business. The Lord has given me a talent for that."

Come to think of it, Sheriff Harpster was pretty casual in the way he ran things, and no question he needed help. The county allowed him one real deputy, Cecil Wells, and two part-timers as old as George Bell.

"I'd be glad to help with the revival. Settin' up chairs and stuff."

Larkin's face lit up. "Oh, it'll be a wonderful blessin'. We've invited the singin' ministry of the Babbit Brothers from Tulsa. They sing all night, and people pray, and receive the spirit, like an ole-time brush arbor meetin'. Joshua County *needs* a revival, Johnny."

Johnny rose to leave. It hadn't been such a bad session, after all. "Yes, sir, I imagine it does. And I want to help if I can. Except . . . Reverend?"

"Yes."

"I ain't my daddy."

Larkin smiled. "I know."

Life wasn't a book. Real people seldom made noble speeches or great sacrifices that changed the world. Still, disasters came hurtling at you, and you played your part the best you could, and long afterwards, when you'd had a chance to think about it, you understood that what had happened *was* like a plot in a novel.

He walked back to the Ogletree place and saw the International, splotched with mud and dead insects. It hadn't been there but for a few minutes because of the waves of heat rising from the hood.

In a book Everett would have been waiting for him, and in life he was, too.

Johnny looked in the broiler house. But as if he'd already read the next page, he knew Everett awaited him in the goat barn. He took a deep breath and plunged toward the awful climax.

"Come creepin' in like a thief in the night?" Everett smashed a cigarette on the cement floor and stood. "Our lover boy."

Johnny shrugged.

"Got it fixed up pretty cozy here." Everett picked up Johnny's transistor radio and threw it to the floor. "Aw, I dropped your radio."

He might as well have stabbed Johnny, but he didn't say, "Oh, no, not my radio." He watched as Everett walked around the room knocking textbooks and papers to the floor. "Sit," Everett said, pointing.

Johnny sat, but with all his muscles tensed and his knees bent, so that he could move in a hurry.

"What happened in the woods, Johnny? On that cot there?"

"I been over this already with Lucy. With Suzanne. Even with Reverend Larkin. Nothin' transpired."

"You lyin' monkey."

"Go fuck yourself."

Everett jumped. "Sposed to be a Christian? I've seen through you. Stand up."

But Johnny stood in a half-crouch, and eyed George Bell's hedge stick leaning against the wall. He remembered the day when he'd cut it, on that cold Arkansas mountain. Somehow the fire hadn't found it. "Don't try to hit me, Everett."

"I'll do what I please." As he moved near, Johnny slid to the wall and placed a hand on the stick.

"We open our home to you, we feed you," Everett said. "Did you run around thout your clothes on?"

He reached to slap Johnny with his big open hand, but Johnny ducked and brought up the hedge stick, aiming without thinking for Everett's head. He hit him solidly on the ear, and Everett dropped to his knees, bellowing in pain but also in disbelief.

Johnny threw matches, pepper, salt, a toothbrush, a towel, a spoon, and his books into a blanket with some soda crackers. He pulled everything together into a crude sack and marched for the door.

All the family had gathered just outside, and they twisted and turned in the dusty air along with the goats. La's head bobbed up.

Suzanne shook her head, tried to form words. She looked at her father, then at Johnny. There was the sorrow of Jesus Himself in her eyes, and already Johnny felt sorry.

Everett staggered to his feet. His ear streamed blood. Somehow, he'd brushed it onto his shirt, too. "I'll get you," he said.

"Daddy—" said Suzanne, breaking the spell. She rushed to her father's side.

Johnny flew the coop.

Chapter Thirteen
On His Own

Long after dark he reached his place, unlocked the shed, and crawled into the Ford to sleep. Rain fell on the tin roof, but he'd climbed up there and pitched every hole a month before and felt comforted and safe. He burrowed into his blankets and dreamed of being in a boat on the ocean. Like the great swells, his fear rose. He woke, shone his flashlight, and could see the glistening walnut trees like the legs of giants. Again, he felt comforted, as though he had friends watching over him through a bout of sickness.

He woke again precisely as the rain stopped. Inside the car, the blackness reminded him of the Ogletree root cellar; outside, where water dripped off the shed and trees, was nearly as dark. Fumbling with matches, he lit the Coleman lantern. Then he built a fire with newspapers and some oily plywood from beneath the Ford, just under the eaves so that smoke would dissipate. He stomped about in the wet grass outside, swinging his lantern, waiting for coffee to boil. Dawn arrived so slowly, and made so little difference, he wondered if the Rapture had come and banished light forevermore.

He drank coffee, ate some cold beans, and sat shivering. Then he jumped up as if he'd heard shooting, and began energetically, demonically, to cut hickory poles with a hand axe, each pole about five feet long. Hickory occurred to him because it was tough and perfectly round. He used the poles as rollers for the kitchen range, finally wrestling the thing into the corner of the shed, fifteen feet or so from the Ford. He shoved flat stones under the broken leg, but still couldn't make a fire because there was nowhere for the smoke to draw.

For two days he scouted for stove pipe, much hampered because he couldn't remember what he was doing for hours at a time. He lay up under bluffs where wet weather springs dripped, listening to the wind in the hollows, and watching the bare trees blow. He climbed to the highest point of ridges and looked far off into the smoky green haze.

Finally, he trekked to a long-abandoned cabin in the state forest, where he found three sections of pipe and an adjustable elbow, all of them rusty, but patchable. There were two sections in the shed that had never been used. He finished the run to the roof with several number ten cans, wiring them together and filling holes with the furnace cement George Bell left, he thought with a harsh laugh, in his will. Then he gathered wood until dark and grew so warm that night he stripped off his coat and propped his bare feet on the oven door. Soon, he'd need fuel for the lantern, but not tonight.

He opened *Tarzan at the Earth's Core* but couldn't read. He talked to himself and pointed angrily at the air.

On the morning of the third day, he had his coffee, and more beans, and walked under the walnuts, hugging the biggest trees. He heard someone shouting and crouched low in the wet leaves, until he realized that the voice was his own.

"Why did you die?" he cried out. "Why did you die and leave me here?"

Then he sat laughing and sobbing. He commanded himself to rise, but minutes later, he was still sitting on the cold, wet ground.

Darkness fell. The International wasn't there and neither was the Caterpillar, but he wanted to make sure Everett didn't come rolling in late, and that chores were done. Finally, the light snapped off at the goat barn, and he could see the outline of a woman returning to the house.

The wind blew from the north, so no animal could know he was coming, but he kept the outbuildings between himself and the kitchen lights as he approached, and shrank in the shadows of the broiler house, listening. Then he slipped over to the garden—surprising a cottontail—and pulled a hundred frosty radishes, eating a dozen or so, and stuffing the rest into his pockets.

Someone had stripped his cot and turned up the mattress, but he found his clothing in a box, washed and folded. He snapped off his flashlight, sniffed at the goat smell, and filled up with sadness again. Lucy *knew* he'd return.

Not Lucy, he thought. Suzanne.

He reached to a ceiling joist and found a pack of Pall Malls. He discovered several cans of Vienna sausages, chicken noodle soup, and sardines. He found his Band-Aid box with its six dollars in change, and a quarter lodged between boards that might have fallen out of Everett's pocket when he decked him.

Something nudged him in the darkness. He swallowed a whoop but it was only La. He knelt and gave her a rub along the ribs. "You miss me, don't you?" he said, and she bleated as if she understood English.

From the worktable he took a worn Crescent wrench, two screwdrivers, and gloves for his cold hands. He thought about grabbing a chicken to boil on his stove, but already he had too much to carry. He took his radio, which someone had pieced together and tied a string around.

La followed him into the barn yard. "You can't come," he said, and tried to escape through the gate, but she grabbed his shirttail with her teeth and yanked.

"You don't belong to me," Johnny told her, but neither did the tools—and in a way, she was his goat. They'd caught her on his land.

"I guess you know a goat roper when you see one," he said, and let her slip through.

Next morning, she pined for the outdoors, and he took her down near the creek and tied her on a long rope, so she'd have water and plenty of grass, even wild strawberries if she wanted.

He ran a scythe along the lane, then shored up George Bell's bridge where some of the ties had sunk over the years. It was a hard job, and afterwards he took a bath in the creek. The transistor radio worked if he set it just right, pulling in a Cardinals spring training game in which Julian Javier had three hits and Lou Brock stole home. He longed for the real season. Perhaps by then he could afford a new radio.

He spent another hour dragging the biggest rocks from under the viaduct, and filling some of the holes in the wash. He rode up and down for a while in the Ford, driving slowly because he didn't want to ruin a tire until he felt he could confront the world.

La bleated when he drove past, and feeling sorry for himself, he waved. La was what she appeared to be. She didn't make sudden moves. He'd never had a better friend.

He parked the Ford down from Noolin Brothers Grocery and walked to the square. School was closed and the town full of traffic, so he reasoned this must be Saturday. He'd been gone from society about a week.

The Democrats were holding a rally, and the candidates sat on the stand, trying to look intelligent while the Piney River Boys, a quartet from the Methodist Church, harmonized around the microphone.

Johnny sat on a bench by a pretty older woman who wore a long granny skirt, except that she wore too much make-up for a granny. She sang along, stomping her sandals in time. When they dragged the sheriff, the man Johnny had come to see, up on the bandstand, she stood and clapped.

Mrs. Koontz! The last time he'd seen her, ten days before or perhaps it was ten years, she seemed beaten-down. Now she looked grand, or . . . *something*. She turned to speak, but then Sheriff Harpster took the microphone.

"Religion and politics don't mix. Is that right?"

Mrs. Koontz clapped hard, and her eyes glowed. "We're with you, Sheriff."

"A person's walk with God is a personal thing. But when I hear these good old songs I think about the old times, how my mom and dad struggled through the Depression, and Dad went off to war—and came back to the Drought. You know what? They always had the Church. And we kids grew up in her bosom and took those dear lessons to heart. I always knew, even in my darkest days in Vietnam, even as my brothers fell before the enemy, that Jesus would guide me through."

He's about as religious as my shoes, Johnny thought, but he out-Larkined Larkin. Johnny studied the sky for the lightning that would strike the man down. All dressed up with a fancy Stetson and string tie, Johnny hardly knew the man.

"Now, I can't sing, though old Reverend Daniels—you remember him, people, had a little church out on Highway J, it burned down?"

"Yes. *Yes*," said a woman carrying groceries, two little girls tugging at her skirt. She took one of the folding chairs, and the girls plopped in the grass.

"He was a good old man, and he tried to get me into a gospel group once. Thought we were gonna be the Chuck Wagon Gang, ha! But I'll give her a whirl with the wonderful Piney River Boys, and you people join right in—and let me say, let me say just this one political thing. I want you to vote for me, but even if you vote for—I forget his name—"

Everyone laughed.

"The main thing is—you know, we're lucky here in America, which I was proud to serve in the United States Army, Americal Division, thank you very much, we are not a bunch of communists or flag-burners—to exercise your right to vote."

And then the Piney River Boys let forth, and the sheriff joined in with a perfect baritone, and something akin to conviction. The crowd grew to several hundred, and you could have sworn it was a revival, particularly with the last number:

Hallelujah! Thine the glory.
Hallelujah! Amen.
Hallelujah! Thine the glory.
Revive us again.

"We miss you in school," Mrs. Koontz said, leaning near. "You came to see Joel?"

"Yes, ma'am."

"He'll be happy to see you," she said, and led Johnny toward the bandstand, falling into him once. He leaned the other way, surprised by her alcohol smell. He placed a hand on her back to steady her, and she gave him a doe-eyed look.

"Did you know?" she whispered and held his eyes.

He reeled back. "Ma'am?"

"That I wrote a play?"

"That's great, ma'am." He was sorry for her because of all the troubles she'd had, but he was used to her in the role of teacher. He didn't know what to make of Mrs. Koontz, woman.

When they neared the bandstand, she stood up straight, and looked serious, as if her being drunk were as much an act as her hillbilly outfit. The sheriff looked serious, too, listening as two men with sober faces gave him the lowdown on something or other. He glanced once over Johnny, but his brown eyes were as remote as the Staked Plains of Texas.

Finally, the two men moved on, and the candidates for director of sewers or dog catcher or whatever they were shook hands with everyone near, and spoke of the chronic need for better sewers, and better dogs—and moved on, too. Mrs. Koontz came near the sheriff as if she'd kiss him but she didn't. They acted as though they'd just happened to bump into each other, but they made a handsome couple.

Pretty soon, Johnny thought, they'd be waltzing across the country club floor—if Baptists allowed waltzing.

They turned and headed up the walk. Harpster hadn't even said hello.

"I got my car on the road." Johnny called out. "I was kinda hopin' to get my driver's license."

The sheriff pointed across the street. "Cecil's on duty."

"Thanks," Johnny said, swallowing. "I couldn't have done it without you."

"Ah huh." Harpster reached for a Pall Mall. "I ran into Everett Ogletree."

"Yes, sir."

"He's all stitched up."

"Yes, sir."

"Sounds to me like there's blame to go around, and he didn't care to press charges."

Johnny nodded.

The sheriff laughed. "In fact, Everett was sorry to lose a good hand, not to mention the payments."

"You paid him?"

"Hell, yes, your government at work. Our wonderful foster care system."

Johnny shrugged.

"You could get into some trouble, behavior like that. You don't *want* trouble with me."

Damn him, Johnny thought, but he hung his head. "No, sir, I don't."

Mrs. Koontz slipped back, staring at him, and then at Johnny. Harpster pulled down the brim of his hat, then wheeled and stalked ahead of her. She smiled at Johnny uncertainly.

The question that Johnny had brought to town remained. "I drove up here to—to ask about that job," he called out.

The sheriff stared in disbelief. "Job!"

"On the bridge. You said they was gonna repair a worn-out bridge, that they'd be hirin'—"

An old couple neared, and Harpster donned that big grin of his. "Don't know what you're talkin' about," he said, and stuck out his hand to the old couple. "How are you?"

"Loved your speech."

"Thank you. Thank you. We try to keep things simple. The old ways are the best, I do believe."

Mrs. Koontz ran back. She grabbed his arm. "I don't understand him, either."

"You guys are . . . together?"

She smiled at him almost sadly, but for answer reached into her purse, and handed him a twenty. "He's just acting," she said. "He'll get over it."

"Ma'am—" he said, and turned away, choking off anger. He almost returned the twenty. He knew he shouldn't take it, but he was hungry.

"The election—it's his high hard one, that's how he puts it. He's *from* here, Johnny, not like us. But you'll be fine, you know why?"

"Why?"

"Because of the play. You're the star!"

Some little school play and she thought Johnny was an actor. Like her dressing up to be a hillbilly and playing at being poor. She didn't understand.

Maybe she did. Her twenty dollars said so. Even an asshole was inspired by a man in a snowdrift; afterwards, everyone called him a hero. But if the snowbound man came to your door, begging food, what was the percentage in handing him a twenty? You had to follow in the steps of Jesus to help at a time such as that.

"I'll pay you back, ma'am," he said.

He could cut some walnut trees. Everyone said they were valuable, but it would take too long. He needed money now.

He parked the Ford in the lane, gave La a bowl of rolled oats, and headed down the tracks to talk to that other candidate for sheriff, Reverend Charles Larkin. He'd promised work, too.

Halfway to the feed mill, Virgil Showalter hailed him. He'd built two high columns out of the wafer-like limestone found everywhere in the woods, and now tried to hoist up a sign. But his sign hung off a cedar log that must have weighed eight hundred pounds. He'd used the scoop on his tractor to hoist the log, but it remained a two-man job. They steadied one end with a chain-hoist, and Johnny climbed into the scoop, rode up, and shouldered the log into place. No need to mortar it.

The sign showed a hillbilly leaning back in a chair, smoking a pipe. It read, "Ozark Village."

"Virgil, what you doin' here?"

"I'm gonna make a zillion dollars, that's what."

His store used to be the place where people went to buy second-hand refrigerators and broken-down couches, one step down from the Salvation Army. But Virgil had cleared out the junk and added a big porch with a tin roof, so that it resembled an old-time Ozark cabin. On the porch stood a dozen oak rocking chairs he'd contracted with an Amish fellow for, and some lawn furniture made from red cedar because it stood weathering, and two concrete angels for the yard.

The inside was filled with galvanized wash tubs, wringer washers, cherry-wood chests of drawers, hard maple dining tables, and crosscut saws with nature scenes painted on them.

A closed-off section brimmed with knickknacks and dolls; and a display of corncob pipes from Washington, Missouri; and a grandpa and grandma carved out of cedar. A mound of fancy embroidered pillows lay atop a bed made of walnut. There were colorful quilts, which Virgil had also bought from the Amish, and cornball sayings to mount on the wall, such as "God gives us nuts, but he doesn't crack them" and "It takes a heap of livin' to make a house a home."

There were some dainty porcelain birds that came from Japan, and packets of sassafras bark and dried fruit, and all sorts of jellies and jams, and pint Mason jars full of herbs and rose petals and red clover.

Virgil grinned. "Patty-Cakes has been savin' this stuff for years."

"Are you kinda makin' fun a the Ozarks here?"

"Naw! We mean to have some fun, but naw, naw, we're celebratin' a precious heritage. We'll have some food. We'll have some gospel groups and fiddlers, and church suppers, and the boys and girls can ride on a gen-u-wine Missouri mule. I been talkin' to them kids at Evangel College, and we're gonna have some play-actin' like at an ole time Literary."

"For free?"

He laughed. "Patty-Cakes and me, we got our lifesavin's in this, and it cain't be for free. The tourists drive for hunnerts of miles down to Branson, you know, and Eureka Springs. They pass through Red Buck and never ever stop, but we got the Ozarks rat here. Chicken business has went all to hell—question is, do we turn over and die? No, sir! Family comes down here from Chicago, they wanna see the simple folk, and the good ole-fashioned, honest ways a livin'. It's all at Ozark Village!"

"Makin' lye soap—"

"Hadn't thought a that. Good 'un!"

"And puttin' up choke-cherry preserves, and butcherin' pigs, and barn-dances, and runnin' a loom, and brush-arbor meetin's—"

"That's the spirit."

"I thought all that stuff was dead as a possum."

"Sure." Virgil smiled. "Ole granny smokin' her corncob pipe, the hillbilly makin' moonshine down in the holler—that kinda thing never really existed. Or it did, I spose, but it wasn't just here. Everybody lived on the farm, see, because they was poor. Wasn't much different bein' poor in the Ozarks from Kentucky or, what the hail, New Jersey, only

in them other places they took off to the city quicker. And
the REA come to us slow, and we didn't have no TV. So
maybe the old ways hung on a little longer.

"That ain't what these ole geezers from Chicago wanna
hear, howsomever. And what I say is, *go with the flow.* They
wanna see Li'l Abner and Jed Clampett. They wanna see a
sad-eyed girl playin' 'Pretty Red Wing' on the dulcimer. They
wanna see the simple folk and feel all warm and homey—
well, we'll give it to 'em, and take their money."

"You need any help with this precious heritage business?"

"Thought a you straight off." His eyes narrowed. "Now
that you and Everett's parted ways."

"Aw, Virgil. I—"

"No reasonin' with the man." He waved a hand. "You
hear he refused his new contract?"

"How come?"

"Not enough money in it. And that's true enough. But
Charley has to keep them houses full, and he cain't help the
prices; he's hurtin' like everybody else. Anyhow, we're 'bout
to open up, and you can be my number-one, all-purpose,
self-risin' Ozarks hillbilly."

Johnny leaned over and spat. Maybe he'd take up snuff.
"Darn tootin'."

"You can start off by scroungin' the back country for
authentic Ozarks souvenirs. Old harness and horseshoes,
them dark green Mason jars with the zinc lids, and some of
'em with porce-lane lids, you know what I mean?"

"Yep."

"Old claw hammers, wood rasps, planes, handsaws with
apple-wood or walnut handles—they gotta have five bolts,
you unnerstand?"

"Five bolts."

"Wooden buckets if they ain't rotten, scrub boards, oak
barrels, sausage grinders, lard presses, straight razors, knives,
scythes—"

"I got one a those but I need it."

"Manure forks with three tongs—"

"Three! The hay would fall through. What good's three?"

"Way they used to make 'em. Cast iron fire shovels, coal scuttles, wood stoves but they got to be in good shape—no rusted-out, home-made barrel stoves. Hickory mallets, rollin' pins—"

"I got a kettle for renderin' lard. One a them big cast iron things?"

Virgil studied his would-be smokehouse. "How big?"

"Oh, it's awful big. Must weigh three hundred pounds."

"Give you ten dollars."

"Worth fifty."

"Twenty dollars if you can get it here, which don't sound likely."

"I'll get it here if you loan me your Farmall H for a day."

"We need that Farmall for rides in the virgin Ozarks forest. You can borrow that little Allis-Chalmers C."

"You gonna hire me for the summer, then? I'd really appreciate it."

Virgil nodded. "Lot a people gettin' outta the chicken business, so the feed mill's gonna be jumpin', too. 'Tween me and the reverend you'll get rich. I pay minimum wage."

"Minimum wage plus a dime? I'll work really, really hard."

"Minimum wage plus a quarter if you sell me some a your walnut trees."

"So you can make tables and sell 'em to the tourists?"

Virgil reached for his snuff and smiled. "Grandfather clocks, too."

The kettle lay half-buried between two tall walnut trees. Johnny cut several roots with a hatchet and then worked under the cast iron with a pike, but it wouldn't budge. Finally, he wrapped a chain around the circumference, connected the chain to the Allis, and yanked the kettle free, though barely. The Allis's tricycle front wheels lifted into the air six inches like they wanted to join the rodeo.

He repositioned the chain and dragged the kettle down the lane until the thing flipped on its side. The chain fell loose and the kettle rolled, wobbling, off-balance, until it flopped upside down. He had neared the bridge and wasn't confident he could pull the thing across without spilling it into Plunge Creek. Now what?

Weeks before, he'd liberated a stout oak pallet from Art's Army Surplus. He brought down the pallet, his pike, and several hickory poles, and at last worked the kettle onto the pallet. Now he dragged the pallet with the Allis, but it kept getting snagged on tree sprouts, and he had to climb down and cut each with his hatchet. But the land sloped downhill to the railroad and if he went slowly, carefully, he could get there.

Some spots were muddy, and pretty soon he was filthy all over, and sweaty even though the temperature was below forty. But at last, he reached the highway and the mown right-of-way, at least on Virgil's side, lay level. A train with 207 cars clanked by, and he knew there wouldn't be another before dawn, meaning the crossing at Virgil's would be clear.

At one point a short bluff pushed out, and he had to drag the kettle down the highway, but midnight loomed and traffic had ceased. At last he parked the kettle directly under Virgil's "Ozark Village" sign and shut off the little tractor, dropping a coffee can over its upright exhaust.

"Hey," he announced to the hoot owls. "All *right*."

He sat to rest. Clouds drifted over the moon, and patches of fog crept along. His sweat dried and he shivered in the wind. He rose on his rubbery legs. He heard a terrible racket coming out of Red Buck, all the scarier because the night was otherwise so silent.

In seconds, a dozen cars roared up Highway 60, took the curve three abreast, and accelerated into the hilly stretch toward Mountain Vale, where they all dropped into the right lane. The drivers were nothing but silhouettes, but he made out Gary Tyrell's big Chevy, running second behind Bobby Sills' two-door '50 Ford.

This was the race that had gone on since the 1930s, the banned race that always seemed to get run. The drivers had chosen this strange time to avoid being caught.

That stretch was a challenge even in the daytime, and at night, when you came down the hill toward Mountain Vale, and banked around the curves by Lake Louise, it was downright treacherous. Johnny felt a burst of anger. He'd worked half the day and most of the night to buy himself something to eat, while those rich fools tanked up on beer and risked their lives, not to mention any deer or human venturing near.

It was past three, but he lit his lantern, stoked the fire, and heated a can of beans that he ate with the last of his bread. Tomorrow, he'd have another twenty dollars. Thank you, Lord, for Mrs. Koontz and for Virgil. He shoved his toes deep into his blankets and slept as if he were dead.

Chapter Fourteen
All's Fair

Gary won the race. He passed Bobby Sills in the last half-mile, dueling Bobby's Ford with his brand-new Chevy, forcing Bobby onto the shoulder in a spot that soon became famous. The road narrowed there, and part of the right of way had washed out. Bobby's right wheel dropped low and he lost control. He clipped a post oak and plunged down the slope toward Lake Louise, while Gary raced on, breaking the old record by twelve seconds. He claimed he hadn't seen the accident.

Two of the racers stopped and scurried after Bobby. His car didn't roll all the way into the lake, and didn't appear to be damaged. But somehow he snapped his neck and died.

Next morning, Mr. Kowalski came on the intercom to announce the accident. He spoke in a wandering, almost tearful manner. He said Bobby might have gone on to be president like Harry Truman. Old Harry started out as a farmer just like Bobby, Kowalski said.

All Johnny could remember was how Bobby had bullied Dick in the locker room and had tried to engineer Johnny's humiliation in a wrestling match. Who could say? Perhaps President Truman had been a bully when he was in high school, too. He *had* dropped that big bomb.

Anyhow, it was the end of the annual race. And there were serious implications for all who had participated, especially Gary. He came to school but didn't make it through the door. Johnny sat in English, looking down on the parking lot as the sheriff and a bald man, who must have been Gary's father caught up with the boy and guided him away.

Everyone saw. Jane began to cry and excused herself. Mrs. Koontz took off her glasses, and rubbed her eyes, and there must have been half a dozen in the class quietly crying, either for Bobby, who could have been Truman, or for Gary, who might be bound for prison.

Hurrying down the hall for algebra, he stopped. Suzanne and he used to stop in this spot near her locker. They'd plan to meet in the library or have lunch. It was the same every day, and didn't amount to much, but he missed it.

He ran back to English. "Is Suzanne sick?"

Mrs. Koontz and he were the only ones in the room. She wiped down the board with a damp cloth, and turned slowly, her eyes big and worried.

"Suzanne Ogletree dropped out of school, Johnny."

"Oh." He plopped down on one of the little chairs that somehow had migrated from the grade school. He couldn't help but think Suzanne had dropped out because she couldn't face him. Or that Everett and Lucy had kept her home, fearing that if she went to school, she'd find Johnny, and never return.

"It's my fault," he said.

"Nonsense." Mrs. Koontz scooted up a kiddie chair herself, and the two of them talked like old friends. It all came out—Everett's mercurial behavior; Johnny's resentment that the sheriff hadn't proved a true friend; and his distress that Suzanne, who *had* been a friend, was in trouble. He told her all about getting washed in the blood of the Lamb, which seemed kind of weird to him, nor had it helped to set his life on a straight and narrow course, because look what happened.

"You can't change people with a magic wand," Mrs. Koontz said. "Leave that religious crap behind just as fast as you can. I'm as upset as you are about Suzanne, but with parents as ignorant as that—"

"Everett saved my life."

"And then exploited you, and beat you."

"Don't you believe in God, ma'am?"

She frowned. "I believe in reaching for your true potential. I believe in being free." She sighed. "Trying to be."

His mind turned over quickly. He could pretend to care about Bobby and Gary, but he didn't. He cared about Suzanne, but even if her predicament was partly his fault, what could he do? Freedom, he thought. How in the world could he define it? It seemed more like an attitude than a thing.

"I want you to be in my play, Johnny. The lead! How can I get through to you? This is no small matter!"

He didn't understand her. Instead, he thought of Jane, leaving class with her face streaked with tears. It was rotten to move in on Gary while he was down, and it was rotten to abandon Suzanne, but he didn't care about Gary, and couldn't help Suzanne. Life was war or at least love was.

"Is Jane Epstein in the play?"

She smiled. "There's a part for her."

"This is the school play?"

"No, Johnny. No. At Ozarks Village. With your friend Virgil."

On Saturday, sick of grubbing in the woods for authentic Ozark treasures, he took a bath in Plunge Creek, bought a Nehi Grape Soda at Noolin Brothers, and drove to Jane's house. He tucked his cigarettes under the seat and combed his hair with his hands and stepped to the door somewhere between a dance and falling on his face. He itched from tick and chigger bites. His palms were blistered and impregnated with grime. Sweat poured down his ribs, but he repeated to himself, all's fair in love and war. As in *Tarzan and the Foreign Legion*, he'd strike like a commando.

He knocked, then stood back so Jane would be sure to see his beautiful car.

It seemed that an hour went by and still no one stirred. The postman walked up, deposited letters, and said hello as if Johnny had always lived in the neighborhood.

"Hi," Johnny said, trying on a grin something like the sheriff's, but afterwards he couldn't arrange his face in any way that wasn't phony. He knocked again, pressed the door-bell, and knocked again, and still there was no answer.

Not so nice, said the Comforter. What did Gary ever do to you?

What do you expect from an ignorant hillbilly?

Something fell and rolled across a floor. More time passed, and a woman parted the curtains, looked out, but didn't open the door.

"You're surrounded," Sheriff Harpster called out on his bull-horn, only it was too late to apprehend the outlaw Johnny Bell, because he was dying in his beloved Jane's arms.

"Why didn't you tell me you cared?" she said.

"How could I? I never knew my father. And my mother was an ape."

Across the street a dog ran toward the curb and barked at Johnny, and then one of those yappy little dogs started barking inside.

At last Jane came around the corner from the back yard, a big paint brush in her hand. She blinked as though Johnny were a Jehovah's Witness. "John."

"I came to—I'm really sorry about Gary—"

She frowned. "John, I'm painting. You should have called first, I look—"

He swallowed. "Beautiful."

Frowning, she pointed toward the Ford. "Where'd you'd get that ugly steering knob?"

A short man with a moustache came around the side and grabbed the mail. He smoked a cigar, and Jane fanned the air to make a point, but he didn't seem to notice. "Nice car," he said, looking Johnny over with hard little eyes. "I owned a '41 once, very similar. All stripped down because of the war, but a fine vehicle. Daniel Epstein," he said, extending a hand. "Which one are you?"

"Father!" Jane smiled apologetically, and Johnny realized she was ashamed of her dad, like sometimes he used to be of his grandfather. "This is John Bell."

Mr. Epstein made a gesture as if he were yanking a rope, and winked, and his hard black eyes were all at once merry. He had bushy eyebrows and slumped shoulders, and with his cigar reminded Johnny of Groucho Marx. "You're the *w-i-i-ild* boy."

Jane was a head taller than her dad, but she seemed to have shrunken back to grade school. "He not so wild," she said mournfully.

Epstein puffed at the cigar. "She talks about you, John. Swingin' from tree to tree—"

"Stop."

"Me Tarzan," Johnny said, and beat his fists on his chest. "Her Jane."

Mr. Epstein laughed and drew Johnny around to the back yard as if he'd been craving an audience. Perhaps it was like this: a long time before, he thought it would be fun to act like Groucho Marx. And he'd forgotten to stop.

Bending over, he strutted back and forth. "Shot an elephant today in my pajamas."

Johnny laughed, but Jane stared into space and pulled at her hair exactly like Suzanne did.

"Want a kosher dog?" her dad asked, working those eyebrows and waving a barbecue fork instead of his cigar.

"What's kosher?"

"Meat from Jewish cows."

Jane rolled her eyes.

"Sure," Johnny said.

"I'll cook, you help my little Janie paint."

"*Pointless,*" Jane said, or rather snarled, as she stabbed her brush at the little back porch.

"What's pointless?" Johnny asked.

"*Him.* He'll go on, and he'll go on, and he'll go *on.*" She closed her eyes, then opened them and painted fiercely, a felony brewing in her eyes. Johnny wanted to say, "Your dad's pretty funny," but he supposed she already knew that. He grabbed a brush and made short work of one side, then moved to hers.

"First *worker* you've brought around," her dad said.

"Either work or a life of crime, sir," Johnny called out.

"Some of these yahoos think they're in the Indianapolis 500."

Jane slammed her brush down and stomped inside, offering Johnny a quick glare. He sympathized: Mr. Epstein had said a cruel thing. He didn't seem regretful or even aware he'd offended. Then again, maybe he wanted Jane out of the way. He handed Johnny two hot dogs, motioning to relish and mustard on a stand. They sat under a maple while he smoked his cigar. "You know the boy who was killed?"

"Not too well, sir."

"When he was little, he'd come into the store sometimes with his mother, but I never talked to him. Don't you hate a thing like that?"

"He coulda been the next Harry Truman."

Mr. Epstein laughed. "Bobby Sills was from humble origins, but that's the only resemblance. Now, Gary, he's been coming 'round eating kosher dogs since he and Janie started kindergarten. And his father and me were in school together. In fact, I'll let you in on a little secret—"

"Sir?"

"We ran that race ourselves."

"Huh," Johnny said, finishing the second dog and hoping he'd be offered another. "When the road was gravel?"

"Not *that* far back." Epstein clamped his fingers on Johnny's forearm, hurting him. "They say this thing was Gary's fault."

Johnny pulled away. "Everybody thinks so."

"Breaking Janie's heart, though I can't talk to her about it. She's *so* grown up." He sighed. "Gary'll be all right. He's got Chevrolets in his future. You trying to move in on him?"

"I—"

"You'd be an improvement. But Janie's college-bound, you know that."

"She's smart—"

"How about yourself?"

"I'm smart—"

"She'll marry some doctor and run him like a toy train. I *will* say, Charley Larkin thinks the world of you."

"Yes, sir," Johnny said. How could this man know so much? Well, it was a small town, and all the businessmen were acquainted, if not through church, then through the Chamber of Commerce and the country club. "He takes a special interest in me. I'll be workin' for him this summer, and for Mr. Showalter, too."

"What's Virgil doing out there?"

"Hard to say, sir. He has some original ideas."

"I think he's on to something. If it was me—"

There was a great commotion, and the back door flew open. After a long moment, a Chihuahua ran out, followed by Mrs. Epstein, dressed in a housecoat. Meanwhile, Groucho returned to his grill and waved his cigar. "What he was doing in my pajamas, I'll never know."

Mrs. Epstein's hair was long and full—like Jane's, Johnny thought, except that it was gray. She carried a bowl of potato salad in one hand, a glass, filled with an orange liquid, in the other.

"Miriam," Mr. Epstein said, almost shouting. "Feeling better?"

She shrugged. "I see Janie has a new friend."

Mrs. Epstein handed Johnny the potato salad, then took his arm and wouldn't let go. She trembled and could hardly stand. An old dog in that kind of shape, Johnny thought, wouldn't make it through another winter.

"Thank you," she said, sitting heavily in a steel lawn chair. "You're a nice boy. Are you Gary's replacement?"

"I—"

"We've decided we don't like Gary, isn't that right, Daniel?"

Groucho lifted his eyebrows.

Then Mrs. Epstein's Chihuahua leaped into her lap and yapped at Johnny. "Now, now, Dooley," she said, smiling at Johnny. "I don't recall Janie mentioning you, John. What does your father do?"

The Chihuahua sounded off again: *Yap! Yap! Yap! Yap!*

"I ain't got no father," he said.

"'Ain't?' Dear me. I thought you said—excuse me, but I overheard—it's your father's car."

"He's that wild boy, Miriam," Mr. Epstein called out.

"Wild goy?"

Yap! Yap! Yap! Yap!

"Boy!"

"Why do they say you're wild?" Merriam asked. "Do you take drugs?"

The back door banged again, and Jane emerged in shorts and a flowery blouse. She'd washed the paint from her cheeks and combed her hair. Her eyes came down on Johnny as if he were property. "Coach Taney has been looking everywhere for you, John. We have a tennis match, our one and only. With Mountain Vale."

"We can go in my car."

She stared for a long time at her mother, who talked to the little dog like Johnny talked to La. The dog sat up as if it understood. Meanwhile, Mr. Epstein dropped Groucho for a whistling routine, never hitting a real tune, his eyes fastened on Jane and Johnny.

Jane sighed dramatically. "OK, we'll take your car. But I'm not your princess, John. I'm not part of some fairy tale where you rescue me or something."

"What's *that* mean?"

She shrugged. "You'll figure it out."

*   *   *

With the school year all but gone, Coach Taney had only been able to schedule an exhibition match, and just with the four of them.

It was plain enough, from the irritability of their players and the indifference of their coach—not a real coach but a student teacher from Springfield—that Mountain Vale regarded the match as an act of charity.

Jane wore creased white shorts, new white shoes, and a green blouse tied high on her stomach. Her hair was buried under a flowery green scarf, and she had on the green eyeliner that always made her seem sophisticated. And she was so cool on the court you'd have thought coolness alone could lead to victory, but it didn't. The Mountain Vale girl took her out 6-3, 6-1.

Myra didn't look nearly so fine, but won two sets, losing her match in five, because she was calm and her opponent felt indignant she even had to play one of those hillbillies from Red Buck. Their match went on almost until dark, and by then the two girls became friends. They cried together over their grueling ordeal. They discovered that they both were going to Central Baptist College in Conway, Arkansas, and decided they'd be roommates.

Dick surprised everyone, including himself, by winning in three tough sets. He'd lost weight, and wore a pair of goggles he'd bought at Art's Army Surplus, making him look like a bomber ace from World War I. His aerodynamic appearance appealed to Myra, who threw her arms around him, and gave him a big, sloppy kiss.

Johnny faced off against a tall, good-looking blond kid named Carson. The coach claimed that Carson had been within one serve of the state championship, and they both seemed to think that Johnny was fortunate even to stand on Mountain Vale's pretty court with him. Johnny wore his green shoes and won the first three games by yucking it up like the goat-roper they thought he was. Carson caught on and nearly killed him with his serves, but Johnny's own serves held up and he squeaked through the first set.

Carson was irritated but ready to play, and knocked off Johnny in the second set 6 to 1. By then the heat had got to them both. But Johnny reached inside himself and asked what Tarzan would do, and Jesus, and ran everything to deuce somehow.

It didn't hurt when Jane sat in the bleachers behind him, like some angel who'd dropped out of paradise. She sipped iced tea and crossed her legs.

"This don't matter nohow," Carson said, and Johnny won the set 8-6, and the match, and the hillbillies from Red Buck had proven they deserved a conference team.

Afterwards, they went to the Dairy Queen.

"Girls lost," said Dick. "Girls have to pay."

"Bullshit," Jane said, but immediately she turned sweet. "You were good, Dick. You, too, John."

"They were both *wonderful*," Myra said, scooting close to Dick.

"You were good, too," Dick said. Bravely, he held out a spoonful of his sundae to Myra. She lapped it up like Mrs. Epstein's Chihuahua.

"You're so sweet to say that," Myra whispered.

"My God," Jane said. "Let me out of here."

But she threw Johnny an encouraging glance.

"That judge was so unfair," he told her. "You were very good."

"Oh, I can't play at all."

She stood to go, cutting their victory dinner short. Still, as he started the car, Johnny thought how far he'd come in the six months since George Bell died. Here he was at a DQ with three nice kids, who came from nice families, more or less, who didn't want for money. He sat with a pretty girl who wouldn't always be in a foul mood. It was a reasonably good imitation of normal.

They neared the place where Bobby Sills had died, and Jane looked down on the water. They might have passed the site without a word, except that while they were playing tennis a crew had arrived to work on the crumbled shoulder. They blocked off the highway, routing traffic onto the bumpy right-of-way on the opposite side. It was dark by then, and a fellow waving a flashlight with a long orange cone on it drew near.

"I hate those guys," Jane said.

"You hate guys with flashlights?"

"You always see them at football games, so cocky. Like a lot of men."

"I'm—"

"Not you, Johnny. Of course, not you. You're sensitive."

She didn't mean it as a compliment. What exactly was a man supposed to be in her eyes? Groucho Marx? Johnny studied the damp imprint of her nipples through her blouse. He should grab her and haul her off to his home in the trees. He'd show her sensitive.

"Did you know Bobby well?" he asked.

"Only since he was born."

In the back seat the slurping sounds stopped. "Me, too," Myra called out.

"How's Gary doin'?" Johnny asked.

Jane didn't answer for a moment. "He won't come out of his room."

"You should go see him."

"And do what?"

"Just . . . talk to him."

"My dad says he'll get off," Myra said.

This had some authority, since her father was a lawyer.

"He never did anything to me," Dick called out.

"He didn't do anything to anyone," Jane said. "I *did* talk to him; it wasn't his fault. And he feels just awful. He knows they shouldn't have had that silly race, and he blames him-self. But he didn't do anything. People don't understand

Gary, they think he's this big dumb jock, but he's kind, and thoughtful—"

He's sensitive, Johnny thought. "He has to go to court?"

"Before a judge. Something. It's not like he's going to jail."

"He'll get off," Myra said.

They passed the final flashlight and picked up speed. The old V-8 throbbed through the wheel, cool air floated up from low places in the woods, and the ride might have been eternal. Jane went silent. She seemed mysterious, and serene, with the moonlight flowing over her.

Sighs and smooching sounds escaped from the back seat, and it seemed likely they'd conceived a child. Johnny felt inspired. He put his elbow on the window and drove with one hand, resting the other on the shift, near Jane's bare legs. She threw him a look that said, don't you dare, or maybe it said, *dare*.

"I like you, John," she said. "But you're so needy."

He used to think that if you connected with a girl she would say nice things about you, and brag about you, and generally be swept away by your rare abilities and wisdom. They passed the lane leading up to his shed, which he didn't point out. Then Ozark Village drew near. "I got a job there."

"Mrs. Koontz mentioned that place to me. Something about a play she wants me in. What's your job?"

"I'm a hillbilly."

She laughed so hard he was afraid she'd choke, but he didn't care anymore. His making a fool of himself was pretty much the basis of their relationship. He wanted to crawl into his hole, make himself some soup, and have a deep, meaningful conversation with La. She was the truest sweetheart he'd ever have.

Mysteriously, as if God had intervened, his radio had begun to work again. He turned it on to Jack Buck. It was the top of the second against the Giants, first game of the year, and Bob Gibson was mowing them down. Five strikeouts in a row—a record, Jack Buck said, in that low, manly voice of his. Not a sensitive fellow.

"You like baseball?" he asked.

"No."

Of course not. Not unless Gary played it. He turned the volume low, but left the game on. Baseball would be there when Jane wasn't, which looked like forever. It would keep him company and explain what life meant. Baseball was like religion, except that you didn't have to do anything.

They let off Myra, who ran up the sidewalk as if she'd won fifty balloons in Vacation Bible School, and then Dick, who staggered in the moonlight, and fell down in the grass drunk with kisses.

Jane began walking toward her front door almost before he'd stopped the car, but he gave it one last try. "Wanna go to the Poultry Festival?"

She turned in disbelief. "You *know* I'm with Gary. You think I'll abandon him because he's in trouble? I'm *loyal*."

"I never meant—"

"Of course, you did. You're obvious."

"I'm crazy about you, that's all. And the Poultry Festival, what would it matter? It would be different if Gary was runnin' around like he usually does—"

"What does *that* mean?"

He eased out the clutch to back away. "Poor choice a words. Listen, I'll just—"

"I guess we can go." She released a tragic sigh. "Since it means so much to you."

What? Unless his ears deceived him, he'd finagled an actual date.

"As long as you're not thinking of it as a *date*."

Chapter Fifteen
The Poultry Festival

High on a pole, a transformer hummed like a floating organ, while below great diesels chugged, blowing off black smoke. They moved a notch higher on the Ferris wheel and arrived among tilt-a-whirls and carousels with their purple and green spirals. Higher still, they could see the concourse stretching out blindingly, like a runway to the stars.

You could shoot at mechanical ducks and win yourself a stuffed bear you'd never know what to do with. You could play bingo with the Catholics and buy a slice of meat loaf from the Methodist ladies. You could jump on a Go-Kart. There was an old car to smash, and a clown in a dunking tank, and a wandering barbershop quartet. Fat women, two-headed infants, and rattlesnakes awaited your inspection, while barkers claimed they'd whisk you away to Borneo, and boil you alive, and shrink your head afterwards.

Men in suits strutted importantly, mingling with men in cowboy boots, over the mysterious business of selling bulls and boars. Tired-looking men in overalls with no shirts sat on benches, smoking plain-end cigarettes. Amish women, wearing black hats, licked at snow cones. Little kids bawled because they didn't know where their parents had gone. Grim-faced women held onto four and five littluns, but might have lost one or two.

Three bad boys ran down the concourse, weaving between legs. They knocked down an old man with a hamburger. A dog grabbed the hamburger and raced toward the stock barns, scaring a prize-winning cow. She fell down and could hardly rise again, her bag was so heavy. She got her purple ribbon all muddy. Then she ran inside the mule barn where she found no sympathy.

Up another notch, and Johnny could see the red light blinking on the water tower, and the headlights on U.S. 60, and the shadowy creek by the highway, overflowing its banks from all the rain they'd had. Late in the afternoon the sun emerged and scalded the puddles. Night fell rough as a canvas, and left you panting, and sweating, and swatting at mosquitoes.

"What you wanna do first?" he asked.

Jane shrugged. "Nothing here but chickens and mules."

Everything was here. They jerked up still another notch and a breeze carried away the stink from below, and the moon sat on Jane's lovely shoulder. She'd cut her hair short and seemed even sassier. Under the neon lights her green eye shadow made her look sultry and wild. Maybe she was a witch.

He reached out to touch her but lost his nerve. "If I never saw another chicken it would be too soon. But I like the mules."

Jane took his hand between hers and kissed his finger-tips. "You're kind of a mule yourself."

Did she mean he was stubborn? Strong? That his parentage was questionable? It didn't matter. He ran his hands up the smooth skin of her back, and her black eyes flashed inside those green circles. He kissed her, then tilted back his head to gulp in the stars. "Ain't no bugs up here!" he called to the Lord above, while Jane reached low to rub his hard, earthly penis.

"Jesus! I thought you hated me."

"Jesus hates you?"

"Oh, no—"

"Would I be here with you, Big John, if I hated you?"

They plunged down into the hot air, picking up snatches of conversation, batting their hands right and left at clouds of gnats. As they shot up again, he put his lips to her ear. "I can't take anymore."

She slid to the far side of the seat. "You can take a *lot* more. You want a corn dog?"

"Not . . . not . . . kosher," he gasped.

She laughed. They landed and he staggered into the sizzling lights. He smelled diesel, French fries, and manure.

"Johnny?"

He blinked because the voice wasn't Jane's. She'd gone off to buy corn dogs. Standing in her place was Suzanne. She tugged at a tall fellow in jeans and an army tee shirt. He had short hair, and quick black eyes that could have been Everett Ogletree's.

"Johnny, this is Max. My brother."

Max stuck out a hand and said "Howya doin'?" but his eyes had already fastened on Jane. "Hel-*lo*," he said.

Jane burnt her lips on her corn dog and pulled back her head as if she'd been struck. A drop of grease spotted her white shorts. But almost in the same movement she handed Johnny his corn dog and gave the soldier-boy half a hug. "Max Ogletree," she said. "I read about you in the paper."

"We—" Johnny began, but Jane and Max had stepped into the concourse, and the only "we" left to him was Suzanne.

Jane turned, her hands clasped behind her, her smile never sweeter. "OK, John? I haven't seen Max since—"

"Since she was wearin' braces," Max said.

Suzanne and Johnny followed, not talking, walking apart across the beaten-down grass. They passed from the bright lights and wandered among new tractors and hay balers.

"Max is a hero," Suzanne called out. She wore a new dress, turquoise, sleek, like a woman in a fancy magazine. Her hair was down. She looked nice, but moments before he'd been riding across the sky, with Jane fondling his private parts. He couldn't wrap his mind around the wonder of it.

"*Are* you a hero?" Jane asked.

"Mostly, I was scared shitless."

"Look at the beautiful chickens," Jane said, running a little ahead, then stopping before a dozen cages of exotic birds, red and white and black, with the old people who'd raised them standing proudly near. Behind them Johnny heard Connie Francis singing "Who's Sorry Now?" and the Beatles "She loves You."

She didn't, not even a little.

"You're the first veteran I've ever met," Jane said. "I mean of the Vietnam War—my dad's a veteran, of course. I don't mean to put you on the spot, Max, but I read in *Time* magazine where lots of people are unhappy with the war. They say it's wrong—what I mean is, all war is horrible, but this war . . . "

"I'm proud I came back," Max said. "And that I'm not all fucked up. Not beyond all recognition, at least. That's all there is to it, beautiful girl."

"I'm sorry you had to go through that," Jane said, so sincerely Johnny could have vomited. Max put an arm around her, and they cruised down among the sows.

Either she was teaching him a lesson—because he'd muscled in on Gary—or he mattered so little that dropping him for Max wasn't worth considering. He thought about jumping Max even if he was a combat veteran; at the same time, he wanted to slip into the darkness, and drive, stopping when he reached the Gulf of Mexico. Then he looked over at Suzanne and saw the hurt in her eyes. He took her hand.

"Mama made me drop out."

"I know. I felt so bad—"

"It's not your fault, Johnny. Daddy treated you like dirt. That fight was just an excuse."

She could have earned a scholarship, he thought. She could have become a famous nurse in a romance novel. He hugged her and felt sadder and sadder.

She drew back, calmer now. "He's here tonight; everyone's here. We used to all come, it was such fun. With Max, in the old days. But Daddy's been drinking."

"Everett's drinkin'?"

"I have the worst parents in the entire world."

He couldn't tell her it wasn't so, so he hugged her again. They walked slowly back toward the lights. Jane stared at him without expression. Suzanne wiped at her tears.

"Whatya think of Suzie's dress?" Max asked. "Bought it on Tudo Street."

"Beautiful," Johnny said.

Suzanne laughed. "He calls me Suzie."

Max clasped Jane's arm. "And this here's the Chicken Queen. Known her since the fifth grade. Only now she's ready to *pluck*."

"You wish," Jane said, aiming a fist at him, but he caught it and turned her toward the bumper cars.

A man chomping on a cigar took their tickets, and they slid out on the floor where old-timey tunes, Bing Crosby and Nat King Cole, played. Johnny found a purple buggy made like a pickup truck, and when the juice came on, he drove as soberly as that drunk, George Bell, used to, because he was thinking about Suzanne, and how to rescue her. Then Max gave him a quick orientation to bumper car driving. He rammed him.

Johnny smashed into Suzanne and drove her to the rail. She wheeled about and ran backwards, and then both Max and Jane hit her and she sat, laughing and crying, with her hands over her ears. But now she had the knack, and drove as fast as she could, gathering speed on the outside. She plowed into Max exactly when Max rammed Jane.

Jane looked up at Max with a snarl. Johnny banged her from the side, bouncing her toward Suzanne, who hit her again. Max took off around the course, gathering speed for more of the same, and Johnny had an idea. Just when Max rounded the far side, he'd strike in a rush, and crack the soldier-boy's head against the support post. It would look like an accident. He'd have to live with the fact he was a murderer, but the Chicken Queen would be his.

He opened the little throttle but didn't have any juice.

"All out!" said the man with a cigar.

In the concourse Suzanne grabbed his hand; Jane gave her a long, empty stare. Max struck a pose like Elvis and combed his hair, what little of it there was, in a funhouse mirror. Jane gave him a long, empty stare, too.

Max offered her a cigarette, and she accepted it as if she were the woman who did the commercials. He struck a Zippo with a Cav horse's head on its side, and she lifted her green-shaded eyes with a dreamy boredom. They blew out smoke, threw deeply mature looks at Suzanne and Johnny, and strode away into the land of glittering generalities.

Suzanne looked up at Johnny gravely. "He's changed some. He uses a lot of bad language. He doesn't seem to care what he says."

"I'll bet he's into it with Everett."

"Not yet."

He pulled her behind the Methodist tent and kissed her again and again, but he was near to bawling. He ran his hands all over her slinky dress.

"Do you love me, Johnny?"

No, Lord help him, he loved Jane! He reeled into the light again, wanting her back, wishing he'd never met her. At a shooting gallery a stout man with a crude haircut pivoted his rifle toward him, and Johnny stumbled, thinking it was Everett.

The man laughed and lowered his rifle. "Sorry, bud."

Sai Baba, Mystic Indian Fakir, the sign said.

"Faker's right," Johnny said.

"You pronounce it 'FAH-KEER,'" Jane announced. "I had to make a speech on world religions."

"I went to somethin' like this in Bangkok," Max said.

"You've been to Thailand?" Jane asked.

"Sho thang, sweetheart. Been to Kansas City, too."

"See Sai Baba perform the holy Monkey God dance," the barker went on, only he wasn't like the other barkers. He had thick black eyebrows and dark eyes and wore a red turban.

He's scary," Suzanne said. "C'mon, Johnny. We'll be late for the program."

An awful moaning came from inside, and they heard music that sounded like a guitar, and also like the handsaw Brother Jones played at church.

"Sitar," Max said.

"*What* program?" Johnny asked.

"Sai Baba, the Monkey God, undergoes the ordeal of fire!" the barker said, fastening his eyes on Johnny. "Sai Baba the Fire Walker!"

"Sounds like fun," Jane said, rubbing up against Max, but smiling at Johnny.

"The annual meeting," Susanne said.

"I remember that," Max said. "The Chicken Follies."

"Johnny, *please*," Suzanne said, tugging at his arm. "We need to talk."

He shook her away. Using all his money, he bought tickets for everyone and plunged inside. He expected a dark chamber, but instead walked onto a section of pasture that had been roped off, and he could see faint stars above. In back was a high wooden fence, like a stockade in the Old West. A great Buddha, staring down with baleful, ruby eyes, lurked in a painting of mountains. Down below stood three little huts that made you think of . . . what? They were made of plywood and chicken wire such as you'd see in a school play. A sign said, "Typical Tibetan Village."

The village street glowed with coals.

"The Monkey God has angered Gautama Buddha," a foreign-sounding voice said. The words blended with the sitar music, as if you'd dreamed them, and the air was choky with a sickening, sweet smell that Max said was incense. A chanting rose.

"Sai Baba, the Monkey God, has traveled many miles through the desert, braving hunger and thirst, bandits and fearsome wild animals, and now he makes his final penance."

"I don't like this," Suzanne said. "I think it's kind of pagan and I don't know why they have it here."

Max guided them through the darkness. "Oh, they had Cleopatra, and Adam and Eve which was pretty good, only they wasn't really nekkid, and one time they even had Hitler. I mean they *said* it was Hitler, and how it has never been proved he died, though it was just this mean-looking guy with a moustache."

"Mama wouldn't let me go in," Suzanne said.

The barker from the entrance materialized out of the smoke, eyes blazing. An anonymous voice announced that Sai Baba would attempt to walk over the coals in his bare feet. "It is a holy act," the voice said, in clipped English. "Please, ladies and gentlemen, show your respect."

Max leaned against the railing at the far end, his arm around Jane. Johnny and Suzanne lost them in the smoke, then drew near. As the holy man stepped forward, wraith-like in the smoke, Max whispered, "We all seek inner tranquility."

"Wow," Jane said.

"I learned about it in Bangkok. Hear that? The chantin'? Say, 'Om.'"

"Om," Jane said, giggling.

"Ah, ooo, um," Max said, drawing his finger across her lips.

"Ah, ooo, um," said Jane.

"Altogether."

"Ah-umm . . . "

Max took on the tone like a priest: "I-am-one-may-I-become-many."

"I am one . . . may I become many? Is that what you said?"

"I-am-one-may-I become-many oh-mmmm . . . "

Johnny couldn't make out anything through the smoke but the glowing path of coals leading up to the Buddha.

Two girls, dressed in long white gowns, danced beside the coals, and threw down water out of tall vials, to make steam rise. Then the guy in the turban, now wearing a mask and a monkey's tail, leaped into the village from out of the smoke. A woman screamed.

"I used to chant that in Vietnam," Max said.

"Really?"

"I'd get all fucked up, scuse my French, with my mind runnin' like a merry-go-round, and I'd say that fifty times, and I could drift right off to sleep. It's sposed to bring you close to the Buddha, but I don't believe in my own God, let alone theirs."

"You don't believe in God?" Suzanne asked.

"Aw, Suzie, we can talk about it." Max looked frustrated. "You don't know what I *seen*."

Several women and a tall Amish fellow at the back of the stockade left in disgust, declaring the entire show to be sacrilegious. Johnny would have left, too, except he'd bought the tickets and wanted his money's worth. His felt nauseated but could hold on.

The sitar and the chanting stopped, and Sai Baba walked solemnly forward. Disoriented by the smoke, Johnny bent at the waist with an inexplicable pain. He saw the man's bare feet sizzling on the coals, his flesh cooking—though he *couldn't* have. It made no sense. Sai Baba's eyes blazed as if aimed at Johnny alone. Was this a vision? Was Sai Baba really Satan? Johnny's stomach flopped, and he couldn't get his breath in such a tight space, smelling that cloying sweetness. He clawed his way toward the back but couldn't see the door.

"Johnny, Johnny!" Suzanne said. "This way—"

She led him outside. He fell on all fours and vomited.

"What is it, Johnny?"

"The fire, that man on fire . . ."

"Oh," she whispered. "Like your grandfather's fire."

Jane and Max joined them. "Poor guy," Jane said, bending near.

"You awright, troop?" Max asked.

Johnny came to his feet but staggered, and the girls grabbed him. For a moment he had his arms around both their waists.

Max broke out laughing. "It's Hugh Hefner."

"You shut up," Jane said. "John's sick, can't you see?"

"Atheist," Suzanne said.

Johnny lay across three folding chairs, shut his eyes, and went hurtling down into a terrible dark place. No mere mortal could withstand such torment, but he thought of Tarzan and sat up. He'd arrived in the big tent, and as his vision steadied, he believed he saw Max at the edge of darkness. He couldn't make out Jane anywhere, but Suzanne sat in front with her family. Seeing Everett again, a chill ran over Johnny, but Everett stared intently toward the stage.

This was Reverend Larkin's chicken show, and a sort of campaign event as well, because signs promoting his candidacy for sheriff hung all around the tent, with lots of bunting and red and blue streamers. Larkin laughed, pumped hands, slapped backs. Children ran up, and without ceasing his talk, Larkin held out a galvanized bucket, so the kids could scrounge for suckers. Every once in a while, someone called out, "Go get 'em, Sheriff!"

Still, this was the Co-op's annual meeting, not a political rally, and a lot of the farmers took it seriously. They went nowhere near the rides on the concourse. They wore their best overalls, clean boots, clean shirts.

Hard to say how they'd vote, or if they'd vote at all.

All the men on the stage, Larkin included, wore bright red sports coats with a cloth rooster pinned to their breast pockets, and the legend, "Chicken of Tomorrow" beneath. A big poster draped from the lectern, featuring a rooster bent back like a baseball pitcher, an egg in his claw.

Larkin sauntered to the lectern with the cheerful countenance of a prosperous Christian. He moved the lectern a little to the right, until his face basked like the light on the disciples in church bulletins. Finally, he ran a finger under his collar, and tapped the microphone. "We got a hot one here tonight," he said. "But don't we thank the good Lord for the rain?"

"That we do, Sheriff," cried Virgil, Larkin's one-man cheering section.

He smiled. "We're here to talk about poultry. The Chicken of Tomorrow!"

"You tell 'em, Sheriff." Virgil lifted both thumbs. "A chicken in every pot!"

Larkin waved his hands and pointed. "Prizes, people. Dinner for two at Don Goodland's Steak House. Nice little Zenith color TV, there'll be a drawin' for that, and this year, for best feed conversion, we have a first prize savin's bond for one hunert dollars. For second, it's fifty, do I hear fifty? Gimme fifty, gimme fifty—"

His imitation of an auctioneer drew some laughs, but Sister Larkin corrected him. "It's twenty-five, Reverend," she called out.

"Sold for twenty-five! That's my wife, people, my darlin' Dorothy. Take my wife—"

A few more laughs.

"Seriously, people, feed conversion is just about the whole shebang when it comes to raisin' poultry—or hogs or beef cattle, far as that goes—and we got Larry Stubbs here outta Bentonville, Arkansas, gonna give us all the latest on chick starter, and cuttin' down on your dead—and a course the Chicken of Tomorrow. It's a White Wyandotte, an All-American bird, crossed with a Cornish—I always thought they was kinda scrawny. But they're gonna give you a pound of meat for two point seven pounds a feed in, it seems incredible, nine weeks. Maybe eight. Maybe even seven! That right, Larry?"

Mr. Stubbs grinned and shuffled some papers, ready to launch into his lecture, but now the reverend took off on the crisis in farming. Who could explain the mysterious thing that happened to politicians when they reached Washington? Why did they forget the hard-working American farmer once they had his vote? He'd founded this country with his muscle and ingenuity, but his very existence—the family farm itself—was threatened by these big companies. You didn't have to look any farther than Arkansas. Was it the wave of the future? Larkin sincerely hoped not, but look what had happened in Russia. Did we want the collective farm right here in Missouri? If all you had was one corporation, telling you what you could raise, setting the prices, was it so different from Communism?

Larkin never mentioned the word sheriff, but in all modesty, he was a proven leader for the Co-op and for business generally here in Joshua County. It was simple, really. People who were privileged to hold a public office needed to apply the principles outlined by Dale Carnegie in his book, *How to Win Friends and Influence People.* Never criticize anyone, Carnegie said, and don't talk about your problems because nobody cares. Ha, ha, when it came to that, but you know what? Sound business principles turned out to be Christian principles. Do unto others as you would have them do unto you, and every little problem would melt away.

Jane and Max slipped into the chairs next to Johnny. "Still sick, buddy?" Max asked.

Somehow, Johnny couldn't hate him. "I'm awright."

Suzanne threw a glance over her shoulder, and Johnny smiled, but her eyes didn't focus. Lucy stared straight ahead. She jerked as Ronnie bounced against her and ran back to jump in Max's lap.

"You gonna behave?"

"'Course."

It was time to go home, Johnny thought, eying Jane, who favored him with a phony smile. She could come with the one who brung her, or not, but he supposed he had to put himself through the humiliation of asking her.

"You goddam crook!"

Johnny had some experience with drunks. Everett was plastered.

Larkin cocked his head sideways, and the crowd, too, shifted its attention. Lucy's face twisted as if she'd swallowed poison.

Everett pulled himself to the stage. His cap fell to the floor, and his ridiculous-looking hair flopped. He squatted, then stood slowly erect as if learning to walk. Larkin stumbled backward and glanced at the crowd.

The Co-op's business meeting might have the most boring thing going on that night in all of Missouri, but still it was news, and the editor from Red Buck's little paper had attended. She came down the aisle, knelt, and snapped pictures. As it turned out, she hadn't had a story such as this since the tornado that killed Kathleen Bell.

The reverend planted his feet. His face wrestled first with sympathy—the preacher side of him—then with contempt. As a businessman, and a candidate for office, he knew he was in trouble. The tent grew so quiet you could hear him whisper, "Everett. Brother Everett, please. We can talk."

"Had enough a your talk, you cheap-ass sonuvabitch." Everett shook his finger, and no question, he had everyone's attention, as much from shock as sympathy. Virgil stood and looked around for allies. Max stood.

"This man is Ananias. A liar who *will* be struck down. He is a moneychanger in the holy temple. You say—you say—he's a-runnin' for sheriff? He better get his heart right with God 'fore he asks for your vote. I gonna tell you, I gonna tell you—" Everett pulled a crumpled sheet of paper from his overalls, waved it, and crumpled it some more. "He talks good. But it all comes down to this: I made fourteen cents an hour with his Goddam birds. How 'bout you people?"

People rose, sat, milled about, and someone went for Joel Harpster. Mr. Stubbs removed himself from the stage, while Virgil and Max ascended it. Lucy rose, took several steps, and stood as though paralyzed.

Reverend Larkin tried to put his arms around Everett, all the time looking out at the audience, but the devil had taken charge, and Everett shook him off. He swung at Larkin and nearly fell. Larkin reached out to steady him and both men fell. Ronnie Ogletree laughed at this, perhaps thinking his father and brother were in a play, but the crowd went silent. Suzanne cried.

A black Plymouth growled to a stop outside the tent, and there was a short burst from a siren. Sheriff Harpster had never been far away.

Everett climbed to his feet, and yelled something, punctuated with curses that eternally damned the notion of feed conversion. Then he spun about, took another swing at the reverend, and stumbled. He hit his head against a chair and lay silently.

Sheriff Harpster's badge gleamed in the lights. He grabbed the microphone—and won the election then and there, surely, if he could restore order at the other candidate's meeting. "All right, people. Everything's fine." As if it were a military operation, he and Max picked Everett up by the shoulders and feet, while Virgil went to comfort the reverend.

"Let me help," Johnny said, grabbing Everett's belt buckle.

The sheriff nodded, recognizing Johnny, but he was a busy man. They hauled Everett down the sawdust aisle like a rejected sacrifice and set him on a picnic table. Suzanne ran for the family car and Johnny found a chair for Lucy. She sat trembling, speechless. Rosie tried to crawl into her lap, but Lucy pushed her away.

The sheriff leaned against the Plymouth. He offered a cigarette to Max and they lit up. Johnny drew near, a beggar, and the sheriff shook out a Pall Mall for him, too. "No better than he is at it, Everett sure gets in a lot a fights."

"He's a fightin' fool." Max grunted. "Emphasis on the fool part."

"Well, he's your dad."

"I think they found me under a bush. Imagine a man so ignorant he makes his kids drop outta school." Max laughed. "Of course, I didn't put up any argument. But my sister—"

"You get your GED in the service?"

"I did."

"Where were you?"

"Down in III Corps. Around Tay Ninh."

"Hunert and Worst?"

"Cav."

"Shit, you just flew around in helicopters."

"More fun than the Tilt-A-Whirl." Max laughed harshly. "What's gonna happen with the old man?"

"I'll see what the Republican candidate for sheriff says. It's trouble if he wants it to be, but I don't imagine he does."

Max nodded. "Appreciate it."

Suzanne arrived with the car and hurried to Lucy's side. Lucy staggered as if she, too, were drunk. She looked down at Everett in wonder, and toward Heaven as if she hoped to be swept up from her worldly cares.

"Mom, it'll be awright," Suzanne said. "He's just, he's just—"

"Of the *Devil*," Lucy whispered.

They moved Everett to the back seat of his car. He grunted and moaned something about an air filter on the International, but never truly woke. The twins squirmed in beside their mother, and Suzanne slid behind the wheel.

"I'll come see you," Johnny whispered.

Suzanne put a hand on his but didn't speak. Lucy's lips moved furiously in prayer.

"Need a ride?" the sheriff asked Max.

Max looked regretful. "I should probably stay with them."

"We can follow 'em home."

"Nice of you," Max said, and climbed into the Plymouth. The sheriff turned on his red light for the benefit of any voters he might have missed.

Johnny slipped under the tent again. Reverend Larkin stood at the podium, mopping his forehead, and presently the expert from Arkansas made his speech. The audience had dwindled to half a dozen. Larkin sat, trying to look calm, but he had to hold a bandage to his forehead. Virgil looked at Johnny and shook his head sorrowfully.

"John, are we going home now?"

Hard to believe, but he'd forgotten about Jane. Their eyes met like two burglars who'd arrived at the same house but didn't know each other.

"You catch all that?"

"Mr. Larkin was trying to talk, but this old drunk—"

"That was Suzanne's dad."

"Poor girl."

Dear Lord, he was blue. He wished he lived in pioneer times, and could ride a mule into the sunset, and live with the Indians.

Jane put a hand on his arm. "John."

He stared at her wearily.

"I just wanted to thank you for asking me out tonight." She smiled sweetly. "I had a really wonderful time."

Chapter Sixteen
Goat Boy

He sat cross-legged before the fire, whispering "Shh" as if the goats were children in a Christmas play. Virgil came across through the shadows and plunked down in his rocking chair. A man coughed, sneezed, blew his nose in his handkerchief. A woman called out "Stop!" and everyone laughed.

Then it was quiet. The moonlight shone through the tall cedars, rippling over the deep scallop in the rock that constituted their amphitheater. You could hear the June bugs buzzing along, knocking themselves out when they banged into the lights, like drunks. Up on the ridge, an owl hooted.

Johnny threw oak chips on the coals to encourage a blaze. This made a real fire, but in several scenes, they had to move it out, so Johnny had built a bowl out of limestone and bricks and then cemented casters onto it. That wasn't all. Since the theater was really the opening to a cave, and a rock shelf hung over everything, they had to park the fire under a crack to draw away the smoke. Over two days he'd piked and picked at the crack, enlarging it into a sort of chimney. He wanted to use dynamite but Virgil thought the whole shelf might fall.

PREACHER GIL: Evenin'. Proud to visit with you. People around these parts call me Preacher Gil, and I'm what they call a narrator. Like the man eatin' frog guts, we're gonna take it easy tonight, and watch this fine story unfold, as the author says. If you need to stretch, or scratch, or use the facilities, you go right on. We ain't what you'd call formal. But listen, we got hot and cold runnin' water, and toilets that flush!

Why, when I was a boy, the "facilities" was a two-holer stocked with Monkey Ward catalogues, and a feller sat there slappin' mosquitoes on his dairy-airy-aire.

Mrs. Koontz didn't enjoy what she called the bathroom humor, but Virgil said he had to act naturally or he couldn't act at all, and his speech always drew a laugh. "If they laugh, they spend money," he said.

The laugh cued Johnny. He looked over the bleachers Virgil and he had built and dug into the uneven ground. Nearly three hundred starlit, upturned faces stared in wonder at that mysterious hole in the darkness.

"Okay, okay," he whispered. He brought himself to one knee and slipped his arm under La's neck. She nodded her head and her bell tinkled just a little. How that girl loved show biz!

PREACHER GIL: Centuries ago, all of the Ozarks was covered with tall, stately pines, refuge to the panther and bear, ancestral home of the peaceful Osage. Then white men came to rip lead and silver from the fragile earth, and to rape the virgin forests. As our story begins, only one piece of the great forest remains, the hideout of a desperate and depraved outlaw band, the last remnant of the legendary Bald Knobbers. It's also home to an innocent wanderer . . . Hiram, the Goat Boy of the Ozarks.

Johnny gave La a little jab behind the shoulder. She shook her head, ringing the bell. The lights came up on the cave, and so did the applause.

GOAT BOY: La la la la la.

It was a goofy line, but La thought he was talking to her, and looked at him through the scene. And the kids in the audience were sure to emit an "Aww . . ."

GOAT BOY: Nobody knows Hiram. But is Hiram sad? No! La la la la!
LA: Braa-aa-aa-at!
GOAT BOY: He has the stars at night and the golden sunshine in the lazy mornin's. He has the mountains and the deep hollers with their sparklin' pools. He has the tall pine trees, where God whispers His love for all livin' things. And he has his friends.

Johnny held out his hands, which the goats knew were filled with apple quarters. They were Everett's goats: Virgil had bought them at auction when the Ogletrees left for parts unknown. The goats gathered around, nuzzling him.

The Goat Boy seemed backward to Johnny, but Mrs. Koontz said oh no, he's a primitive. She even claimed that Johnny was the inspiration for Hiram, since he was an orphan and lived by himself in the woods. Johnny couldn't complain. He was making two dollars over minimum wage and hardly breaking a sweat.

He kneed La in the ribs and she led the other goats off to stage right. He pounded the rock with what Mrs. Koontz called his "staff," which really was George Bell's walking stick. They turned toward the back and exited between two post oaks that grew up through cracks in the cave roof. He parked the goats in a little corral, climbed the crumbling hillside through a clump of cedars, and came down hill again, stage left, to help with moving the scenery.

He hadn't got his breath before Mrs. Koontz drew near and gave him a hug. "Perfect, Johnny!" she whispered.

Her cheeks were rouged, framed in a wig of bouncy sausage curls. She wore a floppy sun bonnet and an old-timey dress. She was the picture of 19th Century virtue, and only he knew that she'd had a drink or two before the play began. He could smell it, and it made him fearful, knowing the broad path George Bell went down. On the other hand, he'd always thought teachers were perfect creatures, barely human. That Mrs. Koontz had turned out to be a sinner made him like her more somehow.

After three performances, tourists lined up in numbers, even after that fellow from the Springfield paper came down and then wrote that they were putting on "an amateurish production that gets history entirely wrong." Mrs. Koontz cried when she read that, but Virgil made fifty dollars one night just from popcorn and was happy.

"Wish me luck, Goat Boy," Mrs. Koontz said.

"Break a leg," he whispered—and on this stage, she might. She disappeared into the darkness, crawling up the hillside. She played Horace Keel's wife in a dramatic and stirring scene.

PREACHER GIL: But let's go back fifteen years, to a time right after the Civil War.

The Piney River Boys began with a fiddle and a mountain dulcimer, real tear-jerky stuff, but it put the crowd in the right mood.

PREACHER GIL: It was brother against brother, and these hills was covered with blood. Didn't matter if it was the Confederates or the Union boys, they stole the food, then burnt the farm. And for long afterwards, it was hard times. Some fellers, even though they took the law in their own hands, stood for justice, but there was others who was nothin' but scalawags.

There was opportunities, too, for an enterprisin' man. Horace Keel packed up his buzz saw and steam engine and followed the James River far into the wilderness. He knew them big Eastern cities was hungry for lumber. He'd heard tell of a stand of virgin pines there for the takin'.

The lights came up on the hillside. Gary Tyrell, who'd taped on a beard to play Horace Keel, clucked to his mules, and rolled the wagon perhaps six feet forward. Some nights, frightened or just mulish, the mules refused to move at all.

SARAH KEEL: (holding the toddler, Peggy) Is it much farther to the cabin?
HORACE KEEL: Twenty miles, still, as the crow flies. Shall we camp here for the night?
SARAH KEEL: Yes, dear husband. I am not concerned for myself, but for your little daughter.
HORACE KEEL: Sarah, you have endured much.
SARAH KEEL: It is the lot of all women.

La delivered her lines with more conviction than Gary mustered, but Jane wouldn't play Peggy Keel unless he played Horace, and he was fine in the action scenes. He reached for his rifle as Nat Kinney, played by the ex-con Clyde Fooch, and his fellow Bald Knobbers spilled down the hillside, dressed in cowboy outfits except for their masks. The masks were gunny sacks with eyeholes in them, and corn cobs, wrapped tightly with black muslin, that stuck up like horns, covered with socks sewn on top. The outlaws shot off blanks. One of them leaped onto the wagon.

HORACE KEEL: Sarah, we are done for!
SARAH KEEL: Better to die at your side, than live a captive among these scoundrels!

The crowd oohed and aahed as Horace fought the good

fight, but at last sank to the ground. The first Bald Knobber searched him, then held up a sack of coins.

PEGGY (as infant): Daddy! Oh, Daddy!
SARAH: Your father is in Heaven, little Peggy. (Looks up at outlaws, in great distress.) Have your way with me. But spare my child!
J. J. BROWN: The woman ain't nothin' but dead weight. I say we knock her and the kid in the haid.
NAT KINNEY: (laughing cruelly): I reckon I got a use for the woman.

Mrs. Koontz wanted to include a scene where Nat Kinney held her down, and she screamed, and the lights went out as the little girl yelled, "Mommy!" She said this would dramatize how women had been treated by men through the ages, but Virgil objected. It was a family show, he said, and you couldn't have rape.

Mrs. Koontz said, "This is a compromise that I am not entirely comfortable with."

"I think the audience will kinda suspicion what went on," Virgil said.

"Understatement, you're saying. Less is more."

"Way I see it, Ruth Ann."

One of the outlaws tried to grab Peggy, but she escaped into the brush. In the darkness the audience heard a woman screaming, and as Virgil said, could suspicion what went on.

More compromise was called for in the drunken Bald Knobbers scene, which took place some years later and showed an older Sarah Keel in the outlaw camp, and a little boy, actually Hiram the Goat Boy, clinging to her leg. Colonel Prather and Nat Kinney danced around the fire, as the Piney River Boys sang "Copper Kettle":

CHORUS: You'll just lay there by the juniper
While the moon is bright,

Watch them jugs a-fillin'
In the pale moonlight.

This was a crowd-pleaser, though Mrs. Koontz didn't approve of all the singing and dancing because she said it romanticized the Bald Knobbers and detracted from her serious intent with the sad story of Sarah Keel, forced to live as a degraded woman with the goat boy at her side. Virgil said that it was important for people from Chicago to see a real Ozarks show. Next year, they'd bring their friends.

"Poetic license," Mrs. Koontz said, almost to herself.

Virgil nodded. "Not necessary out in the county, Ruth Ann. I checked on that."

The audience sang along with the Piney River Boys while Gary Tyrell, alias Horace Keel, climbed on the wagon. The outlaws had left him for dead, but he awakened at last, Preacher Gil explained, and staggered back to civilization with Peggy.

He wore a grey beard now because of all the years that had passed. Beside him was his lovely and talented teenage daughter, Peggy.

PREACHER GIL: Grim years, they was. Prosperity came to Horace Keel even as the trees fell. But he grew ever more bitter as he thought of his lost wife. No woman could replace her in his tortured heart. He returned to the virgin forest, vowin' to fell every tree, and maybe, just maybe, find revenge. But his bold young daughter had other ideas.

As Virgil's all-purpose hillbilly, Johnny supposed he'd have been in the production one way or the other, but Mrs. Koontz had ambushed him. He was coming around the corner of the general store, sweaty, muscles aching, and there she was, rocking placidly on the long front porch. She was already wearing her old-timey outfit. She held out a paper, printed like a bill for a farm auction:

Ozark Village World Premiere!
The thrilling and heart-wrenching tragedy!

Goat Boy of the Ozarks

an original play by Ruth Ann Koontz
performed for you by the acclaimed Osage Players
with musical accompaniment by the
Piney River Gospel Band

Dramatis Personae

Hiram, the Goat Boy, as a child
Hiram, the Goat Boy, guardian of the virgin forest
Horace Keel, a ruthless developer
Sarah Keel, his wife
Peggy Keel, his daughter, as a little girl
Peggy Keel, a young woman who fights to save
the virgin forest
Preacher Gil, an itinerant evangelist, the narrator

The Bald Knobbers:
Colonel Alonzo Prather
Nat Kinney
Yell Frederick
J. J. Brown

Admission $2; children under twelve, twenty-five cents.
Show-time at dusk.

"What does itinerant mean?"
"Wandering."
"Why didn't they just say wandrin'?"

She frowned, but wrote something in a notebook. "Not 'they,' but me. Anyhow, what do you think, Johnny?"

"About what?"

"You, the Goat Boy. You're the lead."

"I could be, maybe, one of the outlaws—"

"Call me Ruthie," she said. "You're a senior, I'll never be your teacher again. We're friends, Johnny."

"Yes, ma'am. But I don't believe I—"

She sighed dramatically. "I put Jane Epstein in it. Just as you asked."

"She plays . . . Peggy? You're sure?"

"I'm the director, aren't I?"

The director hadn't mentioned that Gary would play Horace Keel. She hadn't mentioned that Horace and Peggy would arrive every day in Gary's big Impala with the 8-track thumping out "Satisfaction," of which Johnny wasn't going to get any. Jane seemed to like Gary all the more for his dubious fame.

Johnny liked him, too. The death of Bobby Sills had lodged deep inside him, and he'd grown wistful. "I like that old Ford of yours," he said.

"It gets me there."

"Naw, it's vintage. I have to drive these big Chevies on account of my dad. With the dealership and all."

"Such a cross you bear," Johnny said, and Gary laughed.

Still, this wasn't how the story went in *Tarzan of the Apes,* where Gary would have been the feeble Clayton. Jane loved him, the wild goat boy; she had to. He cornered her when she was coming down the trail between the general store and the theater. He grabbed her shoulders and forced her to look him in the eye.

"I'm crazy about you. And I don't understand what he—"

"You don't know what he's been through."

"What about what *I've* been through? I—"

She looked away. "Gary . . . needs me."

If I had run Bobby Sills off the road, Johnny thought, they'd have strapped me down in chains. And perhaps if the son of the Chevy dealer had strutted and boasted, he'd have been doomed, too. But Gary had seen a light. He'd turned humble and dreamy and sad, a tragic hero.

Jane was always going to be an experiment that fizzled. Pretty girls were everywhere at Ozark Village that summer, and they all had a smile for Johnny because he was the Goat Boy. But he could have driven into Red Buck in a Ferrari red as a bleeding heart, and called himself Paul Newman, and it wouldn't have mattered to Jane.

"Hit's a terrible shame about the poultry business," Virgil said.

It was shutting down in Missouri as big companies such as Tyson took over, and a lot of people would be hurt. Still, someone had to do the dirty work, and Johnny had resolved to pull himself out of poverty. Being a hillbilly was his day job. His night job was catching chickens for Reverend Larkin's faltering Co-op.

The broilers huddled together, making them easy to catch. They'd shit on you and after a while your arms wanted to fall off, because the man on the truck demanded them twenty at a time to fit his cages. In several hours you'd have them thinned out, but the ones that remained were wide awake and knew you wanted to send them to the electric chair. You chased them with a long wire twisted into a hook at the end, kicking up that awful dust filled with ammonia. When you couldn't take anymore, you staggered into the night air, stood by a fire made from busted pallets, and drank Stroh's from tall cans.

You got there a little before midnight because by then the birds were huddled together conveniently, and so deeply asleep they appeared dead. Awake, they flew into walls and bruised the meat.

It took four or five hours to clean out a big house, depending on the crew. Some farms had a dozen houses, and crews went back for a couple of weeks, as if to regular jobs. Still, it was the kind of work no one wanted, and put Johnny beside men who'd been in prison, men otherwise out of work who were turning desperate, and men who could have served as the definition of ignorance, considering how they talked about women and used the Lord's name in vain.

Some he saw only once because all they wanted was enough money for a drunk.

Often, the crews were Mexicans from Arkansas, where the chicken business was migrating. They'd hang a radio from a post and find the Juarez station. Then they all chased after chickens accompanied by mariachi songs and sad ballads. They called the wiliest of the chickens, the ones that ran your legs off or fluttered up to a rafter, *pollos perversos.*

One fellow named Manny came over to Johnny every once in a while as if he meant to bum a cigarette, but instead held up a *Playboy,* dropped down the centerfold, and grinned. Johnny knew some Spanish, but the centerfold was as close as Manny and he came to conversation.

The motels wouldn't rent to the Mexicans, so Johnny didn't know where they went in the daytime, though he guessed they camped somewhere they could cook, because they always took along a stray bird or two. So did Johnny. He kept them by his shed in a rickety rabbit hutch. Come winter, when he didn't have any wages, they'd taste fine.

One day down at the feed mill Reverend Larkin came up to him. "Johnny, I wonder if you could give Clyde Fooch a ride."

Clyde stood off by himself, a tall fellow, bald, with a scraggly beard and a face so thin it reminded Johnny of an axe.

"Brother Fooch is on parole," the reverend said. "But he has paid for his sins, and found the Lord, and needs another chance."

Catching chickens every night wasn't much of a chance, but Johnny supposed it was better than prison. Reverend Larkin seemed serious about it. He was a serious man, now that he was no longer running for sheriff and a big part of his business was dying.

"Sure," Johnny said. "What did Mr. Fooch do?"

"That would be for him to tell you," the reverend said.

Clyde gave him fifty cents for the ride every day, and thanked Johnny gravely. He smoked Chesterfield Kings one after the other, but didn't talk much.

"I got to go to church on Sunday," Clyde announced. "That's the onliest thing."

"Not so painful."

"Charley Larkin give me this job, it's the only kinda work for a jailbird. I had a deprived upbringin' and my education was cut short and they sent me to the penitentiary. They don't teach you no skills there. Young feller like you, you should get your education and a reglar trade."

"That's my plan," Johnny said. "You married, Clyde?"

"Used to be married."

"Kids?"

"Used to have kids."

"I'll bet you're a victim of injustice."

"I never done nothin' to her!" He lit another Chesterfield King. "I told 'em I was in Florida, and I was. Only that humidididdy they got down there does a man in. I have myself a family, I said, and I'm goin' home. Pulled in 'bout three in the mornin'."

They were headed back to Red Buck. It was dawn. "Someone else was there?"

He brought a fist down on the dash. "I run a trouble light out from the garage and was takin' his car apart. I woulda pulled the damn engine he give me another hour, only he worked down at the creamery I reckon, and they start at six. I had all the doors off, and the trunk and the hood and all the lights, and the grill, and the wheels which I rolled into the crick. And the battery, and the bumpers, and one rocker panel."

"What kinda car was it?"

"Corvette. I mean, he was pissed. I wasn't gonna fight him, only he come chargin' out, and screamin', and Vinita right behind wasn't wearin' a stitch, and you think she was sorry? I hit him with the lug wrench in self-defense, only they said I provoked him."

"You killed him?"

"Naw. He hit his head on somethin', put him in a wheel-chair for life. Vinita turned me in. I coulda went on down the road but I stayed there and took my medicine."

"Don't seem fair."

"Fair? I couldn't say 'bout that. I'd settle for 'em jest lettin' me alone."

"Who's 'them?' Reverend Larkin?"

"Naw, naw, he brought me to Jesus. I mean that cowboy Harpster, and my parole officer, and the counselor, and them people at Alcoholics Anonymous. Some days, prison would be an improvement. I don't understand what they're sayin' to me. And they don't leave me time to shit. I cain't hardly even go fishin'."

"You wanna be a Bald Knobber?" Johnny asked.

"What's that?"

"An outlaw. I'm in a play, and they need another outlaw."

"I cain't be involved in no criminal activities."

"This is pretend."

"Why they wanna do that? Bad enough when it's real."

"I don't know, it's for the tourists. It's historical. It's easy money, you could maybe go to the movies once in a while. You'd make a fine Bald Knobber."

Johnny told him where Ozark Village was, and let him off on the square, where he had a room above the dentist's office. In another hour the Howdy Doody would open for breakfast, but Johnny didn't have the strength to wait, and anyhow he stank of chickens. By the time he made it home he was so sleepy he could hardly stay on the road. He couldn't make it to his cot and slept curled around the gear shift.

When he woke he pulled on his overalls and straw hat, walked down the tracks in the punishing sun, and climbed into the dunking tank for his daily bath. It was a high, hot perch until he went under, and sometimes he had to yell out insults to make the suckers bite. All part of the job, Virgil said. Show biz.

"You from Chicago, Mister?"

"How you know?"

"'Cause you look so dumb."

Mostly, he told hillbilly stories he'd stolen from a joke book:

"I know this ole boy doctored himself for twenty years outta the *Capper's Weekly*. He finally died of a typographical error."

No one had made moonshine in Joshua County since World War II, but a corn likker joke or two was required, as well as one about outhouses falling into the river with grandma inside. The idea was to tell such awful jokes that the tourists performed a public service by drowning you.

"This ole hillbilly heads up to Kansas City to sell some hogs and takes along his wife and boy. They're wandrin' around lookin' at all the sights, and the hillbilly and his boy go into this fancy department store. They've never seen an elevator before, and stand there lookin' at this amazin' thing. A big ole woman waddles over, and the door closes. Then it opens again and out steps a gorgeous blonde.

"'Son,' the hillbilly says. 'Go fetch your mama.'"

Johnny had to stay in the tank for two hours, when Clyde took his place. Clyde didn't know any jokes but looked mean and grew angry after he'd dropped into the tank once or twice. He made more money than Johnny.

Afterwards, Johnny shivered no matter how hot the day was. He warmed up by building a fire under that cast-iron kettle he'd sold Virgil. He poured in a pint of oil and a gallon of popcorn and stirred it. The kernels jumped a foot but stayed in the pot. Tourists lined up ten deep for a sackful, as if it tasted better than corn popped on a stove. Corn popped, he begged a sandwich—or whatever remained from the lunch trade—off Patty-Cakes, and fired up Virgil's Farmall H. By late afternoon the old people and honeymooners were ready for a hayride.

He had a regular route headed uphill toward his place, past rustic signs announcing "Moonshine Holler," "Ole Granny's Cabin," and "Osage Camp." He always hit Plunge Creek in third gear, so that everyone had a thrill from the splash.

He pulled his straw hat low, chewed on a match, and did his best to look depraved. Lots of people thought they were visiting a scene of wholesale ignorance and incest. Some hotshot with more money than manners called out, "Where you from, son?"

"Way on back yonder," Johnny said, pointing up the hill more or less in the direction of his shed.

"Has life been hard for you?"

"I cain't complain. Used to live in a cave, where my old pa beat me. Finally, I bested him in a fight, but I had to leave my home and my poor mama. She has a powerful belief in Jesus or she could never endure it. I send her money when I can."

Some people laughed outright at this, but some believed Johnny's story, and upped his tips at the end of the ride.

Toward evening, even after five weeks, he grew excited about the show. He checked on La and her friends and threw them fresh hay. Clyde and he rolled in the still—an authentic piece of equipment Virgil had found down in Arkansas—and fired the boiler. They didn't really make liquor, but it added to the drama if the Bald Knobbers could release some steam as they danced, pretending to be drunk.

Night came, and the cool breezes hit his skin, and his muscles didn't ache anymore from lifting batches of doomed chickens. He felt strong and important. He didn't have many lines but he was the star.

Clyde holed up like an outlaw, chain-smoking Chesterfield Kings. Jane and Gary arrived, a wall of love around them. The Piney River Boys tuned up, cracking their cornball Methodist jokes, and Mrs. Koontz, prissy mother of noble Peggy, drew near the stage, and took a deep breath.

PREACHER GIL: Times had changed in the pioneer Ozarks. Horace Keel was rich, but old and embittered. He drove relentlessly into the virgin pines, drawing ever nearer to the outlaw stronghold. Nobody thought the Bald Knobbers was anything but a scourge of the borderlands now. Most of 'em had drifted back to civilization, but fearsome Nat Kinney remained, and Yell Frederick, and J. J. Brown.

On the dim stage, the outlaws drank from their jug. On the high slope, fully lighted, Horace Keel and Peggy came along in a buggy. There was the sound of axes and saws, growing ever louder.

PEGGY KEEL: Father, will you raze this primeval forest?
HORACE KEEL: Peggy, some matters are for men to determine. Young women should tend to their sewin', and piano-playin', and perhaps visitin' the poor.
PEGGY KEEL: You are wrong, father. It is a new age, and women will climb to unimagined heights! As for these virgin timbers, I don't know how, Father, but I will stop you! Nothing is as lovely as a tree!

(Lights dim and then come up on Preacher Gil.)

PREACHER GIL: Bein' young and spry, Peggy thought she could halt the advance of the woodsmen simply by standin' in their path. Maybe she could have, but she wasn't reckonin' on the outlaws.

(Peggy/Jane, wandering in the virgin pines, came unawares upon the Bald Knobbers. They dragged her away even though she fought valiantly. The stage went dark to her heart-wrenching scream.)

(Lights come up on the outlaw camp. Steam rises from the still. J. J. Brown and Yell Frederick pass their jug.)

PEGGY KEEL: (bound hand and foot) Ruffian! Do you know who I am?
NAT KINNEY: Reckon I do, Missy. I figure your dear ole Daddy will finally stop pesterin' us here in our outlaw fastness. And he'll pay a pretty penny for his beautiful daughter's return.

Clyde never forgot his lines, though he delivered them as if reading a phone book. Still, he was scary. The audience hushed when he spoke.

PEGGY KEEL: Leave my father out of this.
NAT KINNEY: T'aint likely. He's my ticket to Californy.

Unknown to the vile Kinney, the Goat Boy, grown to a stalwart young man, crouched on the bluff above. He watched as the outlaws drank themselves to a stupor, and poor Peggy writhed in her bonds.

GOAT BOY: (holding La) Girl, we must save her.
LA: Brr-aat!

The Goat Boy charged his goats into the outlaw camp, and followed on a mule, six guns blazing. This didn't always proceed as planned. Mrs. Koontz waited at stage left with treats, but sometimes the goats went every which way, even into the audience. And sometimes Johnny couldn't make his mule move and had to come in running. The outlaws fell dead all the same, and then the Goat Boy cut Peggy's bonds. She fell into his arms, looking grateful. Of course, because Peggy was really Jane, it was all an act.

PREACHER GIL: (walking on stage) And so the Bald Knobbers went the way of the buffalo. The last remnant of the pine forest was saved, and love was kindled in Peggy's brash young heart. Alas, it was a love that could not be.

(Lights come up on Goat Boy and Peggy, seated on a log, with goats tethered behind them.)

GOAT BOY: Peggy, your place is with your father.
PEGGY: He is your father, too.
GOAT BOY: (Looking across hills) No, dear sister. My mother, God bless her sweet memory, was also your mother, but I never knew my earthly father (pointing). Their graves lie yonder on that ridge.
PEGGY: It breaks my heart!
GOAT BOY: The only father I ever knew is the One who made these hills. And he has placed me in charge of his great forest.
PEGGY: (sobbing) Ever to wander the whispering pines.
GOAT BOY: (soberly) Ever more.
(Lights fade to sounds of goats bleating.)

When it was time to shut down production and return to school, Mrs. Koontz hosted a cast party. Everyone swore they'd be back for another year, and lavished compliments upon her—and suggestions for rewrites. Perhaps thirty came, but quickly melted away because there wasn't anything to eat but rabbit food. There wasn't any liquor, either, because half the troupe was underage.

Everyone congratulated Johnny. A college girl named Beth, who'd helped with staging, gave him the kiss she said she'd been saving all summer, and said he should look her up if he ever got to the big city of Springfield. Jane caught his eye from across the room and came up slowly as if she had something important to say, but merely shook his hand. Gary, who'd let his hair grow all summer, and sported a beard besides, grasped his shoulders, looked at him soulfully, and said, "Damn!" Then Jane and he went out the door.

The Piney River Boys did two numbers, "Roll in My Sweet Baby's Arms" and "Bonaparte's Retreat," but proved too loud for Ruth Ann's little place. They had a gig in West Plains for Sunday afternoon, they said, and packed their instruments. Their music lingered, then faded like the summer. It had all been great fun, and Johnny wondered if he'd ever be the Goat Boy again.

Clyde was taller than anyone else, and you could see his thin face bobbing as he moved about, eating radishes and celery sticks, and standing with the little groups. He never said anything and no one knew how to talk to him. When he moved to a new group, conversation stopped. He visited the potato chip bowl, made a trip to the kitchen for ginger ale, and finally, came to Johnny with a confession. "I make people nervous."

"No, you don't."

"I been in prison and I make people nervous, but I sure thank you, Johnny Bell, for lettin' me be a Bald Knobber."

"You should thank Mrs. Koontz for writin' the part."

She and Virgil were having a friendly discussion at the door. That is, both smiled and nodded, but Johnny could tell they didn't agree.

Clyde studied Mrs. Koontz for a long time. "She's very nice," he said at last, and stalked out, closely following Virgil.

Johnny went into the bathroom, from where he heard someone fumbling with the record player. *Rubber Soul* started up, and he sang "Drive My Car" as he urinated. When he came out the place was deserted, except he could see Mrs. Koontz flitting back and forth in her bedroom. He caught her reflected in the door mirror, pulling on a blouse. Before he could give the matter much thought, she came into the kitchen again, as if it were a natural thing that he was still in her house, and perhaps it was.

"Johnny, would you do something for me?"

"Yes, ma'am."

She came near on bare feet, and he stood as if paralyzed, not realizing he was where she needed to be. He stumbled away as she stood on tiptoe and retrieved a bottle of tequila from behind some saucepans. It was the brand George Bell used to bring back from Matamoros.

"What do you want me to do?"

"Don't tell the school board." She found ice cubes for two glasses and poured in some Sprite with the tequila. "That I'm a tippler. I drink just a little—to sleep better. Don't you tell them."

"Your secret is safe with me, ma'am." He'd downed a beer or two over summer, but had never tasted hard liquor. He couldn't taste it now. It was nothing but Sprite.

"And another thing," she said.

"What's that, ma'am?"

"Quit calling me 'ma'am.' I'm Ruth Ann. Or Ruthie."

"Ruthie," he whispered.

"Finally," she said. "Listen, I wanted your honest opinion."

About what? She headed off for the couch and put her feet on the coffee table. He stepped toward the opposite end but she shook her head. "Bring the bottle."

After another Sprite drink, the aches in his muscles went away. He kicked off his shoes and danced to the Beatles, sort of, knocking over a lamp. Ruthie rose and put the lamp back, and for a moment they ducked and weaved trying to pass each other, and then she fell back into the couch, laughing. It occurred to him that she was awfully good-looking for an older woman, and maybe that he shouldn't be seen at her house late at night. This was more for her sake than his, because after all he was only a kid.

"About the play," she said, sounding more like Mrs. Koontz than Ruthie, sobering him a little.

"Huh?"

"Your honest opinion."

"It was a great play," he said. "I had the time a my life."

"That damn Virgil undercut me at every turn." She paused. "Was it really good?"

"I like Virgil. He gave me a job when—"

Her eyes glistened. "Of course."

He fell on her ottoman, which had deceived him by being made entirely of foam rubber, so that he sank almost to the floor. "Really good, Ruthie. Everbody laughed, and cried—"

"They did, didn't they? But you know all that stuff, that sentimental stuff . . . I can do better. It's a melodrama. Not a serious genre. You understand?"

He crawled to a straight chair and swallowed more of the Sprite drink. "You sure got a way with words, Ruthie."

She sat up suddenly. "Here's my advice to you."

"Ma'am?"

"Think like a man. I do mean think. But then be bold."

"Yes, ma'am. I mean, Ruthie."

She rattled her ice and reached for the bottle. "You're smart. You're a man, or will be, which we, we—established. Don't be like me and settle for teaching in a little backwater place."

"Red Buck's awright."

"I should be in New York. Or Ireland. Or–or–Spain!"

She held the bottle to the light, then carefully poured out exactly half the remainder. She was crying and her voice sounded like a child's. "I don't wanna go back to that crappy school. I don't wanna be . . . respectable!"

"I never had that problem, Ruthie."

She stopped crying. "You and me. We'll run off to New Mexico!"

"It's kinda like Texas, Ruthie. All just desert."

"Oh, no, no, no, it's beautiful! D. H. Lawrence lived there."

"Who?"

"He wrote *Rainbow*. And *Women in Love*. He was a *great* writer, he wrote about love, he was a feminist!"

She slipped off the couch and went on all fours to her bookcase, where she sat cross-legged for a while, her glasses perched on her nose, leafing through books that Johnny supposed she'd read in college. Meanwhile, little squares of light floated everywhere. After some effort, he started *Rubber Soul* again, thinking he might just be able to afford a stereo now, but on the other hand, he didn't have electricity. When he turned, Ruth Ann was sprawled on the carpet as if dead.

He slid a pillow under her head and she opened her eyes. "They wouldn't give him a chance."

"Who, Ruthie?"

"The fucking Baptists!"

"Who wouldn't the Baptists give a chance?"

"Paul," she said, and didn't seem so drunk. "He'd bid on jobs, but nobody would hire him. They thought he'd take work from the local yokels. As if *we* weren't local. My *husband* . . ." She prolonged the word "husband" almost in horror. Her chest heaved, and she took short breaths as if hyperventilating.

"I'm sorry, ma'am," he said, but already she'd closed her eyes again. She began to snore.

He went into the bathroom again and found aspirins for his confused head. The Beatles sang, "Drive My Car."

He sipped water from the faucet and forced himself to think about going forth in the night to catch chickens. In the living room again, he felt an onrush of pity, and slipped his arms under Ruthie. He carried her to her bed and found a blanket for her.

"Joel," she whispered. "Why won't you ever—?"

"Hush, Ruthie," he said.

"I'm just not—"

"You did great, Ruthie. Go to sleep."

He switched off her lamp and turned the lock as he went out. He leaned against a big maple, and the moon was so bright he could have read by it. Clyde sat on the curb with a Stroh's.

"You been waitin' for me?"

Clyde held up his beer. "Walked down to Noolin Brothers and back."

"Well, I guess we got chickens to catch." Johnny pinched his forehead with his fingers. "Let's ride the truck tonight, I don't feel so good."

He pulled in at the Skelly Truck Stop for coffee and then drove on to the feed mill. They sat in the moonlight, waiting for the Mexicans.

"Tell me about women, Clyde."

"I don't have nothin' to tell." He lit a Chesterfield King. "I used to think the onliest secret was cash, but when I come home from Florida I *had* cash. So that wadn't it."

The truck headed deep into the woods and the Mexicans sang their teary songs. All Johnny could think about was Ruthie, his teacher. He hadn't done anything to be sorry for. Neither had she, not even by Baptist standards, or at least Methodist standards. Well, Catholic standards. He fought back tears with no idea why, and then he thought, through *her* tears, she'd given him some advice. *Think. And be bold.*

Chapter Seventeen
Johnny Good Deeds

"We read in Proverbs that pride goeth before destruction," Reverend Larkin told his little flock, no more than forty, when once there had been two hundred. What was the point in attending a country church such as Larkin's? At worst, the man was a crook. At best, he was nobody, ministering to nobodies. "And a haughty spirit before a fall," he went on.

"Oh, Reverend," Virgil said.

"Lordy, Lordy," said Patty-Cakes.

"Amen!" said Johnny.

"Well, I took a fall, a real tumble. But I was not destroyed. I thought—" He took off his glasses and looked upward. "I thought I was doin' God's work. And I *was* . . . but for my own glory, not His. And the Lord showed me. He said, 'My faithful servant, your reward is in Heaven.'"

"That's so. Lord help us, that's so."

The reverend dropped his voice. "Some people think they can find Heaven on earth, and they chase the almighty dollar, and seek glory in the public arena, and wallow in the pleasures of the flesh."

Johnny had chased after money and felt that it was much better to have than not. He liked the public arena, too. Of course, you could love money, that was the root of all evil, and you could allow the adulation you received as an actor to go your head. He understood. As far as wallowing in flesh, he had a notion what that meant, too, because of the sheriff. He'd seen Harpster in Mountain Vale the week before, in civilian clothes, his hair slicked back, coming out of a restaurant with his arm around Candy Cruz. Ruthie, then Candy—even if you ranged over the two counties, how many women were there? Even more, why did they fall for him?

Johnny had only wallowed in the desire for flesh. Did that count?

"We must help the poor," Reverend Larkin said. "We must do our best to counsel the weary in spirit, even when we are weary ourselves."

The congregation grew quiet.

"We do these things in the name of Jesus and take no credit for ourselves."

No credit! Johnny would need to mull that one over, too.

"Jesus broke me," the reverend went on, lowering his head. "And He set me free!"

Johnny had observed some of that breaking at the feed mill. Broiler prices had fallen so low over summer that people couldn't make back their feed bills. The egg business wasn't much better.

The big companies in Arkansas controlled their business all the way from the hatchery. Integrated production, they called it. Reverend Larkin's Co-op had never done more than to contract for the birds and provide feed. The Arkansas outfits were losing money, too. But they were so big they could run at a loss for a while if they knew small operations such as Larkin's were teetering.

Everett Ogletree wasn't the only one to call Reverend Larkin a crook. "I was better off when I just let them ole hens scratch around in the yard," one fellow said.

"Maybe you were, Peabody," said the reverend.

"I sure as hell shoudna contracted with a wolf like you. Wrong word. I'm slanderin' the damn wolf."

Sometimes, the reverend made his speech about the companies in Arkansas. He said feed prices were determined way off in Chicago because of something called futures, and that producers borrowed money on those futures, and even if your costs went up you couldn't be paid more than the future price you'd agreed to. There was a drought in Nebraska and the Dakotas and corn prices had soared. Combine this with historically low prices for dressed birds, you had a crisis. When it was over, there'd be only two or three operators, integrating their hatcheries with their feed sales with their processing plants with their refrigerated trucks. Some of them had even linked up with restaurants and supermarket chains. How could the little guy compete?

Mostly, the reverend stood there and took it. His face flushed when they cursed him, but he didn't strike back. "I'm sorry for your troubles," he said, his voice growing quieter rather than louder. Since the reverend wouldn't argue, Peabody—and the others like him—went their sad, unprofitable ways.

He'd lost the election before anyone cast a vote, he might have to declare bankruptcy, but still he'd been set free. He didn't stand on high pounding the podium anymore. He sat in front of the altar on a folding chair, and read scripture, and every now and then nodded to that scared-looking factory girl, Sister Celia, to sing another hymn. Testify, he said. Tell the world how the Lord has blessed you.

Sister Larkin testified of her gratitude to the ladies of the church for bringing in fifty empty bleach bottles. Now, she needed scraps of bright cloth, and drawstrings, to make tops for her purses. "Isn't it lovely?" she asked, holding up an example. "It'll be our gift to the missionaries, our humble gift. We have so much here in America, even the poorest of us. Our Kenyan sisters in Christ will be overwhelmed. Their own purses!"

Virgil testified what a blessing the Lord had given him at Ozark Village, and said he hoped he didn't ever grow proud, and forget he'd been raised in a one-room shack by a rail-splitter, and hardly had any education. He meant to tithe, he said. Strictly. He hadn't been so careful about that in recent years; though, in his defense, some of those years had been pretty lean. He hoped the Lord understood.

Clyde Fooch thanked the reverend for providing chickens to catch, praised Brother Showalter for taking a chance on a convicted felon, and praised Johnny for thinking he was a Bald Knobber. Most of all he thanked Jesus, who'd been there all along if only Clyde had picked up his Bible and read it sometime.

There were lots of amens.

Sister Stuart rose slowly to her feet, clinging to the pew, and talked about her stomach problems, and how she had prayed about it and asked Reverend Larkin to pray. She made everybody squirm, and gently the reverend thanked her, and motioned to Sister Celia for a hymn.

But then came the greatest testimonial of them all. It was Brother Griggs, who stood at the head of the aisle for a long moment, then walked haltingly forward. *Walked.* There was silence, as Griggs came halfway toward the altar, then sat heavily in a pew, sweating profusely. He smiled.

"Brother Larry, we're so happy to see you," the reverend said at last.

"He's been healed!" cried Sister Showalter. "Jesus said, the lame and the halt—" Sister Celia sang out in her high, sweet voice. She was well past thirty, a shy spinster who worked at the shoe factory.

Clyde Fooch climbed on the dais and joined her in "The Old Rugged Cross" and "I'd Rather Have Jesus." His rough voice, her sweet one, went together somehow.

Johnny thought, Brother Griggs has been healed. It was a miracle. Not so long ago, a miracle was what he'd been looking for. Miracles proved the gospels were true. A *miracle*!

People sang, and bawled, and hugged each other, and bawled some more. Some knelt, raised their hands like lightning rods to receive the Spirit, and prayed furiously:

blessyoublessyouhowIloveyouLordohJesus!youaremy
BEACONmyanchorohblessyoublessyouIloveyouJesus

.

It was like the chanting when Sai Baba walked on coals, Johnny thought. And very nearly he banished his doubts, but somehow remained unmoved. All this baring of souls was tedious and made his head ache. He preferred a shooting on the first page, a deathbed confession, Tarzan's bold rescues. He found himself staring at Brother Griggs, and wondering why he couldn't walk faster, or less shakily.

He was glad when the congregation filed out onto the bluff, and ate roast beef sandwiches and potato salad, and drank iced tea. Rain dripped from the trees but the sun had emerged, and down below, where the Piney River gurgled past, kids jumped off the bluff into a deep pool. He thought about joining them, but it seemed as though a new generation had taken over, now that the Ogletrees were gone.

Everyone gathered around Brother Griggs, who related in detail his experiences in Tulsa.

"When our pastor threw up his hands," someone said. "Oral Roberts healed you."

"*Jesus* healed me," Griggs said. "I praise his holy name."

Reverend Larkin sat alone with his sandwich. One more burden for the man, Johnny thought, one more failure. "Is he healed, Reverend?"

Larkin smiled. "Why would you doubt it, Johnny?"

"He seems so weak."

"Then we'll just have to pray for him to grow stronger, won't we, Johnny? We've missed you in services."

"Yes, sir, I been meanin' to come." He swallowed. "I like that what you said about good deeds, and never takin' credit. That's a beautiful thought."

In fact, the sermon had given him an idea, how he could go all over the country like Johnny Appleseed, except that instead of planting trees he'd do good deeds. "Here comes Johnny Good Deeds," people would say. "Wonder what good deed he'll do today." A silly notion, but still he kept thinking about it.

"The good works are beautiful," said the reverend. "Not what I said."

"Yes, sir. It made me think about the Ogletrees."

The reverend hung his head. "I failed that family, Johnny. I was too caught up in my own worldly concerns. I couldn't get through to Everett."

"Nobody could. You know, Clyde and me caught the broilers out there, first part a summer. They—"

"I hate even to say the word, but Brother Everett, Sister Lucy, they're divorced, or almost. Everett, I guess he's been to Alaska."

"The Promised Land!"

"Sure sounded like it. He came by . . . to settle affairs. All the way up there, all the way back. He wanted to make amends to me, and I said, well, I too have some fault in this, and him and me, we're fine. But that marriage is tragically shattered."

"Reverend, what could you do? Still, I was sittin' there listenin' to you, and I had a thought. Speakin' of good works, I ought to apologize to Everett. And Lucy. All of 'em."

"You were defendin' yourself, son." Reverend Larkin was astounded. "What did you do wrong?"

"I was mad. I mean, Reverend, I was desperate. But if I was a better person I wouldna hit him, and maybe that family would be together. I set things in motion that—"

"Nonsense. You've done fine, Johnny. Not even a year, and you'd make your daddy proud—make ole George proud. But there's no harm, surely, in visitin' with the Ogletrees. They're in Springfield, Johnny. I'll get you an address."

Chapter Eighteen
The Big City

He read mailbox labels, trying to deduce which apartment Everett lived in. Then a blonde in a bikini darted in front of him and turned the key in her box. Johnny staggered back, crying "Ogletree" as if he were choking.

"Twenty-two," the blonde said, but he couldn't reply, and the girl grinned and trotted off. Johnny had come to understand how clumsy he was around girls, and he wanted to improve, but hadn't yet. Sometimes, girls didn't want anything, didn't even want you around, and sometimes they grew angry because you didn't say the thing they wanted you to say. Thinking about girls used up a lot of time. He wished there were a switch, as if for a lightbulb, that would allow him to think about girls, then stop thinking about them.

Now on the street he saw a black-bearded fellow in a smudged cowboy hat, working on his truck. The man wore a hard look, and a cold fear slid to Johnny's liver, because he knew this man. He'd walked past him twice, so intent on looking for a man he couldn't see him.

It was Everett, more or less. To go with the hat, he wore scuffed black boots and a white Western shirt dingy from grease. His bushy beard threw Johnny off. He resembled a picture Ruthie had of one of the Bald Knobbers, Colonel Prather.

Johnny walked back slowly, summoning an image of himself as Tarzan. "Everett, I know there's been some trouble between us," he meant to say, but couldn't make his voice work. Hard to perform good deeds when you couldn't even talk.

"Gimme that 12-inch Crescent," Everett said, as if the two of them had been working all morning to replace his timing chain. Johnny juggled the wrench and handed it over.

"This would hurt." Everett held the wrench like a throwing knife. "Might be fatal."

Johnny swallowed deep. "Everett, I came to apologize. We had our problems, but you pulled me outta that snow drift, and gave me food to eat, and I shouldn't have behaved in the violent manner that I did."

"That's the God's truth," Everett said, but smiled. "You drove all the way to Springfield just to apologize?"

"To you and Lucy both."

"No problem with me. Hail, I apologize to you, Johnny Bell. I apologize for my entire previous existence. I was a blind man." He grunted. "Cain't speak for her."

Johnny stuck his head under the hood with him, much relieved. "What's wrong with your vehicle?"

"Not a damn thing. I'm just puttin' in a new battery." Everett slammed the hood. He reached for a Lucky, lit it with one long sweep of his match, and drew on it with great satisfaction. "Hop in," he said, motioning toward the cab. "I'll show you a *truck*."

It was a shiny flatbed with a floor shift and four-wheel drive. The cab had blue carpeting. There was an AM-FM radio and air conditioning.

"Old George Bell had a Studebaker truck," Johnny said. "This is nicer."

"Studebaker," Everett muttered, as if it were another word for "sissy." He started the engine and the needles in the big round gauges jerked over right, then hovered as if awaiting blastoff. "Wouldn't let 'em cheat me with them idiot lights," he said. "This truck has *gauges*."

They zipped down to the corner roaring and growling, as if the truck were a stock car, and Johnny shook his head in awe. "It's loaded," he said, remembering a word Gary Tyrell used when describing his Impala.

"Man needs a good truck, where I'm goin'."

"You don't mean—"

"North to Alaska! I can make five hunert a day up there."
He flipped his Lucky out the window like Robert Mitchum
in *Thunder Road*. "Cost a livin's high, but in the summertime
a man can just stay in his truck. I pitch a tent right up on
the flatbed."

"And eat beans?"

"What you mean, beans? Just throw in your line, you
got steelhead for supper."

"Paradise," Johnny said.

"Trucks is in demand. Sold the International to an ole
boy in the loggin' business—more 'an I had in her! This here
truck's worth ten thousand dollars up there. I only paid two,
you believe that?" Everett cut the engine and stared a long
moment, as if Johnny needed convincing of something more.
Finally, he patted the dash. "She don't use a drop a oil."

A little black and white TV sat on a Hiland Dairy crate. *The
Honeymooners* played, but the picture kept drifting slowly
upwards, and arriving from the bottom again. There was a
couch someone had been sleeping on, and also a mattress
flat on the floor. In a corner, on newspapers, lay a drive
shaft with its universals still intact. Beside the drive shaft set
a coffee can filled with U-bolts and end wrenches.

Ronnie watched the TV and played cards with himself.
Three months had passed since Johnny last saw him, but
the boy seemed six inches taller. The kid looked up. His eyes
didn't flicker.

Everett took Johnny into the little kitchen off the living
room, where four steel chairs stood, shoved under a dinette
table with wide strips of Formica peeled off. He offered
Johnny a beer, and Johnny accepted it easily, thinking of
Ruthie. Everybody wanted to give him liquor.

"Coors," Everett said. "Bought it in Montana. Max
still sleepin', Ronnie?"

Ronnie rolled his eyes.

It was hotter in the apartment than on the street, and Johnny drank half his beer quickly to cool himself. Everett pounded the table and stalked into the living room to turn on the air conditioner. Nothing happened, so he pulled out the plug, and stuck it in again.

"Max fucked it up," Ronnie said.

Everett pinched his arm. "There ain't no foul language in this house."

"Ain't a house."

"Don't mock me."

Ronnie stood as if he meant to run outdoors, but sat again. He bit his lip. "We don't got a house. I don't got my own room like you said."

"Gonna cry?" Everett said. "I ain't your mother. I don't see her nowheres, do you?"

Something slammed against the wall. "Tryin' to sleep in here," Max called out.

Bugs Bunny cartoons came on and Ronnie calmed down. Maybe I should apologize to him, too, Johnny thought. He wasn't such a bad kid. He'd fix that vertical hold, and they'd watch Bugs and Porky and Wile E. Coyote.

"Up all night, sleeps all day." Everett scowled at the bedroom door. "'Nother beer?"

"Sure!" The beer was fine. Life was good.

The blonde in the bikini went by, glancing through the wide window that had no curtains. She carried a basket of laundry, perhaps explaining her costume. All her clothes had been in the wash.

Everett handed him a Coors and opened one for himself. "Couldn't take no more a that woman," he said.

For an instant, Johnny thought he meant the blonde.

"She went crazy, Johnny."

On the table, two ants simultaneously reached a tiny pile of sugar. They bumped heads and one fell on its back.

He couldn't have said why this seemed funny, but Johnny began laughing.

"In the hospital three weeks—in the crazy place. They tried to say I deserted my family, but they knowed all along where I was. Tell me, Johnny. Is Everett Ogletree the kinda man shirks his responsibilities in life?"

"Not so's you'd notice it," he said, lapping up beer. He had a strange thought. They'd come to blows more than once, but Johnny was the only one who listened to Everett. His wife had written him off years before. His kids tuned him out. He had no friends, and everyone in Red Buck thought he was a fool.

Beneath all his bluster, Everett liked Johnny because he'd saved his life. Everyone could agree that he'd done a good deed. Every now and then, Johnny became his other son, and if he were lucky, Johnny would call him wise. Johnny looked at him and could have bawled. He did a good deed simply listening to Everett.

"I'd a stood by her better or worse," Everett said, staring at the Coors label. "I was up there makin' my livin', that's all. Gettin' on my feet."

"A dream of yours. But did she share that dream?"

Everett seemed startled. "Well, no. She never did. The thing is, Johnny, I was right! No time atall, I made money!" He hung his head. "She was allus high-strung, I shoulda took it into account more. Only now, only now—it's beyond anything I know how to do."

"You headed back to Alaska?"

"Damn right." Everett brought a fist down on the table, disrupting the long column of ants. "Me and Ronnie, and Max if he wants. It would make a man of him." He drained his beer. "Johnny, you could come, too."

He didn't know what to say. "Suzanne?"

"Not that gal. She don't love her daddy." Everett shook his head. "You know, I hauled the Cat up there, all them miles, but I had work the day I arrived. Couldn't spend all the money! Got a place lined up for the winter—come spring, I'll buy a little farm.

"Meant to write home, I truly did, only then I got a letter from *her*. She said how they'd abandoned the place in Red Buck and was livin' in Springfield, and how she'd been in the hospital but was doin' fine with her church work, and she knowed I was busy but could I come back down, she said, because Suzanne was 'bout to get married to this preacher."

"Suzanne's gettin' married?"

"Who knows, with that bunch?" He eyed Johnny steadily. "I was workin' twelve-hour days and on the weekends but a course givin' my daughter away in holy matrimony—I mean, if she *was* gettin' married—that was important. So I sold the International and got a ride with a long-haul fella down to Montana, where I bought the Chevy. I figured I'd settle up accounts in Red Buck and pay the hospital bills, then everbody could come north. Only turns out Lucy's the one tuck up with this preacher crazy as she is, and she don't want nothin' more to do with me exceptin' a divorce. I don't *believe* in divorce, Johnny. Divorce!

"I do forgive her, despite all the heartache she's caused, and the way she lied. And I don't say I done entirely right, though a man, you know, he has his needs. And that woman never shared my dreams, never believed in me, though I won't say a word against her, I ain't made like that. In the end, I reckon it's between each private person and the Good Lord."

Johnny's elbow slid off the table. It was slippery where he'd spilled beer. "Suzanne, and this preacher—"

"Oh, he's just a runt went to Assembly of God seminary, only Lucy thinks he's Jesus Christ hisself." Everett stepped to the refrigerator. "'Nother Coors?"

Johnny shook his head. "I gotta drive."

"You can drink one more; it ain't like hard liquor."

He had another. He rose to his feet, and spent some time looking into the refrigerator, but couldn't see anything except more beer, and a jar of dill pickles. The blonde girl drifted by with yet another basket of clothes, and locked eyes with him through the window. He stumbled into the living room, drawn by her rare beauty. He slid to the floor with his back against the couch. He heard her laughter like a meadow lark singing, but then she wasn't there.

Far above a light flared, as Everett lit another Lucky. "Johnny, you set me straight," he called down. "Just a kid, lickin' me in a fight. Only the question truly was, not what had you done, but why was I tryin' to fight? I was at that point a pride where I was bound to take a fall."

"Like Reverend Larkin."

He nodded. "I never would have thought it, but that's so. Him and me was walkin' that same broad path that leadeth to destruction. I fell on my face and you run off to the woods and that was the end, see? Couldn't pretend no more. *You* was more of a farmer 'an me, Johnny."

"Aw—" There were knives in his stomach, and he bent to the waist. He tried to focus on Bugs Bunny to show that nothing was wrong. Ronnie laughed.

"Come to Alaska with us, Johnny," Everett said. "We'll have ourselves a time."

He was saved from a decision about the frozen North by a feeling of weightlessness, and a burning in his throat. Everett stared in wonder and reached out his hand to guide him to the bathroom. Johnny barely made it to the stool. Hot beer came rolling up, along with the sausage and eggs he'd bought in Rogersville.

"Yechhh," Ronnie said.

Johnny slammed the door. He soaked a towel, wrung it out, and wrapped it around his head. He heard Ronnie giggling beyond the door and wished he could transport himself to the street as they did on *Star Trek*. All he'd wanted was to apologize, but the Tempter had liquored him up and made him out a fool. Again. That old Tempter never quit.

*   *   *

"You done missed the best part a the day," Everett called out.

"The part with you in it?" said Max. "The fallin' down drunk part?"

Everett mumbled something Johnny couldn't make out.

"I was havin' this dream," Max said. "I was walkin' point—"

"How come you didn't get groceries like I asked? We got a guest here."

"Johnny's almost family; he don't count as a guest. We got eggs."

"And an onion under the cupboard. That's *all* we got."

Johnny staggered from the bathroom, his head full of feathers. Everett looked at him grimly and shoved a chair his way. Johnny sat heavily.

"Hey, dude," Max said. "Want some eggs?"

Johnny tried to smile.

Ronnie poked his head into the kitchen. "Don't give him any, he'll just vomit 'em up."

"This dream," Max went on, as he cracked eggs, and they began to sizzle. "Except a lot of it really happened, that's the strange part. I was on point and we're in the elephant grass, I forget where that was. I see movement up ahead. So I quick motion back to the gunner, and he sets in, and then I mosey forward."

"I'm sorry there's so little to eat, Johnny." Everett said. "We're batchin' it here, but if I'd known you was comin'—"

"He cain't cook at all," Ronnie said. "Is this that story 'bout the buffalo?"

Max picked Ronnie up and set him on the counter. "Yeah, but it came out different in the dream."

"It's a good story."

"Somethin' comes at me fast. It bellows out, and I open up with a burst a twenty."

"Wow," Johnny said, smelling the eggs.

"Big ole water buffalo, and he falls to his knees. I call back to the lieutenant, and he comes up the trotter with that

MexTex Roberto, and zip! Roberto pumps a magazine right in its eye."

"That killed it," Johnny said.

"Yeah, it was dead, but the message didn't reach its brain for a while."

"Pretty dumb," Everett said. "Reminds me—"

"I can't stand how it's bellerin', so I just keep slammin' in magazines. That's how it's a dream. I never really done that. Zip, *brrr-aaat,* the whole squad gathers around, zip, *brr-aat,* we're makin' buffalo hamburger. Then right at the end, it lifts its big ole head, and it has these brown eyes like Mabel's. And that didn't happen, either, but it woke me up. I was all kinda panicky."

"Who's Mabel?" Johnny asked.

"Ole milk cow we had," Max said, glancing away.

"Real gentle ole cow," Everett said.

"We shoulda never got rid a those cows," Max said. "Made a helluva lot more sense than your damn goats."

"We'd a still been on the farm if you'd listened to me about them goats, Max. But hail, I don't wanna argue with you." Everett sighed. "You was tellin' that very intrestin' story, it reminded me. I had kinduva camper on the International. In Alaska."

Max stepped back to light a Kool, then began cutting up the eggs with a spatula, and adding pieces of onion.

"I had some smoked salmon up under my gear, right at the end, there. Long 'bout three in the mornin' there come this thud up agin the truck like a bomb gone off. And there was this grizzly—"

"Wasn't no grizzly," Max said, blowing smoke at the ceiling. "Mighta been a brown bear."

"It was a grizzly, awright. He got up on the bed—"

"Grizzly crawled in bed with you?"

"Truck bed, Max, you know what I mean. I'd forgot to fasten the latch, and he gets the door open and sticks in his ugly old snout. A bear's smart, you know? I had a good look at him there in the moonlight, and he'd a dressed out, easy, a thousand pounds."

Max winked at Johnny. "He stabbed him to death with his Bowie knife."

"Max, why you so hard on me?"

"What you do?" Johnny asked.

"Like I say, he wanted that salmon. All I had was my Harrington-Richardson pistol, nine-shot, double-action—"

"He killed a bar with a .22!" Max said and began to sing. "Like Dav-ee, Dav-ee Crock a Shit."

Ronnie repeated it: "Dav-ee, Dav-ee Crock a Shit," and the brothers laughed, and Johnny would have laughed, too, except that he was sorry for Everett. Compared to these three, George Bell and he made a model family.

Max divided the eggs and dropped them into four steel cereal bowls, and they all passed around pepper and bacon bits. The eggs didn't taste so good.

Everett turned to Johnny. "I never said I killed no grizzly bear. I fired in his face, that's all. It echoed like a cannon in that tight little space, and he lit out, scared as I was."

"Did he get the salmon?" Johnny asked.

Everett laughed. "Yeah."

Max stepped to the sink with his empty bowl. "Rear end went out on that old Dodge. You give me a ride to Red Buck, Johnny?"

"I wanna see Lucy . . . and Suzanne. I can swing back for you."

"Go right now. I can pack in two minutes."

"What you wanna head down there for?" Everett asked.

"Joel Harpster gave me a job. You know that."

"He's gonna be Deppity Dawg!" Ronnie said.

"Well, I guess there's nothin' left to *steal*," Everett said.

"I accounted for every God Damn nickel, asshole." Max turned on the faucet and banged dishes into the sink. "Mom was in the hospital and it wasn't free. Somebody had to be responsible."

Johnny made it to his feet. His stomach still felt queasy. "Maybe we should get goin' then. Everett, I sure wanna thank you—"

"He sold all my tools, Johnny," Everett said. "My Swedish steel ax."

"Thought you didn't wanna argue, old man," Max said. He turned the corner and headed for the bedroom.

"That was your grandfather's ax," Everett called after him.

Everett got himself another beer, then sat in silence. Max came out almost immediately with a suitcase in one hand, an olive drab laundry bag in the other. He took them to the bottom of the stairs, then returned for a fancy amplifier and turntable he said he'd bought in Vietnam. Johnny carried his speakers.

"Let me come," Ronnie said.

"Maybe next time," Max said. He turned to Everett. "Dad, if I don't see you again—"

Everett was almost crying. "Come with me."

"Gotta go," Max said, and was out the door.

"I don't blame him," Everett said. "Except for sellin' my tools. It takes a lifetime to build up your tools. He knowed that."

Johnny stepped onto the balcony. "Good luck to you, Everett," he said, sticking out a hand.

He waved his beer in the air as if bestowing a blessing. "You go with God."

The blonde girl up the steps again. "Max—" she said.

Max smiled but marched on.

At the bottom of the stairs Johnny laid the speakers in the grass and slid into some spirea bushes to heave the eggs.

He looked up blearily. Ronnie leaned over the railing beside the blonde girl, who wore a T-shirt now, and yelled something. Then Everett grabbed the boy around the waist, and both disappeared.

Chapter Nineteen
Bride of Christ

A wind picked up, and to the north dark clouds bunched. Max drove west along Division Street, past freight cars backed up on spur lines, and the pig and cow smell of the stockyards. He turned down a narrow road that twisted into the country, then back into the city, between trailer parks and boarded-up frame houses and vacant lots strewn with worn-out tires. He parked up the grade from a tall brick house with a sagging barn out back. A neon sign read: "Heavenly Light."

"You're right on time," Max said. "For the Reverend Mustard Show." He grabbed his laundry bag from the back seat, tucked it under his head, and slumped back.

"You're not comin' in?"

"I'd have to make too many apologies."

Narrow concrete steps rose into a retaining wall, then became a sidewalk that curved uphill through a grove of tall loblolly pines. The house, some long-dead farmer's idea of a mansion, was white, three stories, with complicated gables and a slate roof. At the very top, a cast iron rooster whirled in the wind, as if he'd flown up there and a conjurer's spell had imprisoned him in rust. Tall windows rose up and up, streaming heavenly light.

Cars pulled in under the pines. Kids, all of them dressed in white, ran across the grass, followed by their parents—dressed in white, too. In the twilight they bobbed in the wind, floating like curls of fog. Johnny slipped behind an old man who didn't observe the dress code: he wore Bermuda shorts, motorcycle boots, and a fatigue shirt. "Howdy, friend," the fellow said, grinning with his yellow teeth.

And here was Lucy. "Brother Bell," she said, no surprise in her voice.

She wore another of those long white dresses. It didn't have buttons or belt hoops, and was drawn with a simple cord. She'd lost weight, and of course she was small, anyhow. Lucy looked like Lucy, only she didn't. Her hair had turned white.

She threw her arms around his neck. He thought of what Everett had done, and the perils of the worldly world in general, and she still hadn't let him go. "God love you," she whispered.

Then Johnny saw Jesus. That is, he saw a slender man with blond hair to his shoulders, and a full beard, and he wore a white robe. He could have been the model for the standard portrait of Jesus in little churches from Missouri to Texas.

His eyes glowed. They grabbed you and threw you into the sun.

Forcefully, Johnny turned away. "You must be Reverend Mustard."

The preacher seemed irritated.

"This is Reverend *Petrie,* Johnny," Lucy said. "Reverend, this is Johnny Bell."

"Mr. Bell," said Petrie gravely, as if talking to Johnny was something he was barely able to do. His devotion to the Lord required it, but he was a great man with many demands on his time. From somewhere out of his robe his hand emerged and closed on Johnny's like bolt cutters.

"Brother Johnny's thinkin' a entrin' the ministry," Lucy said.

"Really," said Reverend Petrie. "What denomination?"

"Oh, Baptist, mostly," Johnny said, but then he remembered Everett talking about the Reverend Mustard and his seminary. Petrie had to be Mustard. "Only I'm kinda leanin' toward the Assembly a God—"

"Heavenly Light is non-denominational," Petrie said sternly. "We are a church of inspired prophecy." He released Johnny's hand but pinched the back of one arm and turned him toward the interior of his church. "Do you know our story?"

"The gospel story?"

Reverend Petrie's terrible eyes bore down on Johnny, and Johnny believed Petrie meant to frighten him, but then one of the prophet's eyebrows lifted about an inch and hovered on his forehead. Perversely, that fearsome eyebrow relaxed Johnny. He imagined the man studying himself in the mirror, trying on various intimidating expressions that complemented the eyebrow. The eyebrow was so scary it wasn't scary at all. Dumb as I am, Johnny thought, I'm not fooled. You'd have to be *really* dumb to be taken in.

The walls and ceiling were white and reflected light so brightly your eyes watered. The great room was nothing but a hollowed-out farmhouse, but it seemed to be another universe. You were on a journey inside God's great ship, and when they opened the doors, you'd step through the pearly gates.

To rest your eyes, you could stare at the altar, where bales of hay were laid on edge, suggesting a manger but without animals. Someone had painted Greek columns on the walls, and a stone street, and palms in the distance. A portrait of Jesus looked down from a still higher place.

Unlike in Reverend Larkin's church, which was full of frail widows and spinsters, kids were everywhere at Heavenly Light. Rosie Ogletree, dressed in white, ran up and threw her arms around Johnny's leg, then ran off with two other white urchins.

Lucy moved to the piano, which was white, too. Johnny found a seat by the old fellow in motorcycle boots, who winked and leaned near as if he had a secret, but all he offered was a stick of Juicy Fruit. Johnny and he chewed in fellowship.

Lucy had improved as a pianist. She didn't seem afraid of the piano anymore and waved her hands dramatically. The congregation grew quiet, and Reverend Petrie sat on one of the hay bales, joining Lucy with a guitar. Finally, with a high, pure voice, he sang about his mansion just over the hilltop, and Lucy backed him up with "silver or gold" and "some day yonder." A woman quietly wept. A bald man fell to his knees and cried out his love for Jesus.

Rising from his hay bale, now and then striking a chord with the guitar, Reverend Petrie began to talk. Those old hymns were sweet, he said, and they fed the soul, but the Lord might return yet this evening. Better get down to business.

"Brothers and sisters, hark ye! Are you prepared for the end?"

Lots of amens and praise the Lords. And now Suzanne stood by Johnny's side. She wore a wedding dress and a veil, but held her skirt up in order to walk. She tugged at him and slowly he stood, looking at this wondrous bride in disbelief.

Johnny's partner, the man wearing motorcycle boots, rose and spoke in a strange tongue. Suzanne yanked at his sleeve but Johnny paused to watch. "*Kohala, kohala, kohala,*" the man said, or anyhow that's what it sounded like. He'd heard that same garbled phrase in Reverend Larkin's church.

Overcome, the man fell across a chair. Reverend Petrie raised both hands and began to interpret what the Lord had said through his humble vessel. It all seemed choreographed, but who could say?

"It is there for us to see," cried the young prophet. "The words of God found in the Revelation of John. Our Lord is the bridegroom, and you, the Church, ye who have remained faithful, are the bride! Let us be glad and rejoice, for the marriage of the Lamb is nigh."

People closed their eyes, held up their trembling hands to heaven and shouted hallelujah. Suzanne was supposed to glide forward at this point, Johnny deduced, and be married to something or other. Instead, she pulled him through a door that opened to a large kitchen with restaurant-sized pots and ladles hanging from the walls. She threw her veil into the sink and led him onward through a back door, down steep wooden steps that rocked in the wind, and toward the barn. Johnny pulled back, confused. "Suzanne—"

She threw her arms around his neck and kissed him. "Did you come to rescue me?"

First, he'd have to catch his breath. But while Tarzan would have slaughtered half a dozen Arabs, thrown his woman over his shoulder, and swung away in the trees, Johnny had no plan. With all his work, he'd saved only six hundred dollars.

"I came to apologize," he said. "That man, is he all right? He—"

"Brother Juicy Fruit? He comes on every Sunday. I think Mustard pays him."

"And he speaks in tongues?"

"Important messages from the Great Beyond. Apologize for what, Johnny?"

"Beatin' up on your dad. For all the bad things that happened. Brother Petrie was about to interpret—"

"He'll get off on death, death, death, and what can material possessions mean in times like these, so give it up, sucker, for the collection plate. I'm fed up with God's work, Johnny. It looks like the devil's work to me, making people miserable."

"What's this bride of Christ stuff?"

"I told him I wouldn't do it anymore, but Mom owes him money. So I said, just this evening, just this once. Apologize? The only thing you did, the *only* thing—"

He braced himself.

"Is going out with Jane Epstein. I don't have her clothes, I don't have her money. I'm just as smart!"

He marveled that Suzanne, with all her troubles, had set aside time to brood on Jane. Woman followed woman, and he made no progress in understanding them. He kissed her. "You're a lot smarter than *I* am," he said.

She kissed him back, hard, but her kiss didn't do much. Maybe it would have been better, more like the movies, if he'd anticipated it, but it seemed more like a duty than a little sample of love. Of course, they both worried about the crazy prophet, but maybe Johnny wasn't much of a kisser. Or maybe those Hollywood-type kisses weren't truly how they were done.

They walked to the north of the house as pines whipped and whined in the wind, and the eternal rooster squawked rustily. "You and Lucy . . . and Rosie—you live with Petrie?"

She dabbed at her eyes with a Kleenex and sniffled. "Woe unto us."

"Why does Max call him Mustard?"

"He works nights for French's Mustard." She laughed. "Max is here?"

"On the street. He says everybody's mad at him about the auction."

She snorted. "I was trying to deal with Mom, and there was rent due, and we couldn't get hold of Daddy. So Max sold the furniture, and all the tools, and the tractor and implements, and the dairy stuff. And he paid Mom's hospital bills, only Daddy thinks he pocketed some money for himself. Mama doesn't care at all. She doesn't know what happened. I put her personal things in some boxes if she ever—" Suzanne paused, "comes to."

"That's so sad," Johnny said.

They reached the front yard and sat on a concrete bench under the pines. "Anyhow, they said she could leave the hospital if she lined up counseling. She didn't even know what that was. She thought it was of the Devil, but then they said she could have *Christian* counseling. So we moved into this house, which is just Mustard's stupid church, only he acts like it's a counseling center, too, so somehow he gets money for it. He's the chief nut."

"You're getting married?"

"No! He'd marry me for real, or I spose he would. I'm scared to be alone with him." She buried her head against his chest. "I gotta get outta here, Johnny."

"And Lucy?"

"Just Jesus, Jesus, Jesus. Twenty-four hour Jesus. Seven days a week Jesus. Three meals a day Jesus."

Possibly because of the absent bride, the service had finished. The faithful appeared under the pines again, their white robes billowing in the wind. Johnny saw Lucy on the porch, praising Jesus, sobbing.

Suzanne turned away. "Why is the world's so full of shit, Johnny?"

Johnny was shocked. Jane could say shit, and Ruthie Koontz, but not Suzanne. "I think it's just money. You could solve a whole lot of things with money. I could give you, maybe, two hundred bucks, Suzanne. How much you make at your job?"

"I'm in housekeeping," she said. "I'm on the bottom with all the other dropouts. Everett Ogletree's career path."

"You're only seventeen."

Her eyes shone. "I'm real good with the patients, and sometimes I help a little when they have to walk down the hall, or want something from the nurse's station, or just need someone to talk to."

"You'll be a great nurse. You saved my toes from frost-bite, didn't you?"

She pressed a cool hand to his cheek. "I have forty-five dollars saved. I won't let Mama see my paychecks, I refuse to tithe, I got a book on the GED, and I'm going to college, Johnny. Burge School of Nursing, right here in Springfield. I can be an assistant in just a year. I'll be a registered nurse if it takes the rest of my shitty life."

The wind fell off but it began to rain, and they returned to the kitchen. He told her about the play he'd been in, how La had been the star. He told her if only because of the law of averages her luck would improve. He held out forty dollars to her. She stared at him intently and then took the money. They kissed again and he liked it better, though it was kind of like his grandmother's kiss or maybe a kindly aunt's.

He wondered about that. He'd never speculated. Somewhere in Joshua County, maybe he had an aunt or a second cousin.

And then Jesus entered. "We missed you in service, Sister," he said, his eyebrow dancing.

What a difference, Johnny thought, between Reverends Petrie and Larkin. Larkin was real, Petrie a cartoon, even if both of them worked as grocery clerks. He gave Suzanne what he hoped was an encouraging smile. "I guess I better be movin' along."

"Drop us a line now and then," she said, striking a tone as phony as his, but he knew she needed to be rescued. How?

They drifted toward the living room, with the Reverend Petrie coming closely behind to make sure Johnny didn't stop drifting. Several of the congregation, or perhaps they were residents, remained. Brother Juicy Fruit winked at Johnny.

Lucy smiled gently. Her white robe reached not quite to her ankles. She wore shower thongs. Johnny couldn't take his eyes from her toes, which were dark-looking and twisted, with cracked black nails.

"I'm so sorry, Lucy," he said.

"For what, Johnny?"

"For all the troubles you've had. For whatever trouble I might have caused you."

"That's kind," she said, nodding. "That's followin' in the steps of our Lord. You allus was a tender-hearted boy."

"And you're awright?"

She looked up adoringly at Petrie. "We're all so happy here at Heavenly Light."

"Good," he said. He shook her hand and then turned

toward the door. Suzanne drew near, kissed his cheek, and whispered, "You'll come back?"

This was too much for Mr. Mustard. "I have a few things against thee!" he cried, and that eyebrow of his rocketed high.

"That's a great trick," Johnny said. "You should get yourself a monocle."

"Because thou are lukewarm, I will spew thee out of my mouth."

"Are you crazy, Reverend?" Johnny asked. "Or just a big phony?"

"Hallelujah!" Lucy said.

Suzanne brought her hands to her ears. "It's a lunatic asylum!"

A cross made of walnut lay on the table by the front door, and Johnny couldn't resist. He held the cross up as if the Reverend Petrie were Dracula. "Quick! Find a wooden stake!"

"Fornicater!" Reverend Petrie cried.

Not so's you'd notice it, Johnny thought. "False prophet!"

"Idolator. Baal worshipper. Nicolatane."

The only words remaining to Johnny were curses, and he refrained. Why would he apologize, if then he had yet another argument, and committed brand-new offenses? If he offended, how could he perform good deeds? He looked the prophet in the eye and said, "I'm sorry, sir. This is your place and it's clear I am unwelcome. I wish you well."

There. He'd turned the other cheek to a preacher.

"You're bound straight for hell," Petrie said, and pointed toward the door, as if it were the quickest route.

"God bless you and keep you, Lucy!" Johnny said.

"I'll write to you, Johnny!" Suzanne called out, even as the great prophet slammed the door.

He stood for a moment on the porch and lit a cigarette. I'm not sure what just happened, he thought. I came to apologize and instead I said goodbye.

It rained harder. Someone had left a newspaper on the porch, and he spread it over his head, and ran to the Ford through the slippery grass. Max threw him one glance and stepped on the starter. They wound interminably through the city streets, coming onto Highway 60 from a farm-to-market road. The wipers sang, *straight to hell, straight to hell, straight to hell.*

"Mission accomplished?" Max asked.

"What do you mean?"

"You apologized. You were forgiven. Do you feel the almost divine sense of redemption and renewal?"

"Oh, shut up," Johnny said.

Chapter Twenty
Back to School

When he woke, he saw that Max had parked down by the tennis courts, transformed into a lake from all the rain. The rain still fell, in sheets that whipped at the dead elms by the cafeteria. He leaped a ditch, slipped once on the grass, and stopped to catch his breath under the awning of a storage building. He could see lights on the second-floor windows and the bobbing heads of students.

A bell rang far off, the heads above disappeared as students slid into their seats, and a fire door clunked open as the janitor stepped out to sneak a cigarette. It gave Johnny an opening, and he slopped through the gravel and vaulted onto the hard maple floor of the gym.

"You're the Goat Boy," the janitor said, stepping back.

Johnny grinned and squished down the floor by the bleachers.

"Don't let Coach see you track on his floor."

He glanced nervously toward the boys' lockers, not wanting to run afoul of Coach Henry, and sat to take off his shoes. He might be the Goat Boy, on his own, with a reliable car, a farm, and six hundred dollars, but now he was back in school, a senior with no Suzanne Ogletree to lean on.

Holding his shoes, he headed down the long hall toward the principal's office. He spotted Coach Taney, his tennis guru, and pantomimed a serve down the hall.

"We're in the conference this year, you hear that?"

"And I'm *numero uno*."

"We'll see," Taney said, with a mock frown.

He strode into the principal's office. The secretary, typing rapidly, didn't look up, though he knew she'd seen him enter.

He reminded himself that in school they valued humility. "My name's Johnny Bell," he said. "I'm kinda late gettin' in to register."

The secretary wheeled in her chair toward a file cabinet, from which she drew out several forms. "I guess some of us just don't feel the need for punctuality."

"Yes, ma'am. Well, I do feel the need, only I been real busy, because I'm on my own and have to save every nickel, and then there at the last I had kinduva personal crisis in my life."

She reared back like a bobcat. "And, of course, you're famous."

"I suppose you are referrin' to my actin' career." Johnny smiled. "But that was an accident, really, and—"

"You are *so* famous, in fact, you can't be reached by phone or by mail."

Something was wrong. "You could have called out to Ozark Village."

"I'm a mind reader? You gave us a phone number, but it's disconnected."

"Yes, ma'am, that would be the Ogletrees, and they have left the country, I'm sorry to say."

"And our letters to you—"

"I got an old mailbox out in the shed, but I just never got around to puttin' it up. You could have contacted Virgil Showalter, or Reverend Larkin—or hell, the sheriff knows me. Excuse me. Didn't mean to say hell."

"No address, how can you register? Are you a vagrant?"

"Ma'am, I'm a solid citizen. Taxes paid, own my own vehicle. I believe the address is Route 2 or you could just say Highway 60. I sure am sorry about the mixup, and I'll get that mailbox up tonight yet."

He grabbed hold of her forms, but she wouldn't let them go, and they had a tug of war for an instant. He stepped back, stunned. She smoothed the forms on her blotter and pinned them with one of those round glass paperweights with snow falling inside.

"I think not," she said.

She turned, and he turned, and Mr. Kowalski ducked his head out of his office. He held a phone to his ear, but clamped a hand over the mouthpiece. "I'll take care of it, Alice," he said, nodding at Johnny.

Johnny trailed after him, remembering those times in grade school when he'd been in a fight or some such, and was delivered a lecture that brought him to tears. Mr. Kowalski went on talking as if Johnny wasn't there, which he knew was supposed to make him feel two feet tall. To hell with these floors, he thought, and leaned down to put on his shoes again. They were wet but no manure clung to them.

Still, he was puzzled, how he could walk down the hall a conquering hero, but in the office shrink to the status of Clyde Fooch. What had he done?

Kowalski hung up at last. "Mr. Bell," he said, and held up a folder with an inch of paper in it. He thumbed through it, chuckling in a phony way. "Some joke you played on us."

"I don't understand."

He pointed a finger like Coach Henry used to. "That doesn't help, young man."

"Sir?"

"Playing innocent. We'll save ourselves some time here, young man, if—"

"Please don't call me that."

"You're not a young man?" But the principal calmed a little and held out still another school form. This one was from Brownsville.

"Oh," Johnny said.

"The bet was you wouldn't even show up." Kowalski's anger got the best of him again, and he pounded the desk with his fist like Everett used to. "Johnny, you're in the ninth grade!"

"Yes, sir."

"At best in the ninth grade. Near as we can determine. You were in seven schools before Brownsville."

"Yes, sir, my grandfather was a restless man, and I'm thinkin' your total for schools is on the light side, only you are overlookin' one thing."

"And what would that be, Johnny?"

"I passed all my classes."

"Yes, you even got one A—in English. Everything else, Ds and Cs, and from what I gather you wouldn't have passed anything without the help of Suzanne Ogletree. What good did you think you were doing, Johnny? What made you think you'd get away with it?"

"People get away with all kinds of things," Johnny said, without much confidence. He supposed it was Suzanne's fault and he should have gone into the ninth grade as Kowalski said, but at the time all he could think of was George Bell being dead and how to deal with the strange family he'd found himself in. Ninth grade, eleventh grade, none of it meant much. What's more, he'd pulled it off. "I'm a foot taller than any of those ninth graders," he said. "I can't go back."

"Maybe not."

"I wasn't thinkin' straight."

Kowalski shifted in his chair, and nodded. "And I guess I can understand why. But you've put us in a dilemma, Johnny. We can't pass you on; we can't graduate you. This is a real school here, and it would cheat those students who've worked very hard to get where they are. That diploma has to mean something."

"So what can I do?"

Kowalski sighed. "Well, if you went into the ninth grade, we might find ways to advance you, but it's hard to get around things like you passed Algebra II with a D, and never took Algebra I. I'm not questioning the fact you're an intelligent young man and could move along fast if you wanted to. And you're only sixteen, am I right?"

"Seventeen in February."

"We might get you out of here by age nineteen, even eighteen with summer classes. Right now, though, you're suspended pending what the school board wants to do."

"Could I talk to the school board?"

"Of course, you could. And I could recommend special courses, an accelerated program."

"What about the play?"

"Play?"

"*Goat Boy of the Ozarks*. I was the star. I brought . . . fame to the community of Red Buck."

"Oh." Kowalski smiled. "*That*. Fame or shame, people are still talking about it. I'm sure you were extraordinary, but it doesn't change—"

"I'm gonna drop out," Johnny said, hoping he'd make the man feel sorry. Hadn't he done well here? The entire town knew him by name. He was the Goat Boy.

Kowalski nodded. "It's a blow to you, of course it is. You know about the General Educational Development test?"

"I'm gonna join the navy."

Kowalski folded his hands over his stomach. "I believe you need to be seventeen, but certainly that's an option."

He wasn't a mean man, Johnny thought. In his way, he was trying to be fair. And maybe, just maybe, the play hadn't been such a big deal as he'd thought. Still—

"It's not fair!"

"Perhaps, in some sense—"

"In some sense?" Johnny stood and tried to think of a clever phrase to make everything right. Kowalski had a half-size baseball bat on his desk that said St. Louis Cardinals on it, and Johnny picked it up and waved it. Kowalski rolled back in his chair and his hand hovered by the phone.

Then on the wall Johnny saw an autographed photo of Stan Musial and realized he didn't know a thing about the principal, but that they were both Cardinal fans. Johnny returned the bat to his desk, and said, "They're goin' to the World Series this year."

Kowalski looked at him in amazement. "Perhaps. If Gibson can come back."

"Oh, he's invincible." With that Johnny marched out almost proudly, but with his insides a seething mess. When the secretary gave him her satisfied look, he picked up her paperweight, smiling ironically. Slowly, the alarm built in her face, but he placed the paperweight carefully on her desk again, and walked slowly, pridefully, through the door. Then he broke into a run with his squishing shoes.

He ran into a girl, knocking her down.

"Sorry!" the girl said, even as her books slid down the buffed floor.

"My fault, my fault," he said, and ran to pick up her books and help her to her feet.

"I'm so late," she said, pulling at her hair, and trying to smooth her skirt.

"You're new?"

She looked up at him woefully.

"Don't you worry," he said. "This is a good school. Who's your teacher?"

She held out her schedule. "A Mrs. Ruth . . . Koontz."

"Oh." Another good deed, he thought. One a day was his goal, and today he'd finish early. "I'll take you there," he said.

He wondered if, a year ago, he'd seemed as pitiful as this little thing. She was pretty enough. Were he still a student here, perhaps he'd rescue her.

Eyes wide, she asked, "Won't you . . . be late, too?"

He'd completely mastered Mrs. Koontz's lessons in irony. The examples life provided were unending. "I'm free this hour."

He stood a moment outside the classroom, watching Ruthie go through her routines. She looked grand, in a crisp blue suit, no cat hairs visible. It hadn't occurred to him that if he could become the heroic Goat Boy, then she might, as the Goat Boy's creator, accrue some fame as well. He knocked softly on the glass door and she turned. Her stern smile grew warm.

"Johnny! Aren't you in the wrong class?"

He motioned to the straggler. "She's new, and I—"

"Yes! Brenda, isn't it? Just have a seat; I'll be with you in a moment." The girl passed, glancing with awe at Johnny as Mrs. Koontz stepped into the hall. "Always the gentleman, aren't we?"

She didn't, he concluded, know that he'd been suspended. "Sometimes, ma'am."

"She's kind of cute." She stepped near and grasped his arm. "Johnny, we have to talk. Soon."

Talking was good. She might try to intervene with his ninth grader's status. Maybe even she felt guilty about their drunken evening together. Luckily, he'd shown restraint. "Yes, ma'am. I don't think there's anything to make a fuss about. It's just that we—what I mean is—"

"It's about Virgil. He wants to come back next year bigger and brassier, but it's his *changes,* Johnny. I don't think he understands how we brought in an audience in the first place. He's a nice man, I know he's helped you, but I swear to God I'm going to kill him. Johnny, you and I need to get together on this. Virgil values your opinion, and we need a united front."

"Yes, ma'am," Johnny said.

She patted his arm and stepped back. "Well, I have a class to teach. Come by after school, will you?"

"Yes, ma'am," he said. "Mrs. Koontz?"

She paused at the door. "Yes?"

"Think. And then be bold."

"That's nice." She nodded thoughtfully. "Did someone famous say that?"

Chapter Twenty-One
The Walnut King

He had a big walnut crop. It was cold work, but he built fires, and drank coffee, and listened to the Cardinals in the World Series. The Red Sox couldn't keep Lou Brock from stealing. Bob Gibson, who'd suffered a broken leg back in July when Roberto Clemente hit him with a line drive, shut down the Red Sox in the seventh game, and even hit a home run.

Then there was no more baseball, and life was without form, and void.

Finally, he'd sold perhaps two tons of nuts and had borrowed Virgil's Allis-Chalmers C and a trailer to haul them. The feed mill was open again, selling pig feed and equipment for raising ducks—and buying walnuts almost as an act of charity.

Virgil didn't work for Reverend Larkin anymore. He'd turned into a corporation. "'Nother year, I think we might employ a hillbilly full-time," he said. "Doin' some woodwork, and maybe in the gift shop. Sorry I ain't got no work at the present moment."

"I'm gettin' by, Virgil."

"I wanna bring you and Ruth Ann together, talk some about the play for next summer. We need more jokes, seems to me. Need a character like Minnie Pearl, you know who I mean? And J. J. Brown, he don't speak no words the way it is, he could be a kinda hillbilly clown, like Festus on *Gunsmoke*. And maybe, you know, there could be a part where the Goat Boy goes to a big church supper. We could work in more songs that way. The kids get restless without the songs."

Johnny couldn't believe he was serious. "And if there's supper on the stage, you could bring up the lights and sell sandwiches."

"That's a dang good angle, Goat Boy. The breakin' bread kinda thing, among the simple hillfolk. You sure got a haid for business."

In November, with Virgil's help, he brought in a crew to cut the walnut trees. The crew worked ten-hour days, trying to finish before snow, and it took them a month even with two-man chainsaws and a hoist on a Caterpillar that lifted the logs to a truck. The men said they'd never seen so many big walnuts—or even white oaks—in one grove, and Johnny made the paper again because of how unusual it was, and because he was about to be rich.

The buyer paid an average of thirty-five cents a board foot—a fair price, Virgil said. A tree thirty inches across, and Johnny had several of those, yielded around seven hundred board feet, or about $250. Virgil insisted he hold out for more with several big veneer trees, one of which was thirty-eight inches across, and the company finally agreed to pay thirteen hundred dollars for it. Later, a man came with pick and shovel to dig out the stumps for burl and paid him thirty and forty dollars each for the ones he took.

The walnut trees were why George Bell had brought him to Red Buck, and at last Johnny understood that the old man had done right by him, and without claiming much credit. He did a good deed even as he plunged into hellfire. He'd done the last thing he needed to.

Johnny appreciated what Clyde Fooch said. "It's like he quit his job."

"What?"

"You can quit, or you can give notice. You shouldn't just quit, because everybody is upset, and don't get no chance to fuss. But it amounts to the same thing."

After the trucks had gone, Johnny burned brush for a week, sawing out a few choice limbs and throwing them up above in the shed. Someday he'd make bowls and table legs.

The hilltop looked like a war zone and made him sad. The trees had been a crop from the first, and like George Bell, they were past their prime. Death wasn't so far away whether by saw or old age. Johnny missed the trees, even so, and he'd deprived a lot of squirrels of their livelihood. And like a squirrel, he planted walnuts all over the smoldering land— perhaps two thousand of them before he was done, because not all of them would germinate.

Then he put up a mailbox in order to receive his checks. When they all came in, he had seventy-nine thousand dollars.

Just before Christmas, Reverend Larkin held his revival, but his finances were much diminished and he couldn't afford the Singing Babbit Brothers. Without the Babbits, Larkin couldn't line up a big-name preacher, either, so he brought the word himself at his church on the Piney. He spoke of a "great harvest of souls."

The truth was that people came to hear Sister Celia Griffin, rather than Reverend Larkin. She's more famous even than me, Johnny thought. She might get a big recording contract, and she doesn't even know it. Once he saw her walking out of the shoe factory, and waved, but she didn't recognize him. Her shoulders slumped and her stubby legs tripped along in a stagger, as if she'd taken a jolt of current. She stared off into another world.

She played the piano as thoughtlessly as he might have shifted gears in his Ford. She didn't attack it, like Lucy; she was part of it. And when the lights shone on her face streaked with tears, she was beautiful. She sang:

> I'm far down that highway
> That hard road of life
> Behind me lies sorrow
> Grievin' and strife

> How I long for that day when
> My trials here shall end
> I'll see my dear wife and
> My mother again.

Johnny's words, but he didn't know where they came from. He wrote the song on a Big Chief tablet one rainy day when he hadn't anything else to do and was thinking about his father. Perhaps he wrote it to please the reverend, who took it as a sign that Johnny was coming around to his father's vocation.

The reverend wanted him to attend a Christian academy a friend of his ran over in Kansas. He said Johnny could earn a high school degree there by the end of next summer, but Johnny found the idea of school disheartening now, and felt reluctant to deepen his obligations to Larkin. He admired the reverend because he lived what he preached, but he hadn't enough faith to become the man's apprentice.

Then there were evenings such as this one, when he took the pulpit, and wondered if perhaps the reverend were right. He lifted his hands to conduct the chorus:

> Oh lonely child
> Oh heartsick brother
> Jesus binds the soul
> Like no other.

Celia's voice rose high, and he wanted to cry out in joy, or perhaps pain. He couldn't stand how lovely her voice was. For a moment, he aspired to be an angel. Of course, his father hadn't been, getting his mother pregnant, then leaving like a thief in the night. Johnny held up Joe Daws's Bible so he'd look official, and on the pulpit itself, where no one could see, he opened the 1947 Greeley, Colorado, school annual to his dad's picture. He wanted to stand exactly as his father had. He wanted to read the passages his father had underlined.

"What the Lord has laid on my heart to talk to you about, dear brothers, dear sisters, is good deeds."

You didn't need a GED to bring the word of God, but he should speak to you in a special way, and Johnny hadn't heard a thing. The question was, did his dad hear something long ago? Was he called by God, or did he call himself? Perhaps he was as phony as Reverend Mustard. If Johnny knew the answer, he'd have a big clue how to live.

"The Lord Jesus," he said, lifting his voice on "Jesus," "gave us a wonderful parable in Luke 10: 30-37. This is the famous story of the Good Samaritan. There was a Jewish man left for dead in the ditch, and a priest passed him by, and a Levite, too." He paused, wondering what a Levite was. "Only the good Samaritan, who was from another land and didn't have any obligations in Judea, he bound up the wounds of the man, 'pouring in oil and wine.'"

Johnny thought of Lucy pouring olive oil over him. Maybe the Book of Luke was where she got the idea. "And then this Samaritan 'brought him to an inn, and took care of him.' What strikes me is that the Good Samaritan didn't require anything in return. The Bible doesn't even give his name."

There were some new people in the congregation, and in the lights, he couldn't see them well. He didn't know if they were listening or had fallen asleep. Up front, he saw Larry Griggs, who'd taken a fall in September, and was back in his wheelchair. He sat with his lips moving in some kind of prayer, eyes closed, tears streaming.

There are no miracles, Johnny thought, in the long silence. There's just hard work and a lot of things you can't be sure of.

At last, Virgil tossed out an "Amen, Brother."

"Amen," Reverend Larkin echoed.

"I believe that is what Jesus wants us to do," Johnny said. "Good deeds because it is a kindness, and not because others will think well of us. Brother Everett Ogletree, bless his troubled path, he pulled me out of a snow drift when I was near death, when he coulda passed me by. He's a good Samaritan."

"He is!"

Johnny stared at Larry Griggs. "Miracles, oh, they are too much to fathom. But what of good works? Selfless good deeds? Can you testify?"

"Yes!" Clyde Fooch stood, and Johnny nodded, grateful to him because he didn't know what more he could say.

"Praise Jesus, I was nothin' but a jailbird. And this man, Reverend Charles Larkin, believed in me. He give me a chance because God was movin' in his life, and had humbled him, and had shown him good works to do. Oh, bless your hearts, I praise Jesus for givin' me work, for givin' me a peaceful heart, for givin' me . . . love."

Clyde pointed at Celia. She blushed, sort of.

"Thank you, Brother Fooch," Johnny said.

"Bless you, Johnny," the Reverend said, coming to the dais and hugging him. Johnny melted away as "Hallelujah" and "Praise the Lord!" rose. It was time to call the sinners home. That was the reverend's job.

"Brother Fooch, I don't deserve your kind words. The point of Johnny's beautiful sermon, I believe, is that good works are their own reward."

"Yes, Lord!"

"Let us sing Reverend Johnny's song."

While everyone whooped and wailed, Reverend Johnny placed a thousand dollars into the collections plate. Larkin might guess where it came from, but he couldn't know for sure.

He grabbed a sack of oranges, the church's Christmas gift to the poor, and slipped out the back. He felt badly leaving the Larkins without wishing them well, but they'd have invited him to dinner, and made a fuss, and he knew he couldn't handle it. He could hear the faithful all down the mountain, accompanied by Sister Celia's tinkly piano. He missed the place already.

He slaughtered his last hen and dropped her in with potatoes and the pinto beans he'd soaked overnight. He waited for the water to boil, then banked the fire, closed the damper, and walked down the slope toward Virgil's. La ran to him without his even calling.

"I sold all those trees," he told her, bending down a wild plum branch where a few withered plums still clung. La chewed thoughtfully and batted her blue eyes.

"Isn't that what I was supposed to do?"

"Brr–aat," La said.

He stood for a long while, petting her, until it began to snow. "If we had any sense, we'd head for a warm climate."

As if she understood, La snorted and trotted up the pasture. She was well fed and had a warm place to sleep, as befitted a famous actress. She was in Goat Heaven.

Back in the shed, he added water to the beans and mixed some cornbread for the Dutch oven, then scrambled around the shed hauling in wood. Twice he fell in the accumulating snow, and before it could drift, he backed in the Ford. Then he ate cornbread and beans, and an orange for dessert.

He hung up two Coleman lanterns for light, then took off the Ford's wheels, leaving the frame propped on blocks. He packed blankets, books, cooking utensils, and his best tools into the car, and rolled up the windows. He wrapped his father's Bible and the Greeley school annual in plastic, placed them in a metal box, and placed the box in the car, too. He locked the car and hid the keys. Then, from bumper to bumper, he stretched plastic sheathing, and taped it down.

As for the trip, he didn't need much. Several changes of clothes. A sackful of biscuits, a jar of peanut butter, the oranges. *East of Eden,* which was fat and would last him for a while, and the envelope full of cash, which was almost as fat.

He cleaned the ashes from the stove and filled it with kindling. He wrapped plastic around his fine new chair and threw several boxes of mouse poison under it. Finally, he slipped out the door, snapping his big brass padlock. The storm had blown out, leaving half a foot of snow. It was just past five in the morning.

He stood on the ridge above the railroad, watching a freight roll by. It wasn't going fast, and he almost jumped into a gondola of finely crushed coal. Tarzan could do it, he thought, but somehow it didn't seem so romantic anymore. It seemed, if not dangerous, then dirty and cold.

He trudged on toward Red Buck, his feet and hands slowly freezing in the snow, and bought a bus ticket.

Rubbing his hands over the station's gas stove, he thought about stepping next door to say goodbye to the sheriff, but in the end couldn't muster the energy. All fall he'd wanted to call Jane and tell her how sorry he was about her mother's death, and even now, at this crazy hour, it occurred to him, but all the speeches he'd rehearsed seemed phony. Mrs. Koontz? Well, yes. He'd drop her a line. I took your advice, he'd say.

He reached Springfield at nine and ate bacon and eggs at a diner by the Kresge's. Then he walked on to Cox Hospital.

The gift shop in the lobby didn't seem anonymous enough, so he walked past Drury College and found a florist's where they were used to working up bouquets for dead people. He bought a box of candy and a card and some Scotch tape. He threw the candy away and taped the box shut several times and taped down the card. It said, "For Suzanne Ogletree." And underneath that, "From a grateful patient."

True enough. She'd saved his toes.

Behind where the candy-stripers sat were two baskets for mail, and he finally deduced the one that was for inside the hospital. He dropped his package there when the candy-stripers were occupied and walked casually on. He figured ten thousand dollars would set her up pretty well. She could get away from the prophet and her loony mother, and find an apartment, and go to school full-time. She could even buy a decent car.

But he couldn't just hand it to her. She wouldn't accept it. She'd think he wanted something in return, and he didn't. Not even—particularly not even—love.

Suzanne would open the box, thinking who in the world would send me candy? Not Reverend Mustard. That shy fellow who worked in laundry?

There wouldn't be any candy. Just an envelope. She'd open it, and pull out all those one hundred dollar bills. She wouldn't comprehend. She'd cry. She'd grow fearful, and maybe even pray. In the end, she'd laugh—and wonder who all over again. Maybe she'd think it was her dad. No, no, it was signed, "A patient." Who?

After some months, after she'd mulled it over with Max and learned that Johnny had come into some money, she'd think of him. By that time she'd be on her way to becoming a nurse.

He had only one more errand. It didn't have to be the navy, his father's branch, but he knew he didn't want the marines. And the air force office was closed.

"How old are you?"

"Eighteen."

"Ah huh." The sergeant stared. "Well, we've got some nice training packages right now, I mean if you don't delay."

"I wanna get my GED."

"Not a problem, young soldier."

The sergeant gave him motel vouchers and told him to return Wednesday at 7:00 a.m. sharp. "You cain't back out now," he said. "You belong to the U.S. Army."

"Great." George Bell would have said, stay out of that war, but Johnny figured the army would make a home for a while. He'd thought about it. It was time to be bold.

The old man was wise in his way, but still he had to walk to Missouri, and he never figured out the meaning of life. It was out there somewhere, and meanwhile, Johnny had money in the bank, and money in his pockets.

And food in his belly. The waitress fed him apple pie and told him her brother was in the army. Her name was Nancy. She gave him directions to the theater, even offered to drop him off once her shift was done. He wanted to walk. Nancy was only a year or so older than he, and he liked to make friends, but tonight he didn't want any company. The theater was showing *Tarzan and the Valley of Gold,* starring Mike Henry. He wanted to sit in the front row like George Bell and he used to, all by his lonesome.

Photo by David Mort

John Mort's first novel, *Soldier in Paradise* (1999), was
widely reviewed and won the W. Y. Boyd Award for best
military fiction. He has published ten other books,
including two literary reference works, four novels, and
four collections of stories. His short stories have appeared
in a wide variety of magazines and journals, including *The
New Yorker*, *Missouri Review*, *Chicago Tribune*, *Arkansas
Review*, and *Sixfold*. He is the recipient of a National
Endowment for the Arts literary grant, the Hackney
Award, and a Western Writers of America Spur for the
short story, "The Hog Whisperer." In 2017 he was
awarded the Sullivan Prize for his short story collection,
Down Along the Piney, which was published in 2018 by the
University of Notre Dame Press.

Mort spent much of his childhood in the southern
Missouri counties of Wright and Texas, where *The Ballad*

of Johnny Bell is set. Mort served with the First Cavalry from 1968 through 1970 as a rifleman and RTO. He attended the University of Iowa, from which he earned a BA in English (1972), an MFA in writing (1974), and an MLS (1976). He worked as a librarian, editor, and teacher. He lives in Coweta, Oklahoma.